UNDERSTANDING JUDICIAL REASONING
Controversies, Concepts and Cases

*To my mother and father
and to Margaret and Jim*

UNDERSTANDING JUDICIAL REASONING
Controversies, Concepts and Cases

Roland Case
Centre for Education, Law and Society
Simon Fraser University

Thompson Educational Publishing, Inc.
Toronto

Copyright © 1997 Thompson Educational Publishing, Inc.
14 Ripley Avenue, Suite 104
Toronto, Ontario, Canada M6S 3N9
Tel: (416) 766-2763
Fax: (416) 766-0398
email: thompson@canadabooks.ingenia.com

This book is published in association with IPI Publishing Limited, Toronto.

Every reasonable effort has been made to acquire permission for copyright materials used in this book and to acknowledge such permissions accurately. Any errors and omissions called to the publisher's attention will be corrected in future printings.

Canadian Cataloguing in Publication Data

Case, Roland, 1951-
    Understanding judicial reasoning : controversies, concepts and cases

Includes bibliographical references and index.
ISBN 1-55077-082-9

1. Judicial process - Canada. 2. Judicial process -
Great Britain. 3. Judicial process - United States.
I. Title.

K2100.C373 1997   347'.012   C97-930494-6

Book and text designed by: Danielle Baum
Cover designed by: Danielle Baum

Printed and bound in Canada on acid-free paper.
1 2 3 4 04 03 02 01 00 99 98 97

CONTENTS

FOREWORD

THE HONOURABLE JOHN SOPINKA,
JUSTICE OF THE SUPREME COURT OF CANADA

The hungry judges soon the sentence sign,
And wretches hang that jurymen may dine;

Alexander Pope, *Rape of the Lock*
(Canto III, L1. 21-22)

This acidic observation from the pen of Alexander Pope is a cynical answer to what remains one of the greatest mysteries of the law: how do judges arrive at their decisions? This example, and others even more extreme with which the literature is replete, highlight the need to penetrate this mystery. *Understanding Judicial Reasoning* is an attempt to do that, not by investigating how judges make decisions in fact, but by analyzing how judges are expected to arrive at decisions. Dr. Case's account is premised on the proposition, expounded by H.L.A. Hart, that legal systems comprise two levels of rules, primary and secondary. The book leads us through Dr. Case's analysis of secondary rules of law—the rules, norms, principles, and modes of reasoning which in his view guide or determine the identification, change, adjudication, and application by judges of primary (or what might be referred to as substantive) rules of law.

An understanding of the processes and patterns of judicial reasoning is particularly relevant at this time. Growing concern with the effective protection and adjudication of human rights worldwide has placed judicial decision making under increasing popular scrutiny, and has prompted examination of the proper role and importance of judges, courts, and the law. This is especially so in Canada, where the relative importance and power of the courts in the national polity has been perceived by many to have increased since the implementation in 1982 of the *Canadian Charter of Rights and Freedoms*. What sets the present book apart from the vast literature on legal reasoning and the philosophy of law is that it addresses directly the manner in which judges make decisions, instead of considering the idea or functioning of law in the abstract. While I do not necessarily subscribe to all of Dr. Case's theories, the book will undoubtedly contribute to an unfolding appreciation of judicial decision making and to the scholarly debate on the nature of legal thought.

FOREWORD

HONOURABLE MR. JUSTICE ALLEN M. LINDEN,
JUSTICE OF THE FEDERAL COURT OF CANADA

The law has become a universal topic of discussion these days. Our newspapers and television report on legal matters like never before. Novels and movies handle justice issues, blending fact with fiction and fiction with fact. Ordinary citizens are more exposed than ever before to our legal system, they understand more about it, they are criticizing it more, and they are demanding reform more. Law has become a political issue.

Much of this is good, for a legal system requires scrutiny and criticism if it is to serve people adequately. However, some of this is also bad, for there is too much ignorance about the law, which ignorance is often exploited by those who should know better in order to advance their political positions. Unfounded and mischievous criticism is sometimes levelled against the legal system. The impression is left with many that the law is "lawless," that courts do whatever they wish to do with cases that come before them. Some criticize "judicial imperialism," "government by the judiciary," and even judicial "dictatorship." While judges have certainly been given additional powers by our new *Charter of Rights and Freedoms*, to say that judges have taken over the government is absolute nonsense and Canadians need to know this.

It is refreshing and truly helpful to have a book, like this one by Professor Roland Case, that explains that courts are not despots, that they are required to follow the law, that they must utilize legal reasoning to reach decisions. Judicial decisions cannot shoot off into the sky like a rocket; rather they must travel well-worn ruts. Judges must always explain themselves according to certain basic rules. If they do not, they will be reversed on appeal and appeal court decisions can usually be altered by Parliament.

Professor Case outlines a sophisticated account of judicial reasoning: reasoning from interpretive guidelines; reasoning from prior cases; and reasoning from principle. During his analysis, he refers to many of the leading middle-of-the-road legal scholars like Hart, Dworkin, Cross, MacCormick, Raz, and Goodhart. He concludes by examining two fascinating case studies from various points of view.

This book is one of great value, not only to non-lawyers, at whom the book is aimed, but also to lawyers and judges interested in a more profound understanding of our legal system.

PREFACE

This book explains the forms of reasoning judges use when deciding how the law applies in particular cases. Judicial application of law is one of the most enduring, important, and contested issues in legal discourse. It has been the focus of immense professional, academic, and public attention. There is, for instance, considerable disagreement within the legal profession about the limits and nature of judges' authority to make law. Intense debates have arisen over issues such as the proper role in judicial decision making of "extra-legal" standards, the breadth and legitimacy of judicial authority to review legislation, and the validity of interpreting the constitution beyond what the original drafters intended. The media and popular press are filled with claims about judicial bias, imposition of personal morality, and usurpation of the legislative function. It is no longer uncommon for newspapers to publish the full text of judicial opinions, due to growing public concern about judicial decision making. This flood of controversy and criticism stems, at least partly, from fundamental ambiguities in the law, the undeniable complexity of the issues, and the incompetence or impropriety of some judges. However, another crucial factor is widespread and profound misconceptions about the basic structure and logic of judicial reasoning. Helping to demystify and, to some extent, reduce unfounded cynicism about the judicial mandate to apply the law are my primary motives for offering yet another a contribution to the "perennial" debate on the nature of judicial reasoning in Anglo-American jurisdictions.[1]

I use the term *judicial reasoning* to refer to reasoning about what the law requires in a particular case. This term could be misleading, since some readers might expect it to include the reasoning followed when establishing the facts of a case. Although trial judges often determine the facts, it is characteristically the jury's responsibility to do so. I exclude considerations involved in fact finding and focus on the justification for judicial decisions on what the law says in a given situation. The central thesis of this book is that judicial application of law, properly conducted, requires that judges conform to prescribed modes of reasoning. When they do otherwise, they exceed their legitimate judicial authority.

My examination of judicial reasoning unfolds in four sections. Section One introduces the general issues surrounding the judicial mandate to apply law. In Chapter 1, I discuss the current, cynical view of judicial decision making—as the exercise of judicial tyranny—and the dangerous implications of this inaccurate perception for the proper functioning of the judiciary. I introduce an alternative picture—the exercise of controlled judgment—that more richly captures the complexity of, and the constraints on, judicial reasoning. In Chapter 2, I outline the basic structure and the rules that govern judicial reasoning. I suggest that these rules establish the standards that judges must rely upon when applying a law. Chapter 3 explains, in general terms, how rules of application allow for judicial flexibility, accommodate controversy, and yet control judicial decision making.

Section Two describes in some detail the three modes of reasoning authorized and constituted by these rules. Chapter 4 examines *reasoning from interpretive guidelines*, which controls application of law by establishing a law's meaning. Chapter 5 focuses on *reasoning from prior cases*, which controls application of law by determining similarities to or differences from previous judicial decisions. Chapter 6 explores *reasoning from principle*, which controls application of law by assessing the acceptability of proposed principles in light of other legal standards.

Section Three features extended opinions in five controversial cases. Chapters 7 and 8 contain two case studies offering close analysis of the reasoning in an American case, *Riggs v. Palmer*, and in a British case, *Davis v. Johnson*. Their purpose is to demonstrate the power of this account of judicial reasoning to represent and explain actual judicial opinions. Chapter 9 contains extended excerpts from judicial opinions in three other controversial cases. These excerpts, classified according to the three modes of reasoning, provide further opportunities to examine the complex, rule-governed nature of judicial reasoning. Readers may find it helpful to consult the appropriate excerpts as they read about the modes of reasoning in Section Two. Similarly, the *Riggs* case study may be considered in connection with Chapters 2 and 4, and the *Davis* case study in connection with Chapters 3 and 6.

Section Four contains a bibliography and other reference aids. I have tried to make the text itself accessible to readers who may not be familiar with the voluminous literature on these topics. The extensive notes in the fourth section provide some of the theoretical justifications, or at least indicate the sources of support, for my ideas. Study questions are included for those who may wish to use this book as a course text.

Much of the research upon which this book is based was carried out with financial assistance from the Human Rights Law Fund of the Department of Justice Canada and from a Social Science and Humanities Research Council of Canada doctoral fellowship.

Various individuals have contributed significantly, and in different ways, to the development of this book. I owe much to LeRoi Daniels, Jerrold Coombs, and J.C. Smith, who were guiding forces during my doctoral studies at the University of British Columbia. It is not clear to me how many of the ideas in this book are mine and how many are borrowed from my advisors, especially from Jerrold Coombs' original exploration of the forms of judicial reasoning. I have had the pleasure of working on this project with three fine editors: Robin Van Heck, Charlotte Coombs, and Julie Zilber. As well, I appreciate the helpful reviews of my manuscript by Wilfrid Waluchow of McMaster University, Steve Wexler of the University of British Columbia, and Joan Brockman of Simon Fraser University. Finally, and most of all, I am grateful to my wonderful wife, Susan Duncan.

Roland Case
Center for Education, Law and Society
Simon Fraser University

SECTION ONE:

THE JUDICIAL MANDATE

1
Judicial Tyranny or Endangered Institution?

As it currently stands there is widespread confusion within the legal profession and among the general public over the "rules" governing the judicial mandate to apply the law. The problem is analogous to the confusion that would arise among umpires, players, and fans if the rules of baseball were not clearly understood. Umpires would not all be operating according to the same rules, players would be uncertain about what is expected of them, and fans would likely be critical of umpires for decisions that might or might not reflect proper baseball practice. The disputes among judges, lawyers, and the public which have fuelled an alarming crisis of confidence in the judicial system are not simply differences of opinion about the precise details of judicial reasoning. Rather, the very nature and legitimacy of judicial application of the law—the most basic "rules of the game"—are matters of fundamental disagreement and bitter controversy.[2]

This book seeks to explain the forms of reasoning that judges are expected to follow in applying law if they are to carry out their duty faithfully—that is, if they do what they promised to do when they were sworn in as judges. My account of judicial reasoning does not report on how judges *actually* reason through a decision—it is not a detailed study of judges' underlying motives, states of mind, prejudices, and so on as they decide cases. Rather I describe how judges are *authorized* to apply the law. I explain the *proper* form of judicial reasoning, *prescribed* structure, and *approved* standards.[3] The distinction between actual and authorized judicial behaviour is an important one to keep in mind. Whether or not all judges actually conform to the authorized norms is an extremely important matter, but one that, for the most part, lies outside the domain of this book. The source of much of the confusion over judicial reasoning is what judges are mandated, and are not mandated, to do when applying law. Knowing the "rules" that judges are expected to follow is exactly like knowing the rules of the road or of a game. Until one understands the permissible actions in games such as baseball or chess, it is difficult to make sense of what is going on. Furthermore, only by knowing how the game is supposed to be played can we determine if and when the rules have been broken. The same is true with judicial application of law: we are in no position to assess whether or not judges are doing their job properly unless we understand the "rules" of judicial reasoning.

In the traditional, and long supplanted, view judicial reasoning consisted in mechanical "application of iron rules"—in other words, judges were restricted to straightforward interpretation of precisely formulated, unambiguous imperatives. This may have been an adequate view when judges felt bound to apply statutes according to a strict, literal interpretation. However, it was never true in applying the common law and, as increasing complexity and changing expectations required more "liberal" approaches to interpretation, the traditional mandate became inappropriate for applying legislation. The mechanical application view cannot satisfactorily accommodate the inevitable problematic cases involving grey areas or borderline interpretations, novel situations that raise issues unimagined by legislators, and hard cases that require choosing between competing legal principles. In addition, application of constitutional guarantees such as equality or liberty requires more than the mere deciphering of the literal meaning of their words. The idea that judges are involved in mechanical jurisprudence is no longer, if it ever was, an accurate portrait of their authorized role.[4]

Numerous accounts of judges' role in applying law have replaced the mechanical application view. The fact that application of law is not straightforward and is often controversial has led many to conclude that judicial reasoning is arbitrary and without standards. It is increasingly popular to regard judges as largely unconstrained in their power to shape the law. For example, American rulings on the U.S. Constitution that deviate from the expressed intentions of the original framers have been labelled as a form of "judicial tyranny" and as "judicial imperialism." A recent American Presidential hopeful referred to judges as "dictators in black robes," and a British legislator expressed great fear of what he described as "judicial sabotage" of legislation. It is said that the *Charter of Rights and Freedoms* has made Canadians vulnerable to the risk of "government by judiciary" or, as another critic claimed, has created "a whole new class of potential dictators."[5] Seemingly, with rejection of the strict mechanical application view, the pendulum of professional, academic, and popular opinion has swung to the other extreme—to a view of judicial usurpation of the legislators' law-making authority. Unfortunately, this current perception is as, if not more, unacceptable than the view it replaces. Characterizing judges as tyrants is both cynical and inaccurate—it requires dismissing judges' own explanations of the limits on their role, and it ignores the legal standards that judges are bound to adhere to when they apply a law.

This first chapter offers a critique of those who claim that judges have unbridled power to shape the law, and discusses the dangers posed by this popular view. For much of the rest of the book I present and defend an alternative view of the judicial mandate which characterizes application of law as judicial exercise of *controlled judgment*. In other words, applying law requires the judging of complex, competing positions according to authorized rules—judges are neither at liberty to impose their preferred personal or social values, nor are they engaged in a straightforward deductive task. The ongoing challenge in avoiding the dichotomy between mechanical application and judicial tyranny is to explain how it is that judicial application of law can be controversial, flexible, and go beyond the words in the text, and yet still be said to be *governed* by law. I attempt to show that the rule-governed account of judicial reasoning presented in this book describes the authorized considerations that judges rely upon when applying *a* law in accordance with *the* law.

THE CYNICAL VIEW

The desire for controlled or rule-governed judicial decision making—with a separation of law-making and law-applying authority—arises because of a belief that the principal legislative agency in a democracy should be elected. Yet, the delegation to the judiciary of the authority to apply the law seems to invest judges with incredible power to shape the law. A somewhat exaggerated statement of the magnitude of this power was voiced by Bishop Hoadly in speaking before the English king in 1717: "Whoever hath an absolute authority to interpret any written or spoken laws, it is he who is truly the Law-giver to all intents and purposes, and not the person who first wrote or spoke them."[6]

The courts' significant role in giving texture and substance to the law has become a more recent preoccupation in light of judges' authority to use general constitutional provisions to review and, if necessary, override laws and government actions. As Justice Oliver Wendell Holmes remarked, "the whole power of the state will be put forth, if necessary, to carry out their judgments."[7] Americans began to appreciate this power in the 1950s, with the controversial decisions about school segregation. Laurence Tribe, a prominent American constitutional expert, argues that judicial decisions profoundly affect individuals' daily lives:

> When parents send their children to parochial schools, when men and women buy contraceptives, when workers organize a union, when friends share their intimate secrets in a telephone conversation without fear that others are listening, they enjoy rights and opportunities that would not exist if the Supreme Court had not secured them for us.[8]

In Canada, the public press and legal scholars have documented the dramatically increased judicial powers resulting from the promulgation of the *Charter of Rights and Freedoms*. In contrast with the courts' limited authority under the *Canadian Bill of Rights* to override federal legislation that interfered with basic rights, since 1982 the courts have repeatedly used the *Charter* to strike down offending legislation and government practices. This significantly enhanced authority profoundly changes the balance of power—the courts now possess wide-ranging powers to override the decisions of elected and non-elected government institutions and officials. Two Canadian writers question what they regard as the paradox of creating a charter that transfers power from elected officials to a "small coterie of unelected bureaucrats." Alluding to Lord Acton's famous saying, they ask sarcastically, "why it is that, while power tends to corrupt, the absolute exercise of judicial power not only fails to corrupt, but actually guards against the corrupt exercise of legislative power?"[9]

The charge of judicial tyranny is not that, on occasion, judges exceed their legal authority and decide a case on "extra-legal" grounds. Rather, it alleges a general lack of legal standards that control judicial decision making, especially in constitutional matters. The argument runs roughly as follows: judicial authority to review and interpret laws affords the courts incredible power, and judicial decisions are seemingly not governed by legal standards, therefore we are ruled by an unelected judiciary. An immense and complex body of literature has developed on this issue and it is impossible here to do justice to the many viewpoints. However, two general lines of reasoning are commonly offered as evidence that judicial application of law is not substantially determined on the basis of *legal* considerations. It is frequently suggested that (1) many judicial decisions, especially in constitutional cases, go far beyond what an interpretation of the words or what established precedent will allow, and (2) the other mechanisms for applying law fail to eliminate individual discretion, merely masking an inevitable imposition of judicial political morality. I will briefly consider each of these claims and raise preliminary doubts about the extent to which they sustain the charge of judicial tyranny.

Going Beyond the Words and Case Law

It has been said that "the Constitution is what the judges say it is."[10] Although this remark is potentially misleading, it is certainly true that all rights protected by the constitution are not expressly set out in the document. There is, for example, no explicit statement in either the American or Canadian constitution giving women rights to abortion; yet the Supreme Court in each country has invalidated statutes curtailing access to abortion. These kinds of decisions, reached without *explicit* direction from either the legal document or established case law, are frequently the basis for complaints of judicial tyranny. For example, Canadian political scientist F.L. Morton suggests that judicial differences of opinion on *Charter* issues often emerge from "the judicial philosophy and political orientation of the judges, not from the text." He offers a pair of cases dealing with legalized abortion—*Morgentaler* and *Borowski*—as "a telling example" of the political nature of constitutional adjudication:

> Morgentaler argues the "principles of fundamental justice" include a woman's absolute right to abortion. Borowski argues the same words protect the right to life of the unborn. Which version is right? *Strictly speaking—based on the text and legislative history—neither is correct* [emphasis added]. But if either one can garner the support of at least five justices, it becomes the new law of the land.[11]

Morton's comments imply that, because the explicit meaning of the words and what is known about the drafters' conscious intentions do not indicate an answer, there is no legally defensible resolution of the abortion question and therefore the judges were imposing their own political morality. This suggestion is unfounded since the two justifications for applying the law that Morton mentions—literal textual interpretation and expressed intentions of the law makers—do not exhaust the interpretive guidelines that the judges actually relied upon when deciding these cases. In the *Morgentaler* decision, the Supreme Court did not decide that abortion was an absolute right, but merely that the existing legislative limits failed miserably to secure equal access to abortion. Statistics presented to the Court showed that because of legislative requirements as many as fifty percent of local hospitals could not perform abortions. In addition, inconsistent interpretations of the vague criteria for deciding whether or not an abortion would be permitted meant that women with identical conditions were treated differently depending upon which abortion approval committee heard their request. These and other documented obstacles made abortion "practically unavailable" to many women living outside of larger urban centres. Since these inequities were seen to be "manifestly unfair," the Court concluded that the existing legislation violated principles of fundamental justice.

In the *Borowski* case, the crucial issue was whether or not the right to life which was guaranteed to "everyone" under the *Charter* extended to the unborn. Relying on several recognized interpretive devices, the Court determined that a foetus did fall within the legal meaning of the concept "everyone." These devices included appealing to the accepted interpretations of relevant concepts found in the common law and in connection with the *Canadian Bill of Rights*. In addition, the Court sought an interpretation consistent with other *Charter* sections that also referred to the rights of "everyone." For example, another section states that "everyone" has the right to be informed of the reasons for their arrest and to be informed of their right to instruct a lawyer. Since it would be odd to claim that these rights extended to a foetus, the Court reasoned that "everyone" did not imply the unborn. As these explanations of the *Morgentaler* and *Borowski* cases suggest, Morton has concluded rashly that judicial decisions in controversial areas are political merely because the conclusions are not immediately obvious from the explicit wording of the text.

Similarly, law school dean (and later federal Minister of Justice) Mark MacGuigan describes several decisions as "blatant indulgence in judicial legislation" because "on the basis *solely of a process of pure textual interpretation* the Judicial Committee could not possibly have reached results so far removed from the clearly expressed structure and meaning of the *British North America Act*" [emphasis added]. Here, too, the assumption underlying this charge—that any deviation from a plain meaning reading of constitutional documents is proof of judicial legislation—reflects a questionable, excessively narrow theory of constitutional interpretation.[12]

Another claim of so-called imposition of judicial morality is found in a *Maclean's* editorial immediately following the Supreme Court decision in the above-mentioned *Morgentaler* case. The magazine's editor wrote:

> ... it is now more evident than ever that the justices will not hesitate to apply their personal opinions to *charter* cases that come before them. As an illustration of that fact, Madame Justice Bertha Wilson wrote in supporting the abortion case: "Women's needs and aspirations are only now being translated into protected rights. The right to reproduce or not to reproduce which is in issue in this case is one such right and is properly perceived as an integral part of modern woman's struggle to assert *her* dignity and worth as a human being." Wilson does not cite case law to support that position: she states it as a simple personal opinion.[13]

The editor was doubly wrong in concluding that Madame Justice Wilson was asserting her own personal opinion since she did not refer to case law. Not only are there are other *bona fide* grounds for justifying a legal decision besides precedent, but a review of Wilson's arguments reveals that she based her legal opinion on relevant case law. The statement quoted above comes after several pages of Wilson's justification that the *Charter* right to liberty "guarantees to every individual a degree of autonomy over important decisions intimately affecting their private lives" such as choosing who to marry and whether or not to have an abortion. In support of this general conclusion Wilson quoted various authorities, including three passages by the Chief

Justice. As well, she referred to nine American cases. The particular point referred to in the above editorial is an aside—not central to the legal opinion that Wilson reached—about the historical neglect of women's rights. In making this point, Wilson paraphrased the conclusions of a human rights scholar at the University of Glasgow:

> the history of the struggle for human rights from the eighteenth century on has been the history of men struggling to assert their dignity and common humanity against an overbearing state apparatus. The more recent struggle for women's rights has been a struggle to eliminate discrimination, to achieve a place for women in a man's world, to develop a set of legislative reforms in order to place women in the same position as men (pp. 81-82). It has *not* been a struggle to define the rights of women in relation to their special place in the societal structure and in relation to the biological distinction between the two sexes. Thus, women's needs and aspirations are only now being translated into protected rights.[14]

It is not controversial to suggest that, historically speaking, women's rights have been overlooked, and Wilson is authorized to refer to legal scholars in supporting this observation. This example illustrates, as do the examples previously discussed, a tendency among critics to impute judicial imperialism whenever judges reach a conclusion that is not dictated explicitly by the law's wording or by precedent. As we will see, there are many diverse and sophisticated legal considerations that guide judges in cases where there is no immediately obvious answer.

Inevitable Judicial Choice

Many who recognize that judges are authorized to go beyond plain-meaning interpretations of the words and direct application of established precedent may nevertheless claim that the mechanisms for applying law do not alter the inevitable political nature of judicial decisions. As a Canadian political scientist recently wrote:

> Perhaps we need to reflect on the implications of the fact that Canada's top jurists can hear the same arguments and read much the same material relating to a particular *Charter* case and yet come to opposite conclusions about the claim. One might wonder what this means for the supposed "inalienability" of the rights enshrined in the *Charter*.[15]

In offering his own answer to this rhetorical remark, the author suggests that the Supreme Court has managed to "camouflage its political calculations behind a veil of legal reasoning, which should lead us to suspect that judges may also disguise their personal values in the formalized rhetoric of judicial pronouncements." Put another way, critics claim that even if we accept broader standards of judicial reasoning, it is inevitable that judges will impose their own political will in deciding controversial cases.

In pursuing this line of criticism, a pair of Canadian law professors referred to judicial "balancing" of competing interests when applying the *Charter* as a "rudimentary methodology" that provides "little more than a convenient device enabling the judiciary to place its political thumb upon the illusory constitutional scales of social justice."[16] So, too, Osgoode Hall law professor Patrick Monahan is unconvinced by judges' explicit disavowals of any imposition of political preference.

He insists that attempts to define the content of *Charter* rights, especially rights to equality and liberty, are inherently political. As he says, these rights "contain little or no substantive criteria; they resemble blank slates on which the judiciary can scrawl the imagery of their choice" and, furthermore, the balancing of individual and collective interests is a legislative, not a judicial, task.[17] Academics and the general public are not the only ones to assert judges' political role; some practicing judges share these sentiments. In his book *How Courts Govern America*, Judge Richard Neely concludes that vague concepts such as equal protection and due process can mean just about anything judges want them to mean. The book's main conclusion is: "When courts apply constitutional law we should not think of them as extracting inescapable meanings from the text of the Constitution but rather as imposing the judges' views of public policy to repair the harm done by legislative inertia, administrative stupidity, or self-interest."[18]

These charges of judicial imposition of political will raise two questions: (1) whether judges overstep their authorized role when they decide a case on grounds other than the most defensible *legal* considerations, and (2) whether it is possible for judges, even if they try, to escape making "political" decisions when applying the law.

An authorized political mandate?

Although there is not unanimity on the issue, there is adamant and widely voiced support among judges for the view that they are *not* authorized to go beyond the law, except possibly in the rarest of circumstances. For example, former Canadian Chief Justice Laskin affirmed that his duty as a judge "is only to the law and to the impartial and expeditious administration of justice under the law."[19] A recent survey of Canadian judges came to the following conclusion:

> Canadian judges seem to see themselves as having little or no legitimate law-making role (and even more so outside of the specific context of *Charter* challenges), and as equally disengaged from the promotion of social or political causes. Any image of judges thirsting to use the *Charter* to turn Canadian law and society on its ear is miles wide of the mark.

One judge in the study observed:

> I am only and definitely an interpreter of the law. This is an important part of the principle of the independence of the judiciary; the legislature makes the law and the judges apply it. This is why the judiciary is independent and the legislature isn't, and any judge who goes beyond this is in error. I do not think that the role is changing over time, or that the *Charter* makes any difference to this principle.

Even the minority of judges who claim a law-making capacity do not necessarily contradict the prevailing view. For example, in the above-mentioned study a judge who identified a law-making role commented: "Only in the most unusual of circumstances would I make law; hard cases make bad law." The reference to the expression "hard cases make bad law" suggests tacit admission that going beyond the law is not a legally authorized exercise of the judicial mandate.[20]

Erwin Griswold, former dean of Harvard Law School, offers the traditional, and I believe correct, view of the judicial mandate. This view implies at most a limited authority to go outside the law:

> We pride ourselves that this is a government of laws, a government under law, and most of us are not willing to give this up as a false ideal. Of course, we know full well that law must be administered by men, and that human judgment is an inevitable element in the application of law. But it is one thing to act according to one's personal predilections or choice, and a wholly different thing to come to one's own best conclusion in the light of his understanding of the law as it has been established by statute, decision, tradition, received ideals and standards, and all the other elements that go to make up our legal system. Of course, no one thinks that any judge decides any case in a capricious or curbstone manner. The question is how far and how hard he seeks to be guided by an outside frame of reference, called for convenience "the law," in arriving at his conclusion, rather than focusing his intellectual effort, perhaps unawares, on justifying his conclusion arrived at somehow or other in some other way. The process is assuredly not a merely mechanical one. But it is a tightly guided process. The scope of individual decision is properly narrow. And the place for individual decision is not reached until the guides of the law have been thoroughly explored and evaluated, with detachment as well as skill.[21]

Although judges may, in unusual circumstances, be forced to reach outside the law, it appears that they are not as a matter of course authorized to exercise a political role. Perhaps the more plausible conclusion is that despite their best intentions judges will unavoidably and frequently be forced to make political choices.

An unavoidable political mandate?

The second line of argument for the cynical view of judicial reasoning is rooted in the belief that, regardless of official expectations, judges are *unavoidably* involved in imposing their political values when applying the law. There is much that needs to be said about the extent to which "extra-legal" considerations are inevitable in judicial reasoning. For the moment, I offer a few observations only.

First of all, it is not always clear what counts as evidence of judicial imposition of extra-legal values. For example, it is sometimes suggested that the mere fact that judges resolve a novel situation proves that they have reached outside the law. Alternatively, the notion of judicial law making—which seems to imply that judges have overreached their judicial law-applying mandate—may mean simply that judges exercise their right to review and, if they find them to be invalid, to overturn legislative and executive actions. It is not obvious that either of these situations establishes judicial resort to extra-legal values. Consider the following remarks by Justice (later Chief Justice) Dickson: "the role of the judiciary is not political nor executive nor administrative. It is adjudicative, but there is of necessity an element of law development in the work." As he explains, resolution of legal problems may require that judges "give meaning to the words of a statute or adapt the law to meet changing social conditions and, in that limited sense, perform a law-making function." However, he emphasizes that this creative dimension of the judicial role is not inconsistent with the court's duty "to proceed in the discharge of its adjudicative function in a reasoned way from principled decision and established concept."[22]

Certainly, constitutional provisions are profoundly normative—equality and liberty represent norms or standards for judging the legality of actions, not mere descriptions of legal behaviour. Although these standards are very general and difficult to define, they are not hopelessly open-ended. As implied by Justice Dickson's comments, judges must appeal to other legal standards for guidance in giving substance to these concepts as they decide the cases before them. These other standards include myriad contextual factors, such as the general point of these kinds of fundamental protections, the intention behind the behaviour under review, the effects of the behaviour, and the implications for other standards that may also pertain to the situation. Judges repeatedly claim that these authorized legal considerations, when impartially and sensitively judged, provide the basis for their decisions in difficult cases.

It is also helpful to explain, because it seems somewhat contradictory, how the law can develop over time and still not involve judges in legislative revision or imposition of personal morality. Judicial development of law is possible because the law allows, in fact requires, judges to apply legal standards to particular situations. As conditions change, the correct legal application of the standards may also vary. Suppose, for example, there was a law stating that it was unlawful for parents to expose young children to dangerous situations. Early on in this century, when airplanes were not reliable modes of transportation, a judge might reasonably have concluded that it was dangerous, and therefore unlawful, for parents to take their children on an airplane. Applying the same standard today would almost certainly result in a different conclusion. Has the law changed? Yes, in one respect—it is not illegal to take young children on airplanes, whereas it may have been in the 1920s. In another respect, the legal standards have not changed—it remains the case that it is illegal to expose children to danger. The fact that a judge in the 1920s may conclude that a particular action is illegal and a judge in the 1990s concludes the opposite does not prove, as our hypothetical example reveals, that judges have reached outside the law in coming to these differing conclusions. Rather, the judges may merely have applied correctly the same legal standard to different conditions.

Further evidence of the supposedly unavoidable political nature of judicial reasoning is the fact that some judges will naturally be more favourably inclined to some political theories than others. For example, in recent years much has been made of the fact that judicial decisions may depend on which judges happen to hear the case.[23] Although some judges may be incapable of putting their prejudices aside, merely because a judge happens to be a liberal or a conservative does not mean that his or her political philosophy will determine the outcome of a case. As well, it is important to recognize that personal preference or predisposition is not authorized practice. As former Chief Justice Laskin observes, impartiality is to be "synonymous with judicial office"—not only must judges be impartial with respect to persons, but judges must also purge their minds "of partiality to arguments, a much subtler matter, for every legal mind is apt to have an innate susceptibility to particular classes of arguments."[24] Certainly it is not easy to be open-minded and impartial when judging what the law requires. However, these difficulties do not relieve judges of their responsibility to be as impartial as is humanly possible. Since it is often very difficult for outsiders to distinguish judges who decide in this manner from those who merely rationalize their decisions, unless we are prepared to disregard what most judges are saying, we have reason to accept that, generally speaking, judges endeavour to decide each case in accordance with the law.

It is often implied, incorrectly in my view, that the mere fact that there are competing political values associated with differing sides in a case establishes that judges resolve the case because of their personal preferences for one set of "political" values. We need to distinguish between the implications of a decision and motives or reasons for the decision. Almost by definition, every constitutional decision has political implications—regardless of which way a case is decided, it will have a differential effect on some individuals or groups. Suppose, for example, a court established strict criteria for approving search warrants. This decision would likely be characterized as pro-libertarian because the consequences of the decision favour the freedom of the individual over the state. However, this label implies nothing about the court's justification for its decision—the reasons which brought the judges to their conclusion is a separate matter. If they were fulfilling their judicial responsibilities, they would have decided as they did because their impartial reading of the law protecting individual freedom required this conclusion, not because they wanted to advance libertarian values. Although it is true that many judicial decisions have political consequences, this does not mean that judges are authorized to, or generally do, decide on "political" grounds.[25]

More extended answers to these challenges to a rule-governed account of judicial reasoning will unfold in subsequent chapters. Before proceeding, it is important to consider the dangers of the cynical view of the judicial mandate.

THE JUDICIARY'S ACHILLES HEEL

The judiciary is the Achilles heel of our legal system—paradoxically, the courts are an incredibly influential and yet vulnerable institution. Despite its considerable authority, the judiciary's ability to fulfill its legitimate mandate is easily endangered. Academic, professional, and public opinion play vital roles in safeguarding the proper workings of the judicature. The roots of the court's vulnerability lie in the potential for political interference to compromise its integrity, and ultimately its ability to function. Paradoxically, the cynical view of the judiciary may simultaneously undermine the court's ability to function and fuel judicial usurpation of legislative powers.

Undermining the Judiciary

The power of judicial review gives judges the authority to invalidate laws that exceed a legislature's jurisdiction or that fail to respect fundamental rights. Although this balance of power is a necessary feature of a constitutional democracy, it creates an "adversarial relationship" between the judiciary and the legislature. There is a danger, as in any power-sharing relationship, that one side will attempt to dominate the other. The proper functioning of the judiciary can by undermined by legislators exploiting their power both to circumvent legitimate judicial authority and to appoint judges on the basis of political ideology.[26]

Circumventing judicial authority

Respect for the judiciary is an important impediment to those who seek to undermine legitimate judicial authority. For example, in the 1980s many legislative proposals were put forward to curtail the jurisdiction of the U.S. federal courts. According to Laurence Tribe, their motivation was to circumvent the U.S. Constitution: "the end being nothing less than the *de facto* reversal—by means far less burdensome than those required for a constitutional amendment—of several highly controversial Supreme Court rulings dealing with such matters as abortion, school prayer, and busing." Faced with court decisions of which they do not approve, governments are more likely to attempt to circumvent or overrule the decisions if the public has a low estimation of judicial competence and integrity. Another writer suggests that U.S. courts have been intimidated from upholding individual rights that are legitimately, if not explicitly, grounded in the Constitution out of a fear that these decisions will be seen as instances of an unelected judiciary running roughshod over "the will of the people." At stake is the survival of judicial review of legislative and executive action by an independent judiciary entrusted to enforce constitutionally entrenched rights.[27]

In Canada, legislatures have considerable authority to overrule judicial decisions on the Constitution without following formal amendment procedures. This arises because of the "notwithstanding" clause (section 33) in the *Charter*, which gives federal and provincial governments considerable power to exclude legislation from *Charter* review. It was initially expected that exercise of this power would normally attract such political opposition that it would be invoked only in extreme situations. Legislators now appear less reluctant to use this power than was first thought. This clause was invoked several times in the first decade of the *Charter*. If the public comes to perceive judicial decisions as arbitrary fiats by non-elected officials, then public pressure—the intended safeguard against excessive use of the notwithstanding clause—may trigger invocation of the clause. Should this power be exercised widely, the effect would be to destroy the very notion of entrenched rights. Constitutions are intended to protect fundamental rights against the whims and insensitivities of the popular mood. It would be gravely unjust if an unwarranted, cynical view of judicial decision making created a political climate that undermined the rights that the constitution and the courts were empowered to safeguard.

Politicizing judicial appointments

The perception that judges are largely unrestrained in the exercise of their duties is pernicious because it fuels calls for partisan appointment of judges by government officials and the resulting expectation that judges will do what their benefactors want them to do.

There appears to be considerable expectation that American judges will support the interests of those who appoint them. In a *Time* article following a 1988 decision on the constitutionality of special prosecutors, the U.S. Supreme Court was said to be acting in a "frustratingly independent" manner by failing to do the "President's bidding." The decision was viewed as a "sweeping repudiation of the White House position" and particularly galling since "the ruling was written by Chief Justice William Rehnquist, the man Reagan had chosen for the court's top job." *Time* also reported that administration officials would regard as ungrateful Reagan-appointed judges who failed to support the President's position. Similarly, the 1987 nomination of Robert Bork as U.S. Supreme Court Justice was seen as a declaration of the Reagan administration's intention to impose its view of morality on law. Significantly, the Senate's somewhat surprising rejection of Bork's nomination was attributed largely to widespread public support for judicial integrity.[28]

Similar aspersions have been cast on the independence of the Canadian judiciary, prompting former Chief Justice Laskin to issue a stirring rebuttal:

> I have to be more sad than angry to read of an insinuation that we are "acting as spear carriers for the federal prime minister" or to read of a statement attributed to a highly respected member of the academic community that "the provinces must have a role in the appointment of members of the Supreme Court in order to ensure that they have confidence that it can fairly represent the interests of the provincial governments as well as any federal government." ... I owe no allegiance, as a judge, to any person or to any interests; my duty, as I have already said, is only to the law and to the impartial and expeditious administration of justice under law. ... Are there responsible persons in our society who see the judges of our courts as spokesmen for special interests, as representatives of some public or private authority or agency? Do they see us as partisan arbitrators rather than as independent judges? ... I know of no better way to subvert our judicial system, no better way to destroy it than to give currency to the view that the judiciary must be a representative agency.[29]

The "ideological screening" of American judges seems to assume that judges will decide not on the basis of law, but in view of their liberal or conservative leaning. This "cynical understanding of the rule of law" is thought to cheapen the judicial process: "More complex questions need to be asked to determine what, besides location on the left/right continuum, goes toward making a wise judge."[30] Although Canadian Supreme Court appointments have not been reduced to political tug-of-wars between the "right" and the "left" as they have been in the United States, there is a history of political feuding between the federal and provincial governments. The *Charter* may increase Canadian politicians' inclination to seek out judicial candidates with "appropriate" political and personal convictions.[31] Significantly, the authors of a recent study of Canadian judges' decision patterns discourage adoption of the U.S. practice of "nakedly partisan attempts" to control Supreme Court decisions by "strategic judicial appointments" because this practice would violate the principles of judicial independence and impartiality. They warn, however, that "Courts that act politically will come to be treated politically."[32]

Usurping Legislative Powers

A second dangerous consequence of widespread acceptance of the judiciary's supposed political role is increased expectations of judges that they should effect social justice. Rolf Sartorius warned twenty-five years ago:

the prevailing view that judges are legislators, were it to be taken seriously by judges, could become self-fulfilling. For judges could generally resort to their own personal preferences in deciding hard cases, could acknowledge that they were doing so, and all this could come to be accepted both by the legal community and the public at large.

Sartorius regarded the prevailing view as mistaken and dangerous. In a similar vein, John Agresto laments the American situation: "To the degree that we have reached the point where judges can legislate, judge, and execute their opinions autonomously, unchecked, the situation is manifestly no longer tolerable."[33]

An example of the pressure on the courts to make political decisions arose over the 1975 Supreme Court of Canada decision in *Murdoch v. Murdoch*. In this case, the Court ruled that Mrs. Murdoch's efforts, which included working for many years with her husband to build a successful ranching operation, did not entitle her to any share of the "family" business. National reaction to the unfairness of the situation was vicious; the judiciary, as the bearer of the news, bore the brunt of the abuse. The Court became the scapegoat for the failure of existing provincial family law to protect women in Mrs. Murdoch's predicament. As one reviewer put it:

While perhaps legally it is the proper function of the Supreme Court of Canada to apply the law as it is, even if it is harsh and inequitable, and to leave it to government to legislate an end to any injustice, nevertheless, the response of the general public to severe judgments is to criticize the Courts for a lack of humanity.[34]

Although court decisions which enforce unfair laws are regrettable, they may be a necessary evil. We cannot have it both ways—the requirements of judicial reasoning which constrain the tyranny of judges who would wish to impose their personal morality on our legal system also curb judges' ability to reverse unjust legislation. As one writer remarked, the rule of law "undoubtedly restrains power, but it also prevents power's benevolent exercise." If democracy—understood as rule by elected officials— is to be maintained, then we must not expect too much or, for that matter, too little from the judiciary. The challenge, as alluded to in the Achilles metaphor, is for double-edged vigilance—to safeguard the exercise of legitimate authority while restricting the exercise of abusive power. In *The Paradoxes of Freedom*, Sidney Hook asks: "If the Court is to serve as the keeper of the community's conscience, who is to keep the Court's conscience?" As it currently stands, thoughtful assessment of judicial performance is severely hampered by widespread disagreement and deep confusion within the legal community about judges' proper role. When exaggerated and unfounded reactions pass for informed evaluations, respect withers and the integrity of the institution is endangered. Recommendations to politicize the judiciary or to institute rigid legal standards are not cures. The former likely undermines the rule of law and the latter likely handcuffs it. If we are to preserve, let alone to improve upon, our imperfect mechanism for applying the law, we must resist proposals that will destroy judicial independence and impartiality. The solution, it would appear, is to "take seriously the judicial duty to uphold the law"—to reaffirm and reinforce the idea that judges are to apply law according to the law. However, we cannot adequately assess the merits of this approach until we understand the authorized "rules" of judicial reasoning and their power to control judicial decision making.[35]

This book is an attempt to give definition and lend credence to the claims made repeatedly by judges and by others that the judicial mandate is to apply law according to the law. I argue that a rule-governed account of judicial reasoning represents faithfully what is generally regarded as *authorized* judicial practice. In addition, I will show how this account accommodates three somewhat paradoxical features of our legal system: (1) that judges are to apply a law according to the law (i.e., judicial decision making is to be controlled by legal standards); (2) that the law is flexible (i.e., the law can evolve over time in rule-governed ways); and (3) that rule-governed judicial decisions can be controversial (i.e., judges are required to decide on complex matters and we should expect differences of opinion, even among impartial judges).

2
Rules of Application

The central thesis of this book is that judicial reasoning is a rule-governed enterprise. In other words, judges are expected to abide by relatively well-established rules when applying the law. These "rules" or "normative standards" are a complex set of legally sanctioned canons, conventions, doctrines, maxims, policies, precepts, presumptions, and principles that provide the legal grounds for deciding how a law is to be applied in a specific case.[36] As we will see, judges must assess varied, flexible, and often competing legal standards in deciding what the law requires. Before we can appreciate how these rules govern judicial reasoning, we must be clear about the general structure and nature of arguments used to justify judicial decisions. This is where I begin the discussion of judicial reasoning. I then introduce British legal philosopher H.L.A. Hart's distinction between primary and secondary rules of law and consider a particular kind of secondary rule, called *secondary rules of application*. I suggest that, in applying law, judges are governed by secondary rules of application which constitute standards for identifying and adjudicating among acceptable reasons for a decision. In other words, judicial judgments must be justified by reasons whose legal validity and weight can be established by criteria set out in rules of application. Because of their importance, I explore in some detail the different types of rules of application. Finally, I argue that we cannot account for judicial reasoning even in so-called easy cases without reference, at least implicitly, to these secondary rules.

STRUCTURE AND NATURE OF JUDICIAL ARGUMENTS

Judicial decisions are generally depicted as requiring the weighing of multiple reasons for and against a particular application of a law. As Hart suggests, "judges marshal in support of their decisions a plurality of such considerations [policies, principles, standards] which they regard as jointly sufficient to support their decision, although each separately would not be. Frequently these considerations conflict, and courts are forced to balance or weigh them and determine priorities among them."[37]

Quebec Association of Protestant School Boards v. Attorney-General of Quebec, a case concerning the right of Quebec parents to send their children to English-speaking public schools, exemplifies the basic structure of judicial reasoning. In an effort to preserve French-language traditions, the Quebec government had enacted legislation requiring that children of new immigrants attend school in French. Several parents and a number of English-speaking school boards argued that this legislation infringed on rights to which parents were entitled under the then newly established *Charter of Rights and Freedoms*. In discussing whether the Quebec law was a reasonable limitation on these *Charter* rights, Quebec Chief Justice Deschenes summarized the government's eleven arguments and the nine arguments put forward by the parents and the school boards.[38] These pro and con arguments were based on a variety of grounds including the authority to interpret constitutional documents broadly, the presumed intentions both of the Quebec legislators and of the federal Parliament, the basic rights of citizenship, the legitimacy of the purpose underlying the statute at issue, and the likely consequences if the restrictions were rescinded. Although most of the arguments presented were independent of each other, some were interrelated, and others countered opposing arguments. In weighing the arguments, the Quebec Chief Justice noted his commitment to undertake "the most objective examination possible" of the arguments on both sides "in light of the criteria which the court has extracted from the foreign and Canadian jurisprudence." In the end, he concluded that the Quebec government's arguments were inadequate to warrant the restriction and of insufficient force to meet the burden of proof, set out in Section 1 of the *Charter,* that limitations on rights be "demonstrably justified." In view of these findings, the Court struck down the offending sections of the language law. (The Quebec government subsequently introduced new legislation that was expressly exempted from the *Charter* under the "notwithstanding" provision.)

This type of justification has been referred to as *conductive reasoning*—where the arguments are conducive to a conclusion, but do not deductively entail it. The conductive structure of judicial reasoning applies in both difficult and relatively straightforward cases. Lawyers for each side have primary responsibility for providing the arguments that judges must assess and weigh. In fact, judges are generally reluctant to address an issue that has not been argued before them and they are expected to reach a conclusion in light of the arguments presented. An easy case would be one in which either there are no legally valid reasons to support a decision in favour of one of the sides or the reasons are clearly outweighed by arguments for the opposing side. Of course, judges are rarely asked to consider cases in which one side has no reasons, or relatively weak reasons, for contesting a case.[39]

In building a case for applying a law one way or another, lawyers and judges are authorized to rely on three kinds of arguments, or *modes of reasoning*. One kind of argument—*reasoning from interpretive guidelines*—appeals to the meaning or interpretation of a law. Put another way, some arguments will be based on how the meaning of the words used in a law are to be interpreted. A second kind of argument—*reasoning from prior cases*—appeals to the relevant similarity of previous cases to the present case. This implies that some arguments will establish whether or not a decision in a prior case sets a precedent for the present case. The final kind of argument—*reasoning from principle*—appeals to the legal acceptability of adopting a proposed principle. Arguments based on principle involve evaluating the implications or consequences of a decision in light of established legal standards.

More will be said about these three modes of reasoning in later chapters. For the moment it is sufficient to appreciate that rules of application regulate how various legal arguments may be justified and the importance or legal weight that each argument deserves. Also, because it is a potential source of confusion, it is important to appreciate that the modes of reasoning are distinguished by the different purposes they serve, and not by virtue of unique sets of rules that apply exclusively to each mode of reasoning. In fact, there is considerable overlap in the sources of legal argument. For example, it is appropriate in all three modes of reasoning to consider decisions reached in previous cases. The particular use to which previous judicial decisions is put will determine the mode of reasoning: the point in considering earlier cases may be to decide on the meaning of words (reasoning from interpretive guidelines), to determine whether cases are relevantly similar (reasoning from prior cases), or to evaluate the legal acceptability of a proposed decision (reasoning from principle).

SECONDARY RULES OF APPLICATION

In his landmark work, *The Concept of Law*, Hart describes law as the interaction of two levels of rules, *primary* and *secondary*.[40] Primary rules specify citizens' obligations within the legal system. These are what lay people typically refer to as "laws," and include rules that prohibit theft and use of violence, or require that motorists drive on the right-hand side of the road and that certain stores remain closed on Sunday. Secondary rules, which are directed primarily at legislators, judges, and other officials within the legal system, regulate how primary (and other secondary) rules are recognized, changed, and adjudicated. Hart discusses three kinds of secondary rules. *Rules of recognition* specify the criteria by which persons within the legal community can identify *bona fide* laws. For example, in Canada, statutes are to be recognized as law once they have been signed by the Governor General, and contracts and wills are recognized as valid legal documents only if signed and witnessed in the proper fashion. *Rules of change*, such as those regulating the steps involved in having legislation pass through Parliament, specify procedures for introducing new laws and amending existing laws. *Rules of adjudication* focus on establishing mechanisms by which disputes over alleged violations of rules are to be settled. Hart offers as examples rules of adjudication that establish the court system, regulate the appointment of court officials, and prescribe courtroom procedures. He says little, however, about the rules that judges are expected to follow in deciding how a given primary rule *applies* in a specific case. Explicating this category of secondary rules of adjudication, which I call *rules of application,* is the main focus in this book.[41]

Whether they involve reasoning from interpretive guidelines, prior cases, or principle, all legal arguments are governed by secondary rules of application. Judges and other officials are expected to justify application of the law according to criteria authorized by these rules. Rules of application are found in various legal sources—in statutes, conventions of judicial practice, classic legal works, and judicial opinions. Although the rules for, say, interpretive arguments will differ in detail from those for arguments based on precedent, three general types of rules of application underlie all three modes of judicial reasoning. I refer to these different rules of application as *argument-validating rules, argument-verifying rules,* and *argument-weighting rules.* The need for the first type of rule of application arises because not every conceivable argument for a decision is legally acceptable: judges must differentiate legally acceptable reasons from the universe of possible reasons for a decision. Argument-*validating* rules provide the criteria for identifying *bona fide* legal arguments. Judges must also know how to verify the truth of claims that are made in fleshing out an argument. Argument-*verifying* rules provide criteria for establishing the legal veracity of claims. Finally, since judges will be confronted with arguments for and against a particular decision, there is need for argument-*weighting* rules, which provide criteria for assessing the relative strength of competing positions.

OVERVIEW OF PRIMARY AND SECONDARY RULES

Secondary Rules	{ Rules of Recognition Rules of Change Rules of Adjudication Rules of Application	{ Argument-Validating Rules Argument-Verifying Rules Argument-Weighting Rules

Primary Rules

Argument Validation

If judicial application of the law is not to be arbitrary or simply discretionary, judges must be limited to only legally sanctioned reasons for their decisions. There will be many "social" or "personal" reasons that judges are not authorized to rely upon when justifying their legal decisions. In order for reasons to be legally sanctioned they must originate from accepted sources of argument—agreed starting points from which valid arguments are developed. Argument-validating rules are the secondary rules of application that provide criteria for recognizing reasons as valid legal grounds for deciding a case. Validity refers to the legitimacy of offering a particular kind of argument as a legal argument; it does not refer to claims about the formal logic of an argument (that a conclusion is necessarily implied by the premises of a deductive argument). In other words, an accepted rule provides the legal anchor for, or establishes the legal status of, an argument. Unless an argument is grounded in law, judges cannot consider it as a reason for deciding a case.[42] For example, conclusions reached in a prior case are grounds for resolving disputes in subsequent cases. This rule of argument validity is part of the doctrine of *stare decisis* (the policy that courts must abide by certain precedents). Another rule, also related to the doctrine of precedent, recognizes the validity of invoking decisions in other jurisdictions to guide the instant case. This rule authorizes judges to look to decisions from courts in other provinces or other countries. Conversely, judges are not authorized to argue on the basis of their personal religious convictions, because there is no rule validating this as a *bona fide* legal argument. In fact, as I suggested in the last chapter, rules on judicial impartiality prohibit resort to these kinds of self-serving arguments. Of course, there are many kinds of arguments within each of the three modes of reasoning to which judges are authorized to appeal in applying the law. The nature and range of valid legal arguments are examined in the chapters on each of the modes of reasoning.

Argument Verification

Other secondary rules of application provide criteria for verifying the claims implied by a legal argument. These argument-verifying rules regulate the means by which the conclusions ascribed to a given argument may be substantiated. For example, while appeal to a statute's purpose is a legally valid argument for interpreting a law in a particular way, not any manner of speculation about that purpose is acceptable. In Britain, and to a lesser extent in Canada, there is a convention that individual politicians' statements about what they were attempting to achieve by a particular piece of legislation are not accepted as evidence of a statute's purpose. Rather, judges are authorized to look to various other sources, including the preamble and any titles used in an act, as evidence of the legislative purpose. Reluctance in some jurisdictions to accept politicians' statements as evidence does not indicate that these jurisdictions consider legislative purpose invalid, but rather that the partisan nature of politics is cause to discount the reliability of politicians' statements. A further example of argument-verifying rules is the admissibility in appeal courts of economic and sociological studies—referred to as Brandeis briefs—to establish claims about existing conditions. Another rule provides authority to take "judicial notice"—to recognize certain propositions as true, without providing any proof, because the claims are accepted as common knowledge.

Although judges rely upon and are bound by argument-verifying rules, these rules are not always explicit. That is, in any given case, judges will not cite all the rules that their arguments rely upon and all the implied rules need not have been previously articulated. Certainly many ordinary language conventions and definitions are implied in determining the "plain meaning" of words and yet they may not be explicitly cited. If pressed, judges would likely cite specific linguistic conventions as evidence for their claim, or they might refer to their authority to take judicial notice of noncontroversial facts.

Argument Weight

The third type of secondary rule of application—argument-weighting rules—establishes criteria for weighing the strength of competing positions. Whereas validity refers to an argument's status as a *legal* argument, weight refers to the relative force or the extent of influence it is accorded. Of course, arguments that are not legally valid cannot correctly be ascribed any legal weight. Assessing the strength of each side's position requires establishing the relative force of competing arguments. At least four factors determine this calculation: (1) the relative weight or legal importance of the *rule,* or of the implied *standard*, upon which the argument is grounded; (2) the magnitude of the *implications* in the given case for the implied standard; (3) the degree of conviction about the *truth* of claims supporting an argument; and (4) whether the minimal requirement about onus of support for one side or the other has been met.

Weight of the rule or implied standard

It was suggested earlier that the validity of every argument is established by a secondary rule. There is, for example, a presumption when interpreting statutes against interfering with personal liberty. In other words, in situations where legislation is ambiguous, judges should lean towards the interpretation that protects the freedom of the individual. Implicit in this rule of argument validity is a relative weighing of importance: other things being equal, preference will be given to individual freedom over the state's interests. However, an interpretation of a statute based on the unambiguous meaning of the terms would typically override an interpretation based on an interpretive presumption. This is because an explicit verbal expression of specific intention has greater interpretive weight than a generalized assumption about legislative intentions. Similar weighting occurs in other modes of reasoning. For example, in reasoning from prior cases weighting is determined in many ways: the *ratio* (i.e., the specific issues settled by the case) may be binding on subsequent judges, whereas *obiter dicta* (i.e., opinions expressed which are not necessary to settling the case) merely have persuasive authority; the higher a court is in the judicial hierarchy, other things being equal, the more authority its decisions carry; a unanimous court opinion carries more weight than a split decision, and so on.

Implied in all primary rules are legal standards—desired states or values that a legal system promotes or protects. For example, laws against murder are intended to safeguard human life, and traffic regulations are intended to promote efficiency of movement and public safety. The relative weight of different standards creates a hierarchical ordering of legal values—the fact that the law authorizes more severe punishments for murderers than for thieves indicates that human life is considered of more important legal value than personal property. Similarly, the freedom to practice one's religion is generally seen to be a more highly valued legal right than the freedom to engage in certain leisure activities—say, playing with a frisbee. Weighting of standards is often implied by constitutional structures: the principle of legislative supremacy means that, in general, standards established by statutory provision will supersede those embedded in judicial decisions, and constitutional paramountcy means that constitutional provisions will be afforded greater weight than statutory provisions. Notice, for example, that arguments based on religious freedoms had less weight prior to the *Charter*, when their protection was not entrenched in the Constitution. The respective weight of conflicting standards is implicit in many court decisions. For example, the U.S. ruling that freedom of expression would yield if there was "clear and present danger" to public safety established that under certain circumstances the physical safety of others has precedence over individual expression.

Implications for the standard

An argument's weight also depends on the degree to which the implied standard is violated or respected in a given situation. For example, an argument would be more compelling (i.e., have greater weight) if the implications for a legal standard were extensive (say, involving complete denial of religious freedoms for large sectors of society) than if the implications were relatively trivial (say, involving a minor inconvenience for the exercise of the religious freedom of a small group). Implicit in this distinction is a rule of argument weight to the effect that, other things being equal, judges should prefer the alternative that most advances legal values. This assessing of the relative implications for legal values is implied by the *Charter*'s "reasonable limits" clause (section 1), which allows that constitutional rights can be overridden provided there is a compelling justification. This calculation was employed in justifying the Federal Court decision in *International Fund for Animal Welfare v. The Queen* which upheld the rationing of media access to the ice floes during the seal hunt off the east coast of Canada. The Court determined that the relatively modest restriction on the *Charter* freedom of information (a limited number of media were allowed access during set periods) was offset by the significant economic disruption to the seal harvest and by the risks to the safety of participants caused by media planes landing on ice floes and disrupting seal herds. The consequences for the fundamental value of freedom of information were judged less severe than were the consequences for other, less fundamental values. As this example illustrates, in weighting the force of competing arguments judges have to assess both the relative weight of the standards at issue and the extent to which these standards are compromised in the particular instance.[43]

Judicial decisions based on the implications for the standard are often erroneously construed to imply a ranking of the importance of the standards themselves. To illustrate, let us take a case where a reason *for* a decision is to protect religious freedoms, and a reason *against* the decision is to protect economic freedoms. Assume, for the sake of argument, that both freedoms are constitutionally entrenched and regarded to be of approximately equal weight. It would be most appropriate to assess the *relative* weight of the two arguments in the case by considering their implications for each standard. If it was decided that the extent of infringement to religious freedoms would be significantly less than the infringement to economic freedoms, the latter argument would have greater weight. This decision, however, would not imply that the judges regard economic freedoms *per se* as more important in law than religious freedoms. It would merely mean that, in this case, the negative implications for one standard were judged to be less severe than the implications for another, equally important standard. Occasions often arise where a small affront to a fundamental principle will be outweighed by the significance of the consequences for an admittedly less fundamental standard. This occurs because no standard has absolute force—if the consequences are sufficiently extreme, even the most cherished legal value may be legitimately overridden.

Degree of certainty

A third factor affecting the weight of an argument is the degree of certainty about the implications for the standard in a given case. If it is questionable whether or not a particular consequence follows, then an argument is less compelling than if these conclusions are clearly supported. As Justice Learned Hand wrote in *Dennis v. United States*, "In each case [courts] must ask whether the gravity of the 'evil,' *discounted by its improbability*, justifies such invasion of free speech as is necessary to avoid the danger" [emphasis added]. Similarly, in *Operation Dismantle v. The Queen*, groups hoping to stop the government from testing cruise missiles claimed that because the testing increased the risk of nuclear war, the government's decision violated the security of persons guaranteed by the *Charter* (section 7). Former Chief Justice Dickson did not accept the appeal because the claimed connection between the testing and the risk of nuclear war was based on conjecture and hypothesis.[44] The reason for considering degree of certainty should be apparent: other things being equal, it would not be rational to attach equivalent weight to two sets of consequences when it is uncertain if one set of consequences will actually arise. Imagine, for example, that a judge must decide whether to allow the government to cut back on established medical services in order to reallocate funds to new types of medical services. Suppose that it could be reliably estimated that cutting back on the existing services would likely result in an additional one hundred deaths per year, and that it could only be surmised that the proposed alternatives might save one hundred lives per year. The certainty of the loss of lives would weigh more heavily than the possible saving of the same number of lives in justifying allocation of medical funds.

Onus of support

A final consideration in weighing competing positions is whether the required onus of support for a position has been met. By and large, a decision in favour of a position is warranted if that position is more strongly supported than any other. However, on some occasions a greater burden of proof is required to justify a finding in favour of one of the parties. Criminal cases are the best-known exceptions to the general rule that it is sufficient that one side provide stronger support than the other. Because of the legal principle of presumption of innocence in criminal matters, it is not sufficient that the Crown establish that its account is more plausible than other theories; the Crown must establish beyond a reasonable doubt that events occurred as it alleges. Similarly, in other areas of law, a greater onus of support is sometimes placed on one party than on the other. For example, the *Charter* requires that parties seeking to place limits on constitutional rights establish that their position is "demonstrably" justified. As we saw in *Quebec Association of Protestant School Boards v. Attorney-General of Quebec*, numerous arguments were offered in support of both the parents' English-language education rights and the Quebec government's right to protect the province's Francophone heritage. In view of the *Charter* onus on those who would limit constitutional rights, the judge upheld the parents' position because the government failed to establish a clear preponderance of support for its position.

Although I have identified three types of secondary rules of application—validating, verifying, and weighting rules—in actual practice, these rules are often not distinguished. A single "rule" of application may specify several types of criteria. Consider the interpretive approach known as the "golden meaning" rule. An early formulation of the rule states that in interpreting legal documents:

> the grammatical and ordinary sense of the words is to be adhered to, unless that would lead to some absurdity, or some repugnance or inconsistency with the rest of the instrument, in which case the grammatical and ordinary sense of the words may be modified, so as to avoid that absurdity and inconsistency, but no farther.[45]

Implicit in this master rule are all three types of rules, including at least five criteria of *argument validity*. In interpreting the meaning of legislation, judges are authorized to rely on (1) the accepted grammatical use of words and (2) the ordinary meaning of words, and to consider exceptions in the event of (3) possible absurd consequences, (4) possible repugnant consequences, and (5) possible inconsistency with the rest of the document. In addition, it can be inferred that grammatical and linguistic conventions would be accepted as grounds for *argument verification*. Also, two criteria of *argument weight* are implied: (1) arguments which avoid absurdity, repugnancy, or inconsistency have priority over arguments which adhere to ordinary meaning but result in absurdity, repugnancy, or inconsistency, and (2) ordinary-meaning arguments have priority over other forms of argument (e.g., arguments from the presumed purpose of the legislation).

ROLE OF SECONDARY RULES OF APPLICATION

Not everyone agrees that it is necessary in explaining judicial reasoning to refer to secondary rules of application. It is commonly thought that, in many situations, the actions covered by a law are clear and uncontroversial and that applying the law involves recognizing whether or not a case falls within the explicit scope or meaning of a law. In other words, judicial decisions, at least in easy cases, can be deduced directly from a primary rule and the facts, without recourse to secondary rules of application. We can see the inadequacy of this rival account of judicial reasoning by considering *Daniels and Daniels v. White & Sons and Tarbard*, a case put forward by Scottish legal philosopher Neil MacCormick as an example of an easy case that can be decided without reference to secondary rules.[46]

MacCormick argues that the application of the law to the facts of the case can be reduced to the following form: In any case, if certain facts occur, then the law has been broken. In the case in question, the specified facts have occurred; therefore, in this case, the law has been broken. More particularly, the relevant statute, the *Sale of Goods Act* (1893), holds sellers liable to purchasers for damages resulting from the sale of goods that are not of suitable, or "merchantable" quality. (This is the primary rule.) In the case in question, a pub owner sold a bottle of contaminated lemonade to Mr. Daniels. (These are the facts.) At trial, the pub owner was found liable for damages stemming from the sale goods of "non-merchantable" quality. (This is the decision.) This account of the application of the law can be summarized in the following deductive argument:

Major premise:	Sellers are liable to purchasers for damages resulting from the sale of goods that are not of merchantable quality.
Minor premise:	A pub owner sold Mr. Daniels a bottle of contaminated lemonade.
Conclusion:	Therefore, the pub owner is liable to Mr. Daniels for damages resulting from the sale of the contaminated lemonade.

This apparent explanation of judicial reasoning without reference to secondary rules of application is deceptive. In completing the deductive argument, MacCormick builds into his major premise an interpretation of "goods of non-merchantable quality" which includes contaminated lemonade. He cites a prior case as a reason for accepting this interpretation. Although characterizing contaminated lemonade as goods of non-merchantable quality may be entirely justified, it assumes that the interpretation of the *Sale of Goods Act* established in the prior case (cited by MacCormick) is relevant, even persuasive, in this instance. This assumption is legally warranted only because of an implicit authorization to use prior interpretations in subsequent applications. In short, a secondary rule about interpreting primary rules is required to justify accepting the proffered interpretation of non-merchantable goods. What is more, additional secondary rules are required to establish that all of the other material facts of the case fall within the primary rule. Consider, for example, the implicit assertion that Mr. Daniels is a "purchaser" under the legal meaning of the term. This is a plausible legal conclusion if we recognize a secondary rule about words being presumed to carry their ordinary-language meaning. However, it is possible that an interpretive provision in the *Act* had established a specific legal meaning for the term "purchaser." For example, the statute may distinguish personal from commercial buyers and, if Mr. Daniels had been acting on behalf of a company, he might not have qualified as a "purchaser." Alternatively, "goods" under the meaning of the *Act* could refer solely to non-edible products. These examples reveal MacCormick's disguised assumptions about the basis for claiming that the specific facts of the case meet each of the conditions contained in the statute. Secondary rules of application provide the necessary legal grounds for concluding that Mr. Daniels qualifies as a "purchaser," that contaminated lemonade qualifies as "non-merchantable goods," and so on. A legal rule is recognized as correctly covering a set of particular situations only if we accept implicitly that second-level rules regulate the scope of coverage, or the *denotation*, of the primary rule. As Hart recognizes: "All rules involve recognizing or classifying particular cases as instances of general terms."[47]

Failure to appreciate the role of secondary rules in deciding whether or not the particulars of a case fall within the authorized meaning of a law encourages naive beliefs about the inherent meaning of a rule. A surprising range of actions can be subsumed under, or excluded from, a rule depending on the understandings ascribed to the categories created by the rule. In one case, for example, a telephone qualified within the category of "telegraph" because the law regulating telegraphs was interpreted to include "all apparatus for transmitting messages or other communications by means of electric signals."[48] Consider also, the implications of introducing a law stipulating that a human foetus will thereafter be understood to be a "person." Although all existing primary rules referring to persons remain unchanged, this new secondary rule of interpretation would alter the range of their application to include unborn babies. These examples suggest why one writer remarked that "the meaning of the terms of a legislative provision does not inhere in the provision itself. Judges do not discover meaning for the words; they assign meaning to the words."[49] Assigning legal meaning, if it is not to be arbitrary, must be regulated by second-order rules.

The extensive role of secondary rules in controlling the meaning ascribed to primary rules is exemplified in the Supreme Court ruling in *Hunter v. Southam*, which considered whether a search of a newspaper office infringed *Charter* protections against unreasonable search and seizure.[50] Resolution of the case hinged on the meaning of the vague term "unreasonable." The judges put forward three criteria for determining reasonableness: the authorization must be made before a search is conducted, the authorizing official must be impartial, and there must be an adequate basis for suspecting that a search is warranted. Significantly, these criteria are not explicitly mentioned in the *Charter* but were explicated and justified by resorting to an accepted interpretive guideline which authorizes consideration of the recognized purposes of the law in applying constitutional provisions. The Court reasoned that the purposes of creating protection against unreasonable search could be achieved only if decisions to authorize searches were made beforehand by impartial officials acting on informed opinion. Thus, the secondary rule of application, not any explicit reference in the primary rule or the purely personal preferences of the judges, provided the Court with the grounds for concluding what unreasonable search should be taken to mean under the *Charter*.

It may be somewhat surprising to learn that many laws are deliberately cast in vague or general terms. Narrowly prescribed laws often fail to cover many unanticipated or novel situations that inevitably arise. The Fifth Amendment of the U.S. Constitution contains a good example of the disadvantages of excess specificity. It states: "In suits at common law, where the value in controversy shall exceed *twenty dollars*, the right of trial by jury shall be preserved" [emphasis added]. In 1791, when the amendment was ratified, twenty dollars represented a significant amount of money; clearly, it is now a trivial sum. If this amendment were taken at face value, individuals could clog the courts by demanding jury trials where the value of the dispute is inconsequential. The benefits of flexibility are not limited to constitutional documents. The widely recognized strength of the common law, where the explicit wording of its rules is not fixed, lies in its adaptability to changing situations. It is useful to imagine laws as having a *specificity threshold*—an equilibrium where the advantages of further specification of what would fall within the scope of the rule is offset by the disadvantages of rigidity. In drafting law, legislators must balance the benefits of precise rules (e.g., predictability, uniformity, certainty, consistent application) against the counterproductive consequences of restrictive rules (e.g., becoming dated, applying rigidly in situations where this is undesirable or self-defeating, increased volume of rules needed). For example, in the previous chapter mention was made of a hypothetical law prohibiting parents from exposing their children to dangerous situations. In place of this general standard, legislators might have enumerated the many specific situations that they deemed to be dangerous for children (e.g., hang gliding, river rafting, bungie jumping). This latter approach would be less efficient and, given changing conditions, in constant need of revision. Clearly, secondary rules of application provide necessary and useful direction for judges when interpreting laws in unanticipated or ambiguous situations.

Thus far, this rule-guided account of judicial reasoning has both explained the open-ended nature of law by showing that application of the law is not limited to the explicitly designated extension of primary rules, and suggested how judicial decisions are grounded in three types of secondary rules of application. However, judicial reasoning is legitimately characterized as a rule-governed practice only if these secondary rules control judicial decisions. Otherwise, judges are free to make up arguments as they go along or to exercise broad discretion in deciding which secondary rules to use in applying a law. As we saw in Chapter 1, the frequency of controversial decisions and the apparent magnitude of judicial discretion cause many to doubt that judicial reasoning can legitimately be described as rule governed. These issues are taken up in the next chapter.

3
Controlled Judgment

Judges commonly disagree in difficult cases. The frequent occurrence of controversy seems incompatible with a rule-governed explanation of judicial reasoning. The following challenge is frequently heard: If judges are merely applying the law—as opposed to making up the law—why are many of their decisions so controversial? In this chapter I explore why a rule-governed conception of judicial reasoning is consistent with contentious judicial decisions. First, I consider an example of conflicting applications of the law. And then, building upon an analysis of judicial discretion by McMaster University's Wilfrid Waluchow, I distinguish between exercising *discretion* and exercising *controlled judgment*.[51] Although there is an inevitable need, given the complexity of the issues judges face, to make judgments when applying the law, this is different from claiming that judges have discretion to determine the law. By considering several kinds of disputes, we can better understand how secondary rules control judicial decisions in controversial cases.

CONTROVERSIAL APPLICATIONS OF LAW

As I indicated in Chapter 1, there is considerable debate over the discretion judges have in deciding difficult cases. Some claim that the high incidence of controversial judicial decisions indicates that, although judges are supposed to "play by the rules," the accepted rules of application do not prescribe a decision in every case. Thus, judges are often required to determine, not simply apply, the law. British legal scholar John Bell has written about a controversial case involving abortion, which he regards as a clear instance of judicial legislation. I use this case, *Royal College of Nursing v. Department of Health,* to launch my explanation of the seemingly paradoxical view that controversial judicial decisions are compatible with rule-governed decision making.[52]

In the 1980s, the British courts were asked to determine whether a statute requiring that pregnancies be "terminated" by a doctor should be interpreted to allow for terminations "supervised" by a doctor. It was argued that if pregnancies were terminated by a doctor, a doctor would physically perform a major part of the actions involved in aborting the foetus; whereas if terminations of pregnancies were merely supervised by a doctor, a doctor need only authorize and take responsibility for the actions of others in aborting the foetus. The effect of the less restrictive interpretation would be to make abortions more accessible and less costly. A key legal issue in the case was the apparent purpose of the legislation. Some of the lawyers and judges argued that its purpose was to authorize safe abortions; others saw it as an effort to establish strict conditions under which abortions were to be performed. Bell concludes that the judges exercised wide discretion in reaching their differing decisions about the best policy to pursue regarding abortion. He suggests that their decisions could not have been rule-governed since the legislative purpose was not specified in law; the judges, of necessity, must have chosen a purpose by assessing the desirability of competing social goals. In effect, the judges acted as legislators.

Bell's explanation of the judges' reasoning in this case is inadequate. The fact that the English Parliament had not expressly announced the legislative purpose and that the judges disagreed about the purpose is not sufficient to support a conclusion that the judges were at liberty to choose what was to be taken as the purpose. To justify his attribution of judicial discretion, Bell must show that the judges did not consider their decisions to be *controlled* by law—namely, that the judges did not decide, and feel bound to decide, the issue in accordance with valid legal considerations. An examination of the opinions offered by the judges strongly suggests that they believed their assessments of the relative weight of the valid arguments for the competing positions required them to reach the conclusions that they did. Although the purposes that the majority and dissenting judges attributed to the statute were not identical, both sides considered them inherent in the statute and apparent in the legislative history. Significantly, one majority justice remarked, "I have reached this conclusion simply as a matter of the construction of the Act."[53] In other words, the judge believed that the evidence about the legislative purpose found in the *Act* and in the rules regulating statutory interpretation was sufficient to decide the case. It should not be presumed, as Bell alleges, that a lack of *explicit* indication of the legislative purpose and the ensuing controversial conclusions establish that the judges failed to *apply* the law. Seemingly, all the judges believed that they were deciding the case in a manner required by the primary rule and by the secondary rules available to interpret the rule. As it turned out, much of the ambiguity surrounding the interpretation stemmed from the fact that the law was a poorly drafted, privately sponsored statute. The judges' commitment to reach the *legally* most defensible resolution of this difficult case is compatible with considerable disagreement over what that resolution should be.

When discussing the extent to which the law regulates judicial decisions, as I suggested in Chapter 1, there is a tendency to view application of the law as a simple dichotomy: either it is a straightforward mechanical operation, or it is a matter of judicial choice. There is an important third option between mechanical and discretionary decision making—one that involves the exercise of judgment, but is nevertheless rule governed. By exploring a distinction between judicial *discretion* and *controlled judgment*, we can see more clearly why controversial judicial decisions are consistent with the view that judicial reasoning is essentially a non-discretionary, rule-governed practice.[54]

DISCRETION v. CONTROLLED JUDGMENT

I will use the term *discretion* to refer to judicial decisions that are not *controlled* by authorized legal criteria—that is, discretionary decisions are not governed by standards articulated in the primary and secondary rules of a given legal system. As long as judges consider themselves obligated to reach the most defensible legal resolution in every case and believe that there are valid legal grounds for selecting one conclusion over the others, their decisions are controlled by law—they are rule governed. On the other hand, the fact that decision making is controlled by legal criteria does not mean that specific laws can always be applied in a straightforward manner. In deciding which of the various alternatives is most defensible on legal grounds, judges must ascertain the legal validity of arguments, verify the implied claims, and assess the weight of competing positions. In short, judges must judge—they must make judgments about what the law requires. I will use the term *controlled judgment* to refer to judicial decisions that are governed by primary and secondary rules, but that involve appraisals on the part of judges. Controlled judgment is not synonymous with what has been called "interstitial legislation," which implies that judges are free to exercise discretion provided they stay within the parameters of settled law (i.e., judges have limited discretion in filling the gaps between laws). I believe that, properly understood, the judicial mandate requires that judges decide all issues *according to* the law, and not merely *within* the law.[55]

Claiming that judicial decisions are governed by primary and secondary rules implies that judges decide, by sincere and impartial determination, the most defensible, *legally grounded* resolution of the case. Being rule governed does not imply a single correct legal answer to every case; different judges may in good conscience "see" the law differently—that is, draw different conclusions about what the law requires in a particular instance. As one writer noted, "The fact that reasonable men may differ in their judgments does not mean that they are merely expressing some personal preference or a mere groundless opinion."[56] Also, it is inevitable that judges will make mistakes. Merely believing that their decisions are the most defensible legal decisions does not make them correct. However, even if mistaken, judges will have met their obligation to apply the law if their decisions are based on conscientiously held beliefs about the appropriate legal grounds for deciding the case. Finally, a rule-governed conception does not imply that judges never exercise discretion. Prominent judges have indicated that on occasion they feel compelled to exercise a free choice, and others admit the possibility that a situation may not be controlled by existing legal standards.[57] It is sufficient to defend against the charge of judicial tyranny if it can be shown that only in the most extreme situations are judicial decisions not controlled by legal considerations.

If judicial decisions are controlled by law, then judges must not be free to select arbitrarily the grounds for deciding a case. Criteria for judging among the alternatives must be presented to, or at least be discoverable by, judges and not be imposed by personal predilection. As I suggested, some critics claim that judges, though not completely free in this regard, still have considerable latitude in the judgments they make—that, in other words, there may not be much difference between the need to exercise judgment in applying legal standards and the exercise of discretion. Even where legal standards control judicial decisions, judgments must be made about controversial issues such as determining (1) which legal arguments form the grounds for a decision, (2) which conclusion satisfies the accepted grounds for a decision, and (3) which "rules" of decision making are valid. What would it mean to claim that judges exercised judgment, as opposed to discretion, in resolving these issues? To answer this question, and better illustrate why the exercise of judgment can be both non-discretionary and controversial, I draw upon an example suggested by Ronald Dworkin, one of the most widely known scholars in Anglo-American jurisprudence. Dworkin's example involves the extent of discretion a sergeant must exercise in carrying out a lieutenant's order to select five soldiers for patrol duty.[58]

Disputed Grounds for a Decision

One source of dispute about the discretionary nature of judicial reasoning focuses on the selection of criteria or the grounds for making a decision. Imagine that a lieutenant's order to a sergeant is to select the five *most experienced* soldiers for patrol duty. It might seem that the sergeant is required merely to exercise judgment in following this command since the lieutenant's order specifies that the sergeant's decision is to be made on the basis of experience. On the other hand, if the lieutenant's order is to select *any* five soldiers, then the sergeant would seemingly be forced to exercise discretion because of the latitude in selecting the criteria upon which to choose five soldiers. Yet such an account of the discretion-judgment distinction would be simplistic: explicit identification of the basis for applying an order does not settle whether or not discretion is required. Under certain conditions the sergeant in the first situation may be required to exercise discretion and, depending on the pool of available soldiers, in the second situation the sergeant may have no discretion. In deciding upon the five most experienced soldiers, for example, the sergeant's selection may be complicated by the fact that some soldiers may have been enlisted in the service longer (i.e., length of experience), others may have spent greater amounts of time on patrol duty (i.e., range of active experience), and still others may have fewer total hours of patrol duty but have participated in a richer range of patrol assignments (i.e., quality of active experience). Since all of these are apparently reasonable measures of experience, it is not obvious that the order controls the sergeant's decision. Without further guidance, the sergeant is left uncertain as to which five soldiers best meet the criterion established by the lieutenant's order.

The capacity of a directive to control a decision does not reside in the specificity of the order (or law) itself. As was discussed in the previous chapter, secondary rules must be considered when deciding upon the application of a law in a given situation. Once we recognize a second level of considerations for resolving ambiguities, then, although the order itself does not specify the relevant criteria sufficiently explicitly to control the decision, the order and second-level considerations collectively may control the decision. For example, in interpreting "most experienced," the sergeant might be authorized to refer to the following considerations: the lieutenant's likely intended meaning, the meaning implied by previous orders involving selection of men, general military guidelines on selection criteria for patrol duty, and the requirements of the specific patrol assignment. These second-level considerations provide grounds for resolving ambiguities or vagueness in the order. Only if the sergeant believes that the order and the relevant second-level considerations fail to sufficiently clarify the basis for interpreting the order will the sergeant need to exercise discretion.

Appeals to second-level considerations in interpreting a senior officer's order are valid only if they are authorized by the "rules" governing military decision making. (In the previous chapter, I suggested that the legitimacy of second-level considerations in applying law is established by argument-validating rules. It is an open question whether or not the second-level rules for military decision making are as extensive and formalized as are those in law.) The sergeant is not required to exercise discretion if the military rules are seen by the sergeant to result in a single, most defensible resolution. In our example, the sergeant must believe that the authorized grounds for interpreting "most experienced" settle which five, and only five, soldiers to select. Perhaps the second-level considerations justify interpreting "most experienced" to mean the soldiers with the *widest range* of experiences. This additional consideration still may not settle the question; some may have a wider range of experiences with varied geographical terrain, but a narrower range of tactical experiences than other soldiers. In this event, further considerations must be found to more precisely define the criterion. If there were a maxim of military strategy suggesting "natural obstacles be treated as posing a greater threat to success than human obstacles," this principle would provide a reason for interpreting "most experienced" to refer to those soldiers with experience of a greater range of geographical terrains. Only when appeals to all the appropriate second-level considerations fail to identify five "most experienced" soldiers might the sergeant reasonably conclude that the order requires the exercise of discretion.

A parallel situation exists with judicial decisions. Only when judges have exhausted all legal considerations and continue to believe that the law fails to provide sufficiently discriminating grounds to support a single, most defensible resolution are they forced to exercise discretion. We have seen that the level of explicitness of a law does not, in itself, determine whether its application involves discretion or controlled judgment. Depending on the particulars of a case, designation in a primary rule of specific criteria for a decision may mask the need to exercise discretion and, conversely, lack of explicit designation of criteria for deciding a case may obscure the fact that a decision is controlled by secondary rules. The anomaly-resolving capacity of secondary rules explains why the judges in *Hunter v. Southam* were able to establish criteria, despite the vagueness of the term "unreasonable," for deciding the legality of the search of the newspaper office. It also explains why, in the "termination" of abortion case (*Royal College of Nursing v. Department of Health*), the lack of an explicit statement of the legislative purpose did not automatically mean that the grounds for deciding the case were at the discretion of the judges.

Disputed Conclusions

A second source of support for the supposedly discretionary nature of judicial decisions stems from disagreement over the most defensible resolution of a case given the accepted legal grounds. Accusations of judicial discretion arise in these situations, since different conclusions may be drawn by individuals relying on seemingly similar grounds. As we will see, because of the need to weigh competing arguments and because of reliance on different arguments, deciding upon the best alternative may be controversial and still not involve the exercise of discretion.

Suppose that the second-level rules of military decision making specify that the pre-eminent consideration in interpreting an order is to effect the issuing officer's wishes, if known. Suppose, further, that the available evidence suggests that the lieutenant *probably* regards *length* of military service as the measure of experience. Let me also suggest that another relevant consideration—what is required for the mission to be successful—strongly suggests that *breadth* of military experience is the most appropriate measure of experience. Faced with these conflicting grounds— the officer's wishes and the requirements for a successful mission—the sergeant must decide whether breadth or length of experience is the most defensible interpretation of the lieutenant's order. Consider three possible lines of argument:

Sergeant A regards the evidence of the lieutenant's wishes to be speculative. Since effecting the merely suspected wishes of the lieutenant about length of service is viewed as significantly increasing the chance of a failed mission, it is seen as appropriate to decide on the basis of the sergeant's knowledge of what the mission requires. Consequently, Sergeant A interprets "most experienced" to mean breadth of experience.

Sergeant B assesses the probability of mission failure if length of service is the criterion, and judges it to be less likely than Sergeant A thought. In view of this, Sergeant B feels compelled to comply with the lieutenant's probable wishes and interprets "most experienced" to mean length of military service.

Sergeant C considers the evidence about the lieutenant's wishes to be very clear and persuasive. Despite believing that the lieutenant's criterion is ill-advised because of the considerable risk of failure if length of service is used as the basis for selecting the patrol, Sergeant C feels obligated to interpret "most experienced" according to the lieutenant's intended meaning, since the "rules" state that this is to be the prime consideration in interpreting orders.

I will attempt to illustrate how these different conclusions and justifications are compatible with a rule-governed account of decision making. For the purposes of this discussion, let us accept that each sergeant decided on the basis of a sincere appraisal of the relevant military considerations (i.e., the order and the second-level rules).

It might be suggested that the discretionary nature of these decisions is evidenced by the fact that, for example, Sergeant C attaches greater weight than Sergeant A to upholding the lieutenant's wishes and less weight to avoiding military failure. This explanation is not convincing since both sergeants accord comparable relative weight to these standards—both recognize that the officer's wishes, if known, are the pre-eminent consideration. It is the degree of certainty of the arguments from these standards that is judged to be different: Sergeant A's assessment of the dubious evidence about the lieutenant's intended meaning requires discounting the weight of that argument. But notice, the two sergeants agree on what the law requires of them, and both have reached their conclusion based on the implications of these considerations for the facts of the case, as they see them. These sergeants are not imposing their own values on the issue before them, and both felt compelled to conclude as they did by the authorized grounds for reaching a decision. Both of these decisions meet the conditions for a controlled judgment.

Another supposed indication of discretion would be to characterize Sergeant C as electing to apply different standards since, unlike the other two, Sergeant C dismisses the implications for military failure. Again, the explanation is not convincing since it is not necessary to entertain this additional consideration if, as Sergeant C believes, the evidence about the lieutenant's wishes is sufficiently compelling to decide the issue on that basis alone. (Remember, the senior officer's intentions were indicated as the pre-eminent consideration in resolving ambiguities.) Again, the different conclusions can be accounted for in a way that does not impute discretion.

This hypothetical example of the three sergeants suggests how different conclusions, all controlled by similar criteria, may be misinterpreted as implying the exercise of discretion. Despite their differences, none of the sergeants *chose* to see the situation the way that they did, nor are their decisions arbitrary; rather, they regard their conclusions as required by the military rules that they are bound to uphold. All three sergeants recognize the validity of the same arguments and respect the same relative weight of the implied standards. The sergeants' conclusions differ because of judgments made in light of their reading of the particular situation. The implications to be drawn about judicial disagreements are that controversy can be attributed to the intricacy of legal issues that must be resolved, and that frequent controversy does not prove that judges are biased or that they impose their personal preference. It may be that, for most judges, they are actually doing what they say they do, which is to endeavour to apply law according to the law.

Disputed Rules for Decision Making

In all of the examples discussed above, disputes about the lieutenant's order were resolved by appeal to second-level considerations. Although these examples explain how disputes involving primary rules may be resolved by appeal to secondary rules, they say nothing about resolving disputes over the secondary rules themselves. This is an important concern: if there is no rule-governed way of resolving disputes about second-order considerations, then we have simply shifted, not eliminated, the source of discretion. Consider the implications, for example, of military officials disagreeing about the appropriateness, when a subordinate is interpreting a senior officer's order, of considering the likelihood of a mission's success. Some sergeants may believe that they are authorized to do so, and others may deny the validity of this sort of appeal. How are disputes over the validity of a second-level consideration to be resolved? Would not the uncertain validity of the rules for decision making lead to the exercise of discretion by individual sergeants? Certainly many judicial controversies hinge on contested secondary rules of application. Whereas it is unclear what are the mechanisms for resolving disputes about the second-level rules of military reasoning, judicial disputes over contested secondary rules are resolved by appeal to other secondary rules.

The *Big M Drug Mart* case, a Supreme Court decision involving Sunday closing legislation, exemplifies how other secondary rules of application are employed to determine the validity of a disputed secondary rule. In this case, the constitutionality of the *Lord's Day Act* depended, in part, on determining its purpose. The *Act,* which required the closing of retail stores on Sunday, was originally enacted to promote observation of the Christian holy day. This objective, since it gave preferential treatment to Christians over other religious groups, was seen to violate a *Charter* requirement that limits placed on rights be consistent with the principles of a "free and democratic society." If the *Act* could be shown to have subsequently acquired a secular purpose— say, to safeguard a uniform day of rest for families to assemble—then it would be less likely to violate the *Charter*. The acceptability of this line of reasoning depended on the validity of an American secondary rule of application known as the "shifting purpose" rule. This rule holds that it is possible for the purpose of an act to have changed significantly if sufficient amendments have been made to it. The Crown argued for the shifting purpose theory by appealing to several U.S. decisions that relied on this argument and by referring to the frequent amendments to the *Lord's Day Act*. Although American decisions have some authority in Canadian constitutional law, the Crown's argument was rejected by the Supreme Court in light of competing arguments: the doctrines of legislative intention and *stare decisis* would be jeopardized if the shifting purpose theory were accepted and these fundamental principles were seen to outweigh the merely persuasive authority of precedents from foreign jurisdictions. In other words, to determine the validity of the shifting purpose rule as a secondary rule of application, the Court assessed competing arguments which themselves were grounded in other, non-contested, secondary rules of application.

This example demonstrates, as do the examples discussed earlier, the law's potential, developed over centuries, to resolve disputes in rule-governed ways. There are abundant second-level considerations, authorized by the rules that govern judicial reasoning, for resolving disputes about the law (primary rules) and about secondary rules for applying the law. The incidence of situations where judges run out of anomaly-resolving considerations, and hence the occasions where judges are left to make discretionary decisions, are rare.[59]

Having emphasized the rule-governed nature of judicial reasoning, it is important not to exaggerate the extent to which a given legal system provides a coherent set of rules that actually control judicial decisions. The fact that rules exist does not mean that they are always followed. Inevitably, there will be mistakes, and some judges will disregard the law. Although they are unlikely to be forthcoming about this matter, some judges openly deviate from the established rules of judicial reasoning. For example, Lord Denning, possibly the most famous judicial "maverick," has on occasion been repudiated by his English superior judges for his apparent rejection of the doctrine of precedent.[60] Ironically, the fact that judges are reprimanded for their failure to abide by the rules is support for the central thesis of this book—namely, that judges are *expected* to conform to relatively well-established rules when applying the law.

(Chapter 8 discusses *Davis v. Johnson*, the case which occasioned Lord Denning's rebuke by the House of Lords, and which further illustrates the capacity of a rule-governed account of judicial reasoning to accommodate disputes over secondary rules of application.)

Another flaw in rule-governed systems of law arises when groups of judges consistently recognize different, and sometimes conflicting, secondary rules. Indications are, for example, that American judges are divided over the weight to be given the intentions of the original framers of the Constitution.[61] The two judicial camps cite rival strands of cases and constitutional principles as authority for their positions. Until this division within the system is resolved, judges will operate according to different standards of judicial reasoning. However, the existence of divisions such as these is compatible with viewing judicial application of law as a rule-governed practice, since decisions by both groups are presumably controlled by their honest reading of the law, as they understand it.[62]

The purpose of this discussion has been to illustrate, in general terms, how controversies arising from the lack of explicit legal direction and from variance in judicial decisions do not automatically indicate that judges are either permitted or forced to exercise discretion. Rather, judges are required to exercise judgment—to identify, assess, and weigh competing *legal* arguments—in reaching decisions that are controlled by legal standards. In the next section I focus on the three modes of judicial reasoning and examine the nature and extent to which the clusters of secondary rules comprising these modes control judicial decisions. Many more instances of supposed judicial discretion will be shown to be accommodated within a rule-governed account of judicial reasoning.

SECTION TWO:

MODES OF JUDICIAL REASONING

4
Reasoning from Interpretive Guidelines

An obvious way in which judges decide what a law requires in a particular case is by interpreting the meaning of the relevant legislation. Literally thousands of secondary rules—more precisely termed "guidelines"—regulate how judges may interpret statutory and constitutional provisions. Before exploring the range of secondary rules that constitute this mode of reasoning, I discuss the meaning of "interpretation" in the context of applying laws. More specifically, I argue that interpreting a law is not simply a matter of discovering what the legislators meant. In the last part of this chapter, I critically examine suggestions that reasoning from interpretive guidelines is not rule-governed and, hence, fails to control judicial decisions.

THE NATURE OF INTERPRETING LAWS

On the face of it, applying a law by interpreting its meaning may seem a straightforward task. In practice, it is far from simple. The very notion of legal interpretation is problematic. It has been called an overworked concept with such a "spectacular breadth of uses" that "its meaning drifts in a most treacherous manner."[63] In ascertaining the meaning of a law, judges have a duty to interpret it in accordance with the "legislative intention." However, legislative intention must be understood figuratively, as a "legal fiction." It is not identical with, and often deviates from, the actual intentions of individual legislators or of a legislative body. The somewhat paradoxical relationship between figurative uses of legislative intention and legislators' actual intentions is equivalent to suggesting that the meaning of a person's statement may not be what the person meant by the statement. Rather than characterizing legal interpretation as discovering what legislators consciously meant, it is better to view legal interpretation as ascertaining what legislation licenses or authorizes. In other words, interpreting law is more a matter of determining authorized "legal meaning" than it is a matter of deciphering an intended message sent from specific legislators to citizens and legal officials.[64]

Authorized Interpretation v. Ordinary Communication

Legislation cannot usefully be conceived of as a form of ordinary communication where any uncertainty over meaning is largely resolved by what a speaker consciously intended by the statement. Formal declarations issued in a legal context authorize interpretations which may not have been intended by the declarers but which, nevertheless, are implied by their statements. These sometimes unintended interpretations are authorized because of the constellation of rules invoked when formal legal statements are uttered. Consider the implications that follow when an individual makes a will or gets married. By virtue of signing a will or making the marriage vow, rights and obligations are implied beyond what is ordinarily meant by the words "I hereby give" or "I do." These statements summon the rules of the institutions of succession or marriage and thereby confer considerable powers and create expansive responsibilities whether or not an individual is aware of them. For example, unless destroyed or replaced in writing, a will remains in effect even if the individual changes her mind and widely communicates this change of mind. Similarly, the bride and groom may be largely unaware of the financial and legal commitments arising from their marital promise. Furthermore, the implications of a declaration may be at odds with many of the declarer's actual intentions: as a result of careless wording, a will may not express the testator's conscious intentions; and a person may marry with no intention of keeping the commitments implied by her vow. Nor is the possibility of implied outcomes restricted to events that the individual could (and even should) have foreseen. Many of the institutional rules invoked when interpreting the declaration may not have been formulated at the time of the initial declaration: subsequent amendments to divorce or family support laws may have established new marital rights and obligations many years after the exchange of marriage vows.

Analogous to situations in which citizens' legal declarations (e.g., signing wills and taking marriage vows) create unanticipated legal obligations and rights, are those in which legislators enact laws. In applying a law, judges must attend to the words used in the legislation, and, to some extent, to what was intended by the drafters of the law; however, many other secondary rules also control legal interpretation. Discrepancies between the meaning of a law that is authorized by these secondary rules and legislators' actual intentions explains why judges may legitimately interpret statutes in ways not imagined by those who drafted the law and even in ways contrary to legislators' actual intentions. Judges *attribute* a meaning to a statute within the limitations prescribed by the text and by the context. As we saw in Chapter 2, the Court in *Hunter v. Southam* relied upon the purpose for having a *Charter* protection against unreasonable search (and not on the conscious intentions of the drafters) in interpreting what was required by this constitutional right. Thus, a law's meaning is not "the conclusion that the legislature would have arrived at, but one which the legislature by the text has authorized the courts to find." Or, as former U.S. Supreme Court Justice Felix Frankfurter suggests, other interpretive considerations "infiltrate the text" as if "written in ink discernible to the judicial eye." For example, when statutory wording is ambiguous, judges rely upon rules called interpretive presumptions—statements about what will be presumed to be the meaning unless otherwise indicated. At one point interpretive presumptions were seen to represent the legislators' most likely intentions; they have long since ceased to be more than *presumed* intentions. Although most legislators (or at least the drafters of legislation) would be aware of these legal presumptions, it cannot be assumed that legislators actually intended that the presumptions be applied in the ways that they are.[65]

Although interpreting legislative declarations is not essentially a matter of determining what the legislators actually intended—it is more a matter of determining the authorized meaning of the legislation given the institutional rules governing statutory and constitutional interpretation—there are important ways in which legal interpretation is closely tied to intended meaning. Most interpretive rules are linguistic and grammatical conventions covering interpretation of the words legislators use to formulate legal rules. Legislators' ability to predict how judges will interpret laws is greatly enhanced by mutually acknowledged, relatively clear interpretive conventions. If legislators know the "rules of the game," they can formulate a law so as to increase the likelihood of its application in ways consistent with their intentions. However, there is an important difference between deciding on an interpretation of the law because the legislators intended it and because the rules of interpretation authorize it.

Rules and Rule Formulations

The role of interpretive guidelines in establishing the meaning of a law can be further clarified by distinguishing between a rule and its formulation. A rule can be understood as a norm or standard prescribing (or prohibiting) a set of actions; the rule's formulation is the set of words used to specify the prescribed behaviour. The same rule (or norm) may be formulated in different ways. For example, the rule prescribing the side of the street on which cars are to be driven may be formulated either as "All cars must be driven on the right-hand side of the road" or "No cars may be driven on the left-hand side of the road." The set of actions prohibited under the first formulation is equivalent to the set of actions prohibited under the second formulation; hence, the two formulations specify the same rule. Significantly, the meaning of a rule is not restricted to its formulation. For example, it is widely accepted that legal rules have implied or unarticulated exceptions.[66] In addition, dramatic changes to a legal rule are possible with no accompanying change in the formulation of the rule. As was suggested in Chapter 2, enactment of an interpretive law stipulating that human foetuses are to be considered to be legal persons would not alter the formulation of a rule stating "All persons have the right to life," but the set of prohibited actions defined by the rule would change. The converse is also true: drastic changes in the formulation of a rule may present no changes to the legal rule. The "plain language" movement, for instance, argues that many statutory provisions and lawyer-drafted documents can be reformulated in simpler language without loss of meaning.

The relation between rules and their formulations accents an important feature of legal interpretation. Law is truly a union of primary and secondary rules. The rule enacted by a legislature is best understood not simply as the expressly formulated primary rule specifically voted upon but also as the constellation of secondary rules recognized within the legal system as regulating this type of primary rule. Secondary rules of application can be seen not as mere indications of the meaning of a legal rule but as *constitutive* of its meaning—they determine the range of situations that can properly be taken to be covered by the rule. Let us now look more closely at the range of these interpretive rules.

RULES FOR INTERPRETING LAW

There are two tiers of secondary rules governing reasoning from interpretive guidelines. At the foundation are what have been referred to as "interpretive approaches" or "basic rules" of interpretation. An interpretive approach establishes the basis for general context within which more specific interpretive arguments are constructed. There are three traditional approaches—the plain meaning rule, the golden meaning rule, and the mischief rule—but other basic rules of interpretation have also been identified. More specific arguments within these basic approaches are authorized by what have been referred to as "minor rules of construction" or "subordinate principles of interpretation." These many minor rules cover an extensive range of considerations from grammar, punctuation, and format to presumed intentions, statements of implied intention, and remarks made by legislators. In a classic work on statutory interpretation, former Dalhousie law professor John Willis described an interpretive approach as a great sun "around which revolve in planetary order a series of minor rules."[67]

Basic Interpretive Approaches

Historically, five different approaches have dominated judicial interpretation. As suggested by the chart which follows, the various approaches fall along a continuum ranging from a strict *letter of the law* focus to a broad *spirit of the law* focus. A letter of the law focus is based on the view that the legislators expressed exactly what they meant and only what they meant in the words used—the ascribed meaning of a law is to be restricted to the meaning of the words. In some cases this meant that the statute's title or preamble, since they were, strictly speaking, not part of the rule formulation, would not be considered when interpreting the law.[68] At the other end of the continuum, a spirit of the law focus implies that the exact wording of a law does not exhaust its meaning and in many situations may be less important than the purpose or objective that a law was intended to serve. In some cases judges following this approach would be willing to contradict what appears to be expressly stated in the wording of the formulation in order to further a law's implicit purpose.

BASIC INTERPRETIVE APPROACHES

frozen concept	plain or literal meaning	golden meaning	mischief rule	originalism or framers' intention	purposive approach

< ——————————————————————————————————— >

Letter of the Law   **Spirit of the Law**

Frozen concept

In an extreme form of the letter of the law focus, the meaning of a law is confined to what the terms meant at the time the law was passed. This approach, which has been referred to as the frozen concept theory, requires that judges limit their interpretation to fixed legal meanings of words. The justification for the frozen concept approach was that strict adherence to the original established meaning of the terms was the only reliable way to interpret the legislators' intention. The Supreme Court of Canada employed this approach in the famous *Persons* case of 1928 when it decided that women could not be senators. The Court reasoned that the term "persons" in the *British North America Act, 1867* did not include women because, at the time this law was passed, women were not allowed to vote in federal elections. It would be odd, so the argument went, to imagine that the law makers intended that women be allowed to become legislators when they were not allowed to vote.[69]

Plain or literal meaning

The plain meaning or literal meaning rule is a less extreme version of the letter of the law focus. The Canadian and British version of this rule requires that, if the language is clear, judges confine their interpretation to the explicit meaning of the words but allows them to accept the contemporary legal and ordinary meanings of terms. Unlike the frozen concept interpretation, a plain meaning reading of "persons" would mean that women qualify as persons for the purposes of Senate appointments. However, under this approach, judges must adhere to the ordinary meaning of the terms even if the interpretation has absurd or manifestly unjust consequences. A 1955 case involving the *Income Tax Act* illustrates the limits of this approach. According to the *Act*, a tax deduction could be claimed for the expenses of caring for a physically disabled person only if the person was *necessarily confined to a bed or wheelchair*. In this particular case, a woman who was confined to bed by a serious heart problem and had to be carried by her husband or by a hired nurse to a rocking chair did not qualify for this deduction because when she left her bed she was not placed in a wheelchair. The meaning of the words were clear: a rocking chair is not a wheelchair.[70]

Golden meaning

Closer to the middle of the continuum is the golden meaning, which requires that the plain meaning rule be followed except in cases where it results in obvious incongruities. The classic statement of this rule is as follows: "the grammatical and ordinary sense of the words is to be adhered to, unless that would lead to some absurdity, or some repugnancy or inconsistency with the rest of the instrument, in which case the grammatical and ordinary sense of the words may be modified, so as to avoid that absurdity and inconsistency, but no farther."[71] In the case mentioned above, the absurdity of disallowing the income tax exemption merely because the woman was confined to a rocking chair, not to a wheelchair, would likely have resulted in a different ruling had a golden meaning approach been followed.

Mischief rule

On the other side of the mid-point in this continuum is the mischief rule, which allows that the *explicitly* articulated objectives of a law be used to interpret its meaning. In earlier times, the preamble to each piece of legislation would typically specify the "mischief" or "defect in the common law" that the legislators were attempting to prevent. Although judges could not override the plain meaning of terms, they could appeal to these explicit statements of intention in resolving uncertainty or ambiguity. Before the eighteenth century, the mischief rule was the basic approach to statutory interpretation in British courts. Because modern-day statutes rarely specify the "mischief," this approach, at least as it was originally conceived, cannot often be followed.[72]

Originalism or framers' intention

Slightly further along the continuum is originalism or the framers' intention approach. While interpretations following this approach may deviate from the letter of the law, they must be compatible with what is known to be the original drafters' intentions. A broader range of evidence than is allowed under the mischief rule can be used to determine the actual or likely intentions. Statements such as those appearing in the records of legislative debates or in government reports are permissible, especially when interpreting constitutional provisions. A call for "originalism" is currently popular in the United States among conservatives who regard many principles enunciated by the courts to be inconsistent with the wishes of those who originally framed the U.S. Constitution.[73]

Purposive approach

The most liberal of the basic interpretive rules is the purposive approach, which does not restrict interpretation to actual intentions but allows judges to consider a wider range of historical, philosophical, and linguistic evidence about purpose when interpreting laws. The Canadian articulation of this recent rule of constitutional interpretation was stated in a leading *Charter* case, *R. v. Big M Drug Mart Ltd.*:

> the purpose of the right or freedom in question is to be sought by reference to the character and larger objects of the *Charter* itself, to the language chosen to articulate the specific right or freedom, to the historical origins of the concepts enshrined, and where applicable, to the meaning and purpose of the other specific rights and freedoms with which it is associated within the text of the *Charter*. The interpretation should be ... a generous rather than a legalistic one, aimed at fulfilling the purpose of the guarantee and securing for individuals the full benefit of the *Charter's* protection. At the same time it is important not to overshoot the actual purpose of the right or freedom in question, but to recall that the *Charter* was not enacted in a vacuum, and must therefore ... be placed in its proper linguistic, philosophic and historical [sic] contexts.[74]

It has been suggested that the difficulty of imputing and discovering the intention of a collective body has motivated the transition from talk of the *legislative intention* to the *purpose of the legislation*—"purpose is to be elicited from the Act and its context, not from the minds of the legislators."[75]

As implied by the reference to a continuum, following the letter, as opposed to the spirit, of the law is more a matter of degree than it is a choice between discrete alternatives. Judges need to have some understanding of the meaning of the words to determine a law's purpose, and, in turn, the meaning of the words depends partly on the context in which they appear and their general purpose. In addition, evolution of the basic approaches changes the range of acceptable minor rules. For example, as indicated above, the mischief rule required interpretation in light of expressly formulated accounts of the mischief that was being remedied. Thus statutory interpretation was still restricted to "the four corners of the printed act" although not limited to the wording of the provision. Additional minor rules pertaining to an implied legislative purpose were not acceptable. The continued use of the basic rule, in a more extended sense of "mischief," refers to what might now be called a purposive approach. A further blurring of the approaches arises because the same approach is not applicable to all areas of law: interpretive guidelines differ between constitutional and statutory provisions[76] and between criminal law statutes and other types of ordinary legislation.[77]

Minor Interpretive Rules

The basic interpretive approaches provide the parameters within which the many minor interpretive rules operate. The similarities and differences between any two basic approaches can be explained in terms of the overlapping range of minor interpretive rules that are authorized within the approaches. For example, both the framers' intention and purposive approaches consider evidence about the legislators' intentions to be important. However, the latter approach regards it as only one of a number of arguments and therefore attaches less authority to it than the former approach, which considers it compelling. Judges adopting the plain meaning rule, at least according to some proponents, would be unlikely to entertain information about legislative intention. And, as was suggested earlier, a strict plain meaning approach would prohibit resort to a statute's preamble and heading. Despite these differences, the vast majority of minor rules would be applicable regardless of which basic approach was authorized—most rules of grammar and punctuation, and many other textual aids, are common to all interpretive approaches.

Minor rules have traditionally been classified under four categories: (1) intrinsic aids; (2) extrinsic aids; (3) interpretive presumptions; and (4) general stylistic, semantic, and grammatical rules.

Intrinsic aids

Intrinsic or internal aids refer, as the name suggests, to rules which direct judges to sources within an act for guidance in interpreting a particular provision. Judges are authorized to use interpretive and definitional sections contained in many acts. For example, section 27 of the *Charter* stipulates that provisions "shall be interpreted in a manner consistent with the preservation and enhancement of the multicultural heritage of Canadians"; section 30 explains that the term "province" shall be taken to include "territories." Judges are also authorized to look for guidance in other parts of an act so as to avoid conflicting or inconsistent interpretations. In the first Supreme Court case involving the *Charter,* the title of the general cluster of rights—mobility rights—was used to clarify the purpose of a specific provision which guarantees the right "to pursue the gaining of a livelihood in any province." As suggested by the title, the purpose of the cluster of rights was to safeguard freedom of movement between provinces. It was not, as a surface reading of the specific section suggests, a general right to work in a particular province; rather, it was a prohibition against using provincial barriers to prevent someone from working.[78]

Extrinsic aids

Extrinsic or external aids refer to rules that direct judges to sources which are not part of the legislative document but are assumed to be extensions of the document. These rules authorize resort to documents dealing with legislative history, legal commentaries or reference materials, and other domestic and international legislation and agreements. As part of legislative history, published drafts of legislation may be useful in interpreting law. For example, two early versions of the *Charter* freedom of expression provision contained the phrase "media of information." The eventual change to the broader phrase "media of communication" and the explanatory notes accompanying the revised version suggest that freedom of expression should be interpreted to include non-verbal forms of expression, such as the performing arts, which are not normally considered to be sources of *information*.[79] Reliance on international covenants was helpful in deciding whether the *Charter* freedom of religion provision implied the freedom not only to hold, but also to act on, religious opinions. The Court looked to the United Nations' *International Covenant on Civil and Political Rights*, which Canada ratified in 1976. Article 18 of this document clearly indicates that freedom of religion extends to the freedom to *manifest* religion or belief in worship, observation, practice, and teaching. Because Canada has an obligation to support this covenant in its domestic law, this was a valid reason for interpreting freedom of religion to include the right to practice one's religion.[80]

Interpretive presumptions

Interpretive presumptions refer to an extensive repertoire of generic assumptions about what any legislation can be presumed to include or exclude. There is a presumption in favour of the rationality of legislation. It asserts that, unless proven otherwise, legislators shall be presumed to have acted reasonably in crafting the legislation. There is a presumption against retroactive effect: judges will generally not apply a law to events which occurred before the law was passed even if the law is in effect at the time of the court proceedings. Another presumption is against radical change. This presumption is a reminder to the Courts that if legislators had intended to alter the law drastically, they would likely have communicated that intention in clear and unambiguous language. The presumption against taking away property without compensation implies that, unless otherwise stated, legislation should be assumed not to take away individuals' ability to enjoy their property without some form of repayment.

Stylistic, semantic, and grammatical conventions

The final category of interpretive rules includes a wide range of stylistic, semantic, and grammatical conventions used in drafting legislation. One of these conventions is that no words are redundant. Section 2 of the *Charter* guarantees the freedom of conscience and religion. Inclusion of both "conscience" and "religion" suggests that these terms are not identical; conscience obviously extends the freedom to deeply felt, non-religious ethical beliefs—those of atheists, for instance. Another convention suggests that where a word has the same meaning as a phrase, the word should be used. This implies that if a phrase is used it should not be interpreted to have the same meaning as a word that might otherwise be seen to be synonymous. For example, section 15 of the *Charter* mentions that individuals are not to be discriminated against on the basis of "national origin." The use of this phrase rather than the term "nationality" suggests that a different meaning is intended. An Irish immigrant to Canada who eventually becomes a naturalized citizen would have a Canadian nationality and an Irish national origin. Presumably, the equality section is intended to prevent discrimination on the basis of national background regardless of current citizenship.

To this point, I have emphasized the useful role that basic approaches and minor rules play in interpreting law. It would be misleading, however, to leave this discussion without considering criticisms that have been directed at this mode of reasoning. Critics have commented harshly on the apparent inadequacy of interpretive guidelines: "Looking at these rules and approaches today one finds a maze of conflicting, mutually inconsistent prescriptions, a veritable jungle;" "the principles of statutory interpretation are one of the less stable, less consistent and less logically satisfying branches of jurisprudence."[81] These comments are particularly relevant because they challenge the appropriateness of characterizing reasoning from interpretive guidelines as a rule-governed enterprise. Let us consider some of these concerns about the extent to which interpretive guidelines control judicial decisions.

JUDICIAL DISCRETION AND INTERPRETIVE GUIDELINES

Three explanations are frequently offered by those who believe that judges have considerable discretion when interpreting law: (1) since minor rules invariably conflict with or oppose each other, judges are at liberty to rationalize any decision by electing to follow one rule over another; (2) since basic interpretive approaches often produce inconclusive results, they license any interpretation that the judge prefers; and (3) there are no established rules of interpretation since different judges appeal to changing, often conflicting, basic interpretive approaches. I will argue that these objections can be resolved in ways that are consistent with a rule-governed account of reasoning from interpretive guidelines.

Before proceeding, it is important to distinguish criticisms about confused or improper practice that are consistent with the rule-governed conception of judicial reasoning from those criticisms which challenge this conception. As I suggested in the previous chapter, rule-governed practices are not always well understood, perfectly obeyed, or entirely consistent. Although these defects may impair the workings of the practice, they do not necessarily undermine the essential rule-governed nature of the practice. The fact that judges often disagree about the validity of a rule or the conclusion it suggests does not mean that judges regard themselves as unconstrained by rules. On the contrary, to a considerable extent disputes over these issues are implicit affirmations that the practice is essentially rule governed. The distinction between poorly conducted rule-governed reasoning and non-rule-governed reasoning is not trivial. If judicial reasoning is properly characterized as rule governed, then any defects will be addressed by working with judges to increase their understanding of and adherence to the authorized forms of reasoning; on the other hand, if the root of the problem is that judicial reasoning is not controlled by secondary rules of application, then new rules are necessary to combat judicial tyranny.

Conflicting Minor Rules

It is often claimed that many minor rules conflict with each other—"they tend to hunt in pairs" and "there are two opposing canons on almost every point"—allowing judges to rationalize whatever interpretation they prefer.[82] The apparently offsetting directions provided by these rules is suggested by the following pairs of interpretive guidelines:

(1) The meaning of a word may be ascertained by reference to the meaning of words associated with it; and (2) A word may have a character of its own not to be submerged by its association.

(1) Where design has been distinctly stated no place is left for construction; and (2) Courts have the power to inquire into real—as distinct from ostensible—purpose.

(1) A statute cannot go beyond its text; and (2) To effect its purpose a statute may be implemented beyond its text.[83]

Despite the apparently contradictory directions these interpretive rules suggest, it is a misreading of their proper role to claim that the guidelines invariably cancel each other. Most of the so-called "paired canons" negate each other only in a subset of the contexts to which they apply. Consider the first pair listed above. These are obviously permissive rules; that is, they allow, but do not require, judges to consider arguments drawn both from the broader context and from the words in isolation. In short, they permit judges to consider a range of arguments, many of which may or may not be relevant in a particular case. Regarding the second pair of interpretive guidelines, on occasions where there is no explicit statement of design, judges are left to follow the second rule and inquire into the "real" purpose. In situations where the rules produce conflicting conclusions, such as in the third pair, the prevailing view is that these rules must be presumed to be inconclusive (i.e., to allow judges to entertain competing lines of argument). Although both canons serve as argument-validating rules for interpreting the meaning of a law, further reasons for and against these competing interpretations must be considered before a decision is justified.

The basic interpretive approach operating in the particular area of law may determine which line of argument is persuasive—a purposive approach would clearly give greater weight to going beyond the text. As one Canadian expert explains, interpretive conventions "represent valid points of view—competing values to be taken into account before reaching a conclusion. As in all balancing exercises, it is the cumulative weight of all relevant considerations that is significant rather than the conclusive influence of any one of them."[84]

Recognition that interpretive guidelines authorize opposing arguments is not a repudiation of the rule-governed nature of this form of reasoning. Rather, it means that the cumulative weight of these interpretive arguments must be considered and, in cases where there is no clear best conclusion, other forms of argument must be relied upon to decide the case.

Inconclusive Direction

Not all criticisms about the inadequacy of interpretive guidelines are answered by explaining the cumulative nature of this form of reasoning. Numerous cases can be cited where judges have not made obvious errors in following a common interpretive approach and yet have reached differing conclusions. For example, a panel of judges hearing a particular case will accept that a law should be interpreted according to its plain meaning and yet each judge offers a different interpretation; or, the definition under the golden meaning rule of what counts as an "absurdity" will vary from judge to judge; or, a purposive approach will seemingly require judges to choose between competing purposes.[85] Typically the argument about the inconclusiveness of interpretive approaches is as follows: Even after weighing similar factors, in many situations no one interpretation will be more defensible than the rest; thus, when judges interpret the law they must often decide cases on other grounds, possibly disguising the real reasons for their decisions behind the pretext of appeals to interpretive guidelines. I will briefly consider two responses to this challenge: (1) many critics may mistake controversial application of interpretive guidelines for judicial discretion, and (2) the fact that interpretive guidelines fail to produce a conclusive result does not mean that *other* legal standards do not control judicial reasoning in these cases.

As I argued in the previous chapter, it is conceivable that judges are acting in a rule-governed manner even though they disagree about the most defensible interpretation of a law. Since an interpretive approach is essentially a constellation of complex competing arguments, judges following, say, the plain meaning approach may plausibly reach different conclusions about a law's plain meaning. It need not be, as some infer, that the basic rule is inconclusive; rather, it may mean merely that individual judges, acting in good faith, often reach conflicting conclusions because of the need to weigh competing arguments. As we saw when discussing disputes over interpretation of an officer's order to select five soldiers for patrol duty, the need to exercise judgment and the likelihood of differences of opinion are to be expected in complex rule-governed practices.

The second suggestion, that interpretive approaches fail to control judges' decisions because they do not indicate a single most defensible resolution of the case, was also discussed in the previous chapter. The fact that reasoning from interpretive guidelines does not settle every legal issue is not, in itself, troubling. There are two other forms of reasoning—from prior cases and from principle—that judges are authorized to use in applying law. Only after judges have exhausted these avenues and still do not have a legally warranted resolution have legal standards failed to control their decision. As will be seen in the next two chapters, the other forms of reasoning, and especially reasoning from principle, provide abundant grounds for deciding cases when the law seemingly has run out.

Shifting Basic Rules

A final challenge to a rule-governed conception of reasoning from interpretive guidelines is the claim that judges regularly follow different or disputed interpretive approaches in justifying their decisions. The argument is not that some judges get it wrong, but that there is fundamental inconsistency in the so-called "rules" that judges recognize as valid. For example, some authorities misleadingly treat the three historical principles (i.e., the plain meaning, golden meaning, and mischief rules) "as if, having been enunciated by a court, they remain equally valid at all times," and the author of a standard Canadian textbook suggests that in determining legislative intention judges may resort to any one of these three approaches. Another example of inconsistency is the refusal of American courts to abandon the supposedly discredited plain meaning rule despite its apparent repudiation in a Supreme Court decision.[86]

The rule-governed explanation for this challenge requires some understanding of how changes occur in statutory interpretation. Consider, for example, the move towards the spirit of the law approach, beginning in the twentieth century, as judges resorted to legislators' actual intentions and, more recently, to legislative purpose. As legislation increasingly became directed to lay persons rather than to lawyers, statutes tended to be framed in less technical language. However, plain meaning interpretations of typically "wide and general language" regularly fail to resolve disputes about intended meaning. The traditional interpretive approaches were inadequate since they required that judges interpret statutes within the "four corners of the act" (notice, a plain meaning approach in *Hunter v. Southam* does not reveal if the search of the newspaper office is "unreasonable"). Consequently, so the theory goes, the mischief rule was extended to allow judges to consider extrinsic factors, such as legislative history, when addressing the "object" of the legislation. In other words, the "strict" approaches which were adopted initially to ensure that judicial interpretation respected legislative intentions had to be supplanted because, in their original formulations, they produced interpretations that failed to comply with the legislators' wishes.[87]

I explore the legal grounds for changes in rules of application and, in particular, the possibility of these being rule-governed changes in the chapter on reasoning from principle (Chapter 9). However, the U.S. case where legislators' remarks were first admitted as an interpretive guideline provides some insight into how secondary rules change in rule-governed ways. The apparent turning point for recognition of legislative history as a valid interpretive argument was *Holy Trinity Church v. United States*. In this 1892 U.S. Supreme Court decision, a statute prohibiting groups from importing aliens for "labor or service of any kind" was held not to prohibit a church congregation from obtaining an ordained minister from abroad. Although the wording of the statute prohibited importing all forms of labour, the Senate Committee responsible for drafting the legislation explicitly stated that the committee would have recommended that the wording be changed to reflect the clear purpose of the bill, which was to prohibit importation of *unskilled* labour, if it had not been concerned about delaying passage of the bill until a later session. The obvious inconsistency of the statute's specific wording with the more sensible solution unambiguously supported by the legislators' comments, by the obvious purpose of the Act, and by other interpretive aids made it unacceptable for the Court to ignore this argument. Thus a precedent was set for the admissibility of extrinsic evidence in cases where the plain meaning produced manifestly undesirable results—among other arguments, the broad interpretation which would preclude clergy was seen to be inconsistent with the pervasive commitment to religious expression.[88]

Notice how this change to secondary rules of application occurred. The particulars of the case forced a choice between two legal standards—between consistency with fundamental legal principles (i.e., respecting the clear and reasonable intentions of the legislators, and the commitment to religious expression) and a less fundamental rule (i.e., a reluctance to use legislative history). The judges, quite reasonably, felt bound to uphold the more fundamental principles and accordingly made an exception to the lesser rule. Over time, additional exceptions were seen to be legally warranted: subsequent U.S. courts justified the admission of extrinsic evidence because of the unreasonableness of categorically excluding evidence that provided reliable assistance in settling an ambiguity. The inevitability of legitimate exceptions to rules explains, even within a rule-governed conception, an important source of change in judicial standards. A prior case establishes authority for an exception to the general rule and, if reaffirmed repeatedly and extended with application, the exceptions may eventually "eat up" the older rule.[89]

The evolution of primary and secondary rules occurs as judges are inevitably faced with "hard choices"—situations that pit established legal rules and principles against one another. The need to decide these dilemmas means that some feature of the received law will change. However, as I have repeatedly stressed, these "hard choices" are controlled judgments that must be reached by deciding which option best accords with the law, all things considered. The evolutionary nature of secondary rules also explains why there may be considerable uncertainty among judges about the validity of a given rule. Consider, for example, noted Canadian scholar Elmer Driedger's remarks about the status of the plain meaning, golden meaning and mischief rules of interpretation:

> After struggling with these so-called rules for many years, I have finally come to the conclusion that, although they may have been separate and distinct "rules" at one time, they have been fused into one, which I have expressed as follows: The words of an Act are to be read in their entire context in their grammatical and ordinary sense harmoniously within the scheme of the Act, the object of the Act and the intention of Parliament.[90]

Driedger's observation helps to explain the concern that the three traditional rules seem to be accepted as equally valid—in the general move towards a spirit of the law focus, the traditional rules have, it would appear, become a single more complex rule. Lingering references to the golden meaning and mischief rules are, as Neil MacCormick suggests, "simply to express in terms of standard justifying reasons the justification for departing from the more obvious meaning."[91]

The above discussion has shown how disputes over the validity of interpretive rules and concerns about the failure of interpretive guidelines to control judicial decisions can be explained within a rule-governed account of interpretation. Although shifts in the basic interpretive approach and the introduction of new minor rules create uncertainty as to the acceptable standards for interpreting statutory and constitutional provisions, these changes in interpretive guidelines and the accompanying inconsistent application of them are compatible with a rule-governed account of judicial reasoning.

5
Reasoning from Prior Cases

Judges not only make use of interpretive guidelines, in applying law they also rely on precedent. In other words, judges decide the relevance of conclusions reached in prior cases in determining what the law requires in the case before them. Although reliance on precedent has been a feature of our legal tradition for centuries, current understanding of this mode of reasoning has, somewhat surprisingly, been described as in a "primitive" stage: "if one were to ask law students, lawyers, judges, or legal academics what following precedent entails, one would almost surely get a variety of inconsistent answers."[92] Much of the inconsistency is rooted in confusion over how precedent is to be used in deciding subsequent cases. Does it involve reasoning by analogy or application of a judge-made general rule to particular cases? If reasoning from prior cases requires analogous reasoning, then judges must determine relative parallelism—whether two cases are sufficiently similar in relevant respects to warrant accepting the prior case as having settled the issue in the subsequent case. Alternatively, if reasoning from prior cases involves applying a general rule, then a prior case must establish a rule broad enough to cover or subsume all cases that subsequently follow the precedent-setting case. In practice, there are countless instances where a decision reached in a prior case is clearly not sufficiently general to subsume a subsequent case, yet the former is nevertheless accepted by the courts as a precedent for the latter. These instances cause many legal practitioners and theorists to conclude that judges make new law, rather than merely follow or apply existing law. The implication is that reasoning from prior cases is not a rule-governed practice but a form of discretionary judicial legislation. In this chapter, I argue that if reasoning from prior cases is properly seen as analogous reasoning, then these countless instances of apparent judicial legislation can be explained in terms of rule-governed judicial behaviour.

I begin by describing the nature of reasoning from prior cases and by showing how this mode of reasoning is connected to, yet differs from, reasoning from interpretive guidelines. I sketch an account of reasoning from prior cases as analogous reasoning by describing the secondary rules involved in (1) determining the "rule" established by a case, (2) deciding whether or not the rule applies in subsequent cases, and (3) establishing the authority or weight of a decision in subsequent cases. Finally, I respond in some detail to three general challenges to the view that reasoning from prior cases is a rule-governed enterprise.

THE NATURE OF REASONING FROM PRIOR CASES

Both reasoning from prior cases and reasoning from interpretive guidelines are concerned with applying pre-existing rules, but each uses different criteria in applying the rules. Interpretation focuses on the ascribed meaning of legislative language. Interpretation is carried out in light of a constellation of basic and minor secondary rules which control the scope of a primary rule by regulating what it can be taken to mean. On the other hand, as suggested by the doctrine of precedent or *stare decisis*, reasoning from prior cases is concerned with deciding whether or not a decision reached in a prior case settles the issue raised in a current case. The full Latin version of the doctrine is *stare decisis et non quienta movere*, which translates as "to stand by decisions and not to disturb settled matters." If there are no compelling legal reasons for distinguishing between the significant circumstances surrounding a decision reached in a prior case and the significant circumstances in a subsequent case, then the prior decision is taken to have also settled the issue in the subsequent case. This is what is referred to as reasoning by analogy—establishing the parallelism or relevant similarity between two cases. Analogous reasoning differs from reasoning from interpretive guidelines, which focuses on whether or not the particular facts of a case fall within the scope or ascribed meaning of a law. Although judges must "interpret" judicial opinions in prior cases to ascertain what was decided, reasoning from prior cases is not "interpretation of common law" in the way that reasoning from interpretive guidelines seeks to ascribe meaning to statutory and constitutional law. Reasoning from prior cases seeks to determine whether or not the circumstances of a prior case are analogous to those of the current case by establishing that the significant or *material* facts of the cases are not different in any legally relevant way.

Reasoning from prior cases and reasoning from interpretive guidelines are sometimes confused with one another because often judges reasoning from interpretive guidelines will appeal to previous judicial decisions. It may be helpful, in understanding judges' different uses of prior decisions, to distinguish between *reference to precedent* and *reasoning from prior cases*. Reference to precedent is the direct reliance on a rule enunciated in a previous case, which is assumed (i.e., is taken as a given) to be relevantly similar to the present case. For example, in a case involving a person's will, the interpretation of the word "heirs" may be raised as an issue. If an earlier case had ruled that "heirs" means "all descendants related by blood" then a judge may refer to the earlier case as evidence of the meaning of that word. In other words, the validity of that definition (i.e., the validity of the interpretive guideline which states that "heirs" mean "all descendants related by blood") is defended by referring to a prior case that established or applied that guideline. Similarly, in the previous chapter, I suggested that legislative history was first relied upon to interpret a U.S. statute restricting immigrant labour. In subsequent cases, this decision was used to confirm the validity of relying on legislators' remarks to interpret legislation. As these examples indicate, previous judicial decisions are one source for identifying interpretive guidelines as valid rules of application. However, there is a difference between referring to prior cases to confirm rules, and *reasoning from* prior cases. An appeal to a prior case qualifies as reasoning from prior cases whenever questions are raised about the relevance of differences between the circumstances of the prior and current cases. If no questions about relevant differences are raised, reference to the prior case is offered merely as evidence of the validity of a particular rule. Consider the above-mentioned examples about the definition of "heirs" and the use of legislative history. In a subsequent case involving a contract, instead of a will, the meaning of "heirs" may also be raised as an issue. If the lawyers argue for acceptance of the definition developed in the context of interpreting wills *on the grounds* that the circumstances are relevantly similar to contracts, they are reasoning from prior cases. Similarly, in a subsequent case involving interpretation of a constitutional provision, as opposed to an ordinary statute, questions might be raised about the appropriateness of relying on legislative history. Deciding whether the earlier case, which dealt with an ordinary statute, establishes a precedent for the use of legislative history in constitutional cases requires reasoning from prior cases. Judges in the subsequent case would not know if appeal to legislative history is appropriate until they decide upon the relevance, in this context, of differences between statutory and constitutional interpretation. These examples, which require that judges *establish* the relevance of an earlier decision, are to be contrasted with situations where a prior case is cited merely to *confirm* the validity of a particular rule.

RULES FOR REASONING FROM PRIOR CASES

I will now explain how secondary rules of application provide the criteria by which judges reason from prior cases. As stated above, reasoning from prior cases involves deciding whether a decision reached in an earlier case settles the issue raised in a current case. In applying this form of reasoning, judges must resolve three main issues: (1) What is the rule or, as it is more commonly called, the *ratio* established by a decision in a prior case? (2) Are the cases legally analogous? and (3) If the cases are relevantly similar, what is the authority or weight of the prior ruling in the current case?

Determining the Ratio

A crucial step in reasoning from prior cases is identifying the *ratio* of a case. The full Latin term is *ratio decidendi,* which means the grounds or reason for a decision. Questions about definition and methods of determining the *ratio* comprise volumes of legal literature. Rupert Cross, the leading English authority on precedent, offers what he calls a "tolerably accurate" definition of the *ratio* of a case as "any rule of law expressly or impliedly treated by a judge as a necessary step in reaching his conclusion, having regard to the line of reasoning adopted by him." Others refer to the *ratio* as the principle or rule necessary for the decision.[93]

Determining the *ratio* is a matter of formulating a rule from the key relevant facts, called the *material facts,* and the judgment of the case. For example in *R. v. Therens*, a *Charter* case involving the right not to be arbitrarily detained, the issue arose whether a police officer's request that an individual accompany the officer to the police station constituted detention. The material facts of the case are that an individual was asked to accompany a police officer and that the individual could be punished for refusing to comply with the officer's request. The Court decided that this situation amounted to detaining the individual. Thus, the *ratio* established in the case *might* be summarized as follows: individuals are detained if they are liable for punishment should they fail to comply with a request to accompany a police officer. I suggest that the *ratio* might be characterized this way, because the wording is likely to undergo revision—the words of a *ratio* are not in "fixed verbal form" but are an approximation subject to continual refinement. A judge's formulation of a *ratio* is not authoritative; that is, the specific words used by a judge do not fix the *ratio*'s formulation in the way that legislators specify the precise wording of a statutory provision.[94]

The most common difficulty in determining the *ratio* lies in identifying and describing the material facts of the case. The material facts are those details of the case that are seen to be *the* relevant factors in deciding the issue before the court. Consider the case just mentioned. I implied that a factor in the decision was that the individual was liable to be punished if he did not comply with the police officer's request. A judge who dissented with the majority opinions queried whether the detention arose because the individual was *actually* subject to punishment if he refused to comply or because he merely *believed* (perhaps erroneously) that he would be punished. In other words, there is a second plausible interpretation of the *ratio*: individuals are detained *if they believe* that they are liable for punishment should they fail to comply with a request to accompany a police officer. The dissenting judge's speculations about the alternative interpretation is not an acceptable *ratio*—the *ratio* is always limited to that which is necessary to decide a case. Since the detained person was actually subject to legal sanction if he refused to accompany the police officer, *Therens* cannot be taken to decide that individuals need only suspect that they may be punished. In subsequent cases, the courts might decide that there is no legally relevant difference, in the context of detaining individuals, between actually being liable and merely believing that one is liable to be punished. But this conclusion would require establishing the analogy between the two predicaments; it is not the *ratio* established by *Therens*.

It is also important to note that a single case may establish more than one *ratio* on different points of law. For example, in addition to finding that a request for an individual to accompany a police officer to the police station counts as detention, *Therens* may be taken to have established that, under normal circumstances, evidence obtained from a detained person who has not been informed of a right to counsel is not to be admitted in court. Both *rationes* were necessary to the decision reached in *Therens*, and thus both are taken to have been established by the case.

Establishing Analogous Cases

A second, and often more difficult, task in reasoning from prior cases involves deciding whether a new case is analogous to the prior case and, thus, whether the *ratio* established in a prior case settles the issue in the subsequent case. Since it is inevitable that there will be at least minor differences between any two cases, the key issue is whether or not the differences are of *legal* significance. Judges are authorized to treat cases as relevantly similar only if there are no legally recognized differences between the material facts in the cases. In order to appreciate how secondary rules govern this form of reasoning, we must understand what is involved in deciding to *follow* or *distinguish* a case. I will then consider how application of established common law principles is a form of rule-governed analogous reasoning.

Following prior cases

If judges establish that a prior case is relevantly similar to a current case and accept the prior case as a precedent, they are said to *follow* the prior case. The considerations involved in establishing relevant similarity can be illustrated by two hypothetical cases with the following material facts:

Case #1:   A man kills his wife by deliberately firing a loaded rifle at her;

Case #2:   A woman kills her husband by deliberately firing a loaded pistol at him.

I will assume that the statements above fully describe the material facts of the two cases. Because Case #1 can be held to determine only the issues as they apply to the facts in that case, reasoning from prior cases here may be said to involve a judgment about the legal appropriateness of a *proposed* expanded (or restricted) formulation of a *ratio* established in Case #1 to include (or exclude) Case #2. Put another way, judges will consider whether or not recognized relevant similarities between the prior and subsequent case justify broadening the initial *ratio* to cover the material facts of both cases. In deciding whether Case #2 is analogous to Case #1, a judge would, *in effect*, match the proven, material facts of each case to assess whether classifying them in more general terms contradicts relevant legal distinctions. For example, is it significant, legally speaking, that the weapon in Case #1 is a rifle and in Case #2 a pistol? Or can both weapons be classified, more generally, as guns without blurring relevant legal considerations? Distinctions between pairs of facts would be relevant if they had a bearing on establishing legal responsibility in this type of criminal situation. The need to ground a distinction in law—that is, to provide a legal reason for establishing the similarity or difference between material facts—explains why reasoning from prior cases is rule governed. The constellation of legal norms within the appropriate area of law provide the basis for deciding whether the material facts are, legally speaking, relevantly similar. Although judges do not actually list the pairs of material facts and specify the more general descriptions or classifications, the underlying logic or formal structure of reasoning from prior cases is reflected in the following chart:

CLASSIFICATION OF MATERIAL FACTS

	Case #1	Case #2	Encompassing classification
Agent	man	woman	adult
Effect	kills	kills	kills
Victim	wife	husband	spouse
Means	rifle	pistol	gun
Intention	deliberate	deliberate	deliberate

Establishing relevant similarity involves deciding whether broadening the description of each category of material fact (i.e., the agent, the effect of the agent's action, the agent's relationship to the victim, the means used, and the agent's intention to use the weapon) contradicts legally accepted distinctions. In this straightforward example, the new encompassing classification of each category of material facts is an acceptable extension of the facts in the prior case (Case #1). That is, there is no apparent reason related to the legal justification for holding persons culpable for killing that would warrant distinguishing between, say, the genders of the agents or the types of gun used. Since there are no obvious legal standards that preclude extending these classifications, the material facts in Case #1 are to be regarded as relevantly similar to those in Case #2, and the former can legitimately be accepted as setting a precedent for the latter. The new formulation of the *rationes* established by Cases #1 and #2 might refer to "adults who deliberately kill spouses with a gun." It is easy to appreciate why Edward Levi, in his classic book on legal reasoning, refers to reasoning from prior cases as a "moving classification scheme."[95]

A famous English case, *Steel v. Glasgow Iron and Steel,* provides an example in which the court stated its justification for treating a pair of material facts as relevantly similar.[96] In this case, the widow of a railway guard sought compensation for the loss of her husband, who was killed while attempting to avert a serious train collision. An earlier case had established a right to compensation for losses arising in an attempt to save another's life. A key issue in the *Steel* case was whether the right to recover damages while attempting to save a life extended to a right to recover losses while attempting to prevent catastrophic damage to another's property. In other words, was there a legally relevant difference between saving a life and averting horrific property damage? According to the judges, the answer depended upon the justification for compensating losses while attempting to avoid disaster. A majority of the judges in the *Steel* case agreed that the law regarding compensation was based on the reasonableness of the risk incurred considered in light of the magnitude of the consequences to be avoided. With rescuers of lives, the justification for compensation resides in the considerable value attached to human life: risking personal danger is reasonable if it can avoid almost certain loss of human life. By analogy, if the extent of potential property damage is catastrophic, as it was in the *Steel* case, then it is also reasonable to incur risk in attempting to protect property, because it too is recognized as an important legal value. The law's interest in avoiding immanent disaster provided the justification for classifying attempts to save a life and attempts to avoid catastrophic property damage as relevantly similar kinds of attempts to prevent disastrous consequences.

Distinguishing prior cases

To this point I have focused on how judges establish that cases are relevantly similar. I now explore cases that are *distinguished* or found to be relevantly different from one another. Consider a third hypothetical case with the following material facts.

Case #3: A child kills a passer-by by deliberately firing a pea shooter at her.

In deciding whether the earlier two cases can be taken to be precedents for this third case, judges, in effect, would need to consider the legal appropriateness of describing the pairs of material facts under even more general classifications. The extension of the earlier encompassing classification to include Case #3 might look as follows:

FURTHER CLASSIFICATION OF MATERIAL FACTS

	Cases #1-2	Case #3	New Encompassing classification
Agent	adult	child	any person
Effect	kills	kills	kills
Victim	spouse	passer-by	another person
Means	gun	pea shooter	dangerous object
Intent	deliberate	deliberate	deliberate

Establishing relevant differences between Case #3 and Cases #1-2 involves deciding that further broadening of the description of even one category of material fact contradicts a legally accepted distinction. In this example, it is unlikely that the earlier cases would be accepted as relevantly similar to Case #3 because extension of at least two of the categories—agent and means—flies in the face of relevant legal distinctions. The extension of the agent category to "any person" would likely be unacceptable because the legal culpability of accused persons depends on their capacity to make rational choices. In criminal law, adults are often held responsible for their actions in ways that children are not. Thus, in this context, an adult is relevantly different from a child. Also, legal culpability may depend on the means, since the level of care that should be expected from a responsible person will differ. Pea shooters, which are essentially toys, albeit potentially dangerous ones, are a different order of dangerous object than guns. A person who fires a gun at another person should expect consequences that would not normally be expected from firing a pea shooter at a person. Thus, there is a relevant difference between the type of means employed in the cases. For both these reasons, despite considerable similarities between the cases, the prior cases would not set a precedent for a decision in Case #3.

An important point to note is that establishing relevant differences is governed by the legal considerations and distinctions that operate in the legal area or domain under consideration. Pairs of material facts may legitimately be regarded as relevantly similar in some contexts and not so in others. For example, section 28 of the *Charter* states that protected rights and freedoms are to extend equally to male and female persons. This clause may be cited by judges to argue against distinguishing between males and females with regard to constitutional rights. However, this general principle against drawing distinctions along gender lines is expressly overruled in section 15 of the *Charter* to permit affirmative action and other programs whose purpose is to overcome systemic inequality. In these latter contexts, distinguishing material facts on gender grounds may be legally warranted. For example, a decision that found no injustice in providing special employment incentives available only to women may be distinguished from (i.e., found to be relevantly dissimilar from) an otherwise identical program that provided special employment incentives available only to men.

Reasoning from prior cases is not simply a matter of deciding whether to follow or distinguish decisions reached in *individual* prior cases. Over time, many cases may cluster around key points of law. After repeated consideration of similar or nearly similar situations, principles of common law often emerge. It is instructive to see how reasoning from these broader principles continues to be in terms of reasoning by analogy.

Application of common law principles

It is frequently suggested that the reasoning involved in deciding to follow or distinguish individual cases is different from the reasoning involved in applying principles of common law, which are based on an accumulation of case law. I will respond to this suggestion by examining how case law evolves from a single *ratio* established in an individual case to a common law principle grounded in many cases. Then I will explain how application of common law principles in particular cases involves analogous reasoning.

As indicated previously, case law evolves continually as judges extend and qualify *rationes* in successive cases. For example, the evolving principle established by the three hypothetical cases cited above might be stated as "a mature person who kills another person through deliberate use of an inherently or obviously dangerous object is legally culpable." Issues raised by subsequent cases typically require reworking old cases—judges may re-express the initial *ratio* provided it can still justify the decision reached in prior cases. For example, the "agent" in Case #1 was a man and in Case #2 was a woman. A judge deciding whether these two cases are relevantly similar would consider the appropriateness of classifying both agents as "adults." It would be acceptable, however, to narrow this formulation to "adults of normal mental capacity" should a subsequent case involve a mentally handicapped adult, and still later to expand the formulation to "adults and mature adolescents of normal mental capacity" should another case involve a teenager. The fact that these distinctions did not occur to, or were ignored by, judges in the first three cases does not alter what can legitimately be declared as the *ratio* established in these prior cases. Cases have binding authority only for what is required to resolve the issues under consideration. The earlier cases did not consider mental ability or young adults, therefore they cannot be said to have decided these issues. Judges are restricted to deciding the specific case before them because it is considered unrealistic and unwise to expect judges to formulate a complete rule covering all possible cases. Lord Wright, an English judge, provided a graphic metaphor for the gradual evolution of case law through narrowly focused judicial decisions when he suggested that the courts proceed "from case to case, like the ancient Mediterranean mariners, hugging the coast from point to point and avoiding the dangers of the open sea."[97]

Despite the fact that cases are taken to settle only the issue before the court, judges regularly claim that they merely announce or declare a principle that was, until then, immanent in the law. The earlier discussed distinction between a rule and its formulation can help to further clarify the relationship between a principle underlying a body of cases and the *rationes* of individual cases: a *ratio* is a partial formulation of a more extensive, underlying, or immanent rule. The *ratio* of any single case is a "rule fragment" or "point of law," and only after repeated application and extensions do the accumulated *rationes* become a "complete rule" or common law principle. Although cases which subsequently follow or distinguish the initial case will alter the formulation (i.e., extend or restrict the initial *ratio*) they are, if correctly reasoned, based on an implicit rule underlying the initial case. Because of the doctrine of *stare decisis*, which requires that all relevantly similar cases be treated alike, the rule established implicitly in the initial decision consists, at least hypothetically, of the *ratio* of that case and the cumulative *rationes* of all other possible cases that are relevantly similar to it. Of course, that rule can never be completely formulated, as it is impossible to anticipate all the cases that might correctly be seen to be relevantly similar, and the actual judicial decisions may not all be correct. Nevertheless, the rule is, hypothetically speaking, implicit in the decision in the initial case, even though the formulation of the rule is imperfectly and very slowly enunciated through subsequent cases. One way to make explicit this point would be to imagine the following phrase added to every *ratio*: "and the *ratio* formulated from the material facts in this case includes all yet-to-be-determined situations whose material facts are relevantly similar." The practice of deciding only the matter before the courts is consistent with what judges have widely claimed; namely, that there is an unannounced rule driving the evolving judicial formulations.[98]

Acceptance of the notion that there is a nascent rule or principle underlying the evolution of case law fuels the impression that application of case law does not require analogous reasoning; that instead, it requires determining whether or not the rule or principle established in prior cases *subsumes* the facts of a subsequent case. I will examine this challenge in connection with one of the most famous cases in English common law, *Donoghue v. Stevenson* (extended excerpts of this House of Lords decision are presented in Chapter 9). In this case, a manufacturer of ginger beer was held responsible for personal injury to a woman caused by the presence of a dead snail in a bottle of ginger beer. The principle articulated in *Donoghue*, referred to as the "duty of care" principle, is often stated as follows: "manufacturers have a duty of care to their consumers." It is not the simple *ratio* established by the facts in *Donoghue* (i.e., a manufacturer of ginger beer is liable for damages caused by the presence of a snail in the bottle), but the more general common law principle enunciated in *Donoghue* that, presumably, has been applied in a "straightforward way" in subsequent cases. It is suggested that this application is a matter of determining if the material facts of subsequent cases fall within the scope of the established principle and not a matter of extending or restricting the scope of the principle by establishing relevant similarity among the material facts of the cases.[99]

The problem with this view is that it treats common law principles as formal declarations of a law (as are statutes and clauses in legal agreements) and not as approximate summaries of a body of case law. The mistaken view holds that repeated applications of a principle alter its legal pedigree and the manner in which it is to be applied. I contend that, properly understood, even repeatedly applied common law principles are necessarily tentative, evolving formulations of their accumulated *rationes*. Appeal to precedent, whether with reference to a single *ratio* or to a body of *rationes*, requires analogous reasoning. For convenience, since numerous judges have repeatedly and widely upheld a duty of care, it may be useful to refer to these many decisions in summary form as "the duty of care principle," rather than attempt a detailed cumulative formulation of individual *rationes*. Nonetheless, a duty of care has only been held to extend to those situations in which the courts have established a duty. Significantly, a 1970 English case stated that the duty of care principle articulated in *Donoghue* "is a basic and general but not universal principle and does not in law apply to all the situations which are covered by the wide words" used to describe the principle.[100] A case falling within the gap between the accumulated *rationes* and the formulated principle is to be resolved by deciding whether or not to distinguish the current case. Since repeated adoption of a principle in wide-ranging cases makes it increasingly remote that new cases with very similar fact patterns will be seen to be relevantly different, judges often seem to assume that the principle covers the new situation. However, this does not alter the judicial need to employ analogous reasoning should the question of relevant difference arise. As Lord Wilberforce observed in stating the duty of care principle in a 1978 English case, it remains necessary to ask "whether there are any considerations which ought to negate, or reduce or limit the scope of the duty or the class of person to whom it is owed or the damage to which a breach of it may give rise." This comment affirms that legally relevant differences should be considered, even in the case of common law principles, whenever the relevant similarity of circumstances is questionable.[101]

Contrary to what others have argued, reasoning from prior cases is not the direct subsumption of a current case under a rule established in prior cases. I have tried to show how the application of common law principles and of individual *rationes* both require analogous reasoning.[102]

Ascertaining the Authority of Relevant Cases

Reasoning from prior cases is not solely a matter of analogous reasoning. There is another consideration besides establishing the relevant similarity of prior cases to a current case that judges must entertain: they must also consider the weight to accord to prior decisions that are found to be relevantly similar. As discussed in Chapter 2, secondary rules of argument weight govern this calculation by determining the relative authority of the court issuing the decision and the relative authority of particular comments within a given judicial opinion.

The authority of a decision depends in part on the relative place within the judicial hierarchy of the courts in which the case is heard. In the Canadian system, all provincial and federal courts come under the jurisdiction of the Supreme Court of Canada. The decisions of this Court are binding (i.e., have compelling weight) on all other Canadian courts. A superior court has the power to overrule decisions reached by lower courts in its jurisdiction. Decisions by courts at the same level or lower are not binding, although they are recognized to carry some weight. Courts in different provinces are not bound by each others' decisions, although courts in one province would give greater importance to a decision of superior courts in another province than they would to lower courts in another province. Even the decisions of courts in other countries, but especially in Commonwealth countries and the United States, would have some weight or, as it is more commonly called, persuasive authority.

The nature of the judges' remarks and the context in which they are offered also affect the weight they will have in subsequent cases. Not everything that judges write in their *opinions*—their reasons for the decision and other related remarks—is afforded equal weight by other judges in subsequent cases. Only that part of the opinion that is necessary for the decision—those comments pertaining to what is seen to be the *ratio* of the case—is binding on future decisions. Other remarks, that are not necessary for deciding the case in the way in which it was decided, are called *obiter dicta* or "sayings by the way." For example, judges may speculate about the legal implications had the facts of the case been somewhat different. These additional comments, though not binding, are potentially persuasive, especially when expressed by a superior court or by judges known for their sound legal reasoning. Another factor affecting the weight of opinions is the degree of unanimity of the court. Often a single case will contain several opinions written by different judges. Decisions that are supported by all judges hearing the case have more authority than split decisions. Even *dissenting opinions*—opinions that are not supported by the majority of judges hearing the case— will carry some weight in subsequent cases. In relatively rare cases, a relevant prior case will be dismissed because the decision is *per incuriam*—the conclusion in the prior case is held to be mistaken because the judge neglected to consider essential questions of law in reaching the conclusion.[103]

Although the authority of the court and the comments within an opinion influence the weight that conclusions reached in prior cases will carry in subsequent cases, the heart of reasoning from prior cases is deciding the relevant similarity of cases—and this involves analogous reasoning.

JUDICIAL DISCRETION AND REASONING FROM PRIOR CASES

In this final section I examine three interrelated challenges to the view that this mode of reasoning is rule governed. Critics suggest that reasoning from prior cases inevitably requires exercise of judicial discretion for the following reasons: (1) difficulties in determining the rule that a prior case can be taken to have settled; (2) inherent inadequacies in the guidance offered by analogous reasoning; and (3) evidence of indisputable *law-making* power in judge-made case law.

Difficulties in Determining the Ratio

One common challenge to a rule-governed account of reasoning from prior cases is based on the observation that a given case can stand for several *rationes*. This challenge has at least two versions: (1) judges are frequently ambiguous or inconsistent in stating the *ratio*, and (2) there is inevitable arbitrariness in formulating *rationes*. For these reasons, it is suggested, reasoning from prior cases involves considerable judicial discretion.

Ambiguous or inconsistent rationes

Inconsistency between judges deciding the same case and ambiguity in individual judges' reasoning may cloud what a case can be taken to have established. Confusion arises most often when there are multiple judicial opinions offering conflicting accounts or when a judge has not explicated the issues with sufficient care. It is thought by some that the existence of ambiguous or competing *rationes* for a single case undermines the rule-guided nature of reasoning from prior cases.

Although the problems described above make judges' work more difficult and increase the likelihood of judicial errors in applying case law, it is not obvious that they require the exercise of judicial discretion. In dealing with ambiguous and inconsistent situations, judges endeavour to identify the most plausible *ratio* or otherwise resolve the confusion with maximal deference to the prior judges' reasoning. Since there is a clear rule that judges are not to be taken to have resolved any questions of law beyond those necessary to decide the issue before them, if resolving an ambiguity in a prior case is not required to decide a current case, judges will avoid drawing conclusions about the ambiguity. If deciding whether or not to accept the prior case as a precedent requires resolution of an ambiguity, judges will either offer what they regard as the most plausible account of the prior judges' reasoning, or they will conclude that no binding *ratio* can be extracted and the prior case cannot be presumed to settle the issue.[104] These ways of dealing with ambiguous or inconsistent statements are not a repudiation of the obligation to follow the *ratio* established in a prior case; rather, such ambiguities and inconsistencies impede its application. Although some judges will take advantage of ambiguities to rationalize their conclusions, it is not correct practice to do so. Judges are expected, to the extent possible, to resolve uncertainty about *rationes* in an impartial manner in light of the legal considerations outlined above.

Arbitrary rationes

Judicial latitude in identifying and characterizing the material facts of a case may mean that the determination of *rationes* is discretionary. The problem is not a matter of uncertainty over *the* correct *ratio,* but the apparent authorization to adopt any of a variety of *rationes* on a single point of law. *Donoghue* is frequently cited as an illustration of extensive latitude in formulating the *ratio* of a case—the material facts can be characterized across a wide spectrum ranging from a very specific to a very general description. For example, does *Donoghue* establish that liability arises if the source of harm is a dead snail? Or, can it be any snail; or any foreign, noxious object; or simply any noxious object? If a precise characterization of each material fact is offered, the *ratio* is very narrow. If broad categories are used, the case establishes an expansive *ratio.* It is claimed that judges exercise considerable discretion in determining the breadth of a *ratio* and this latitude determines what the case is taken to have established.[105]

Considerable looseness in the level of generality of formulated *rationes* does not necessarily imply exercise of judicial discretion. Much looseness on the part of judges in categorizing material facts may mean simply that, at the time, the judges perceived no plausible grounds for asserting a relevant difference between the descriptions of the material facts. For example, in delivering the decision in *Donoghue,* Lord Atkin rephrases the *ratio* in different words throughout his opinion, referring to it as a duty held by manufacturers of an "article of drink" and at a later point by manufacturers of products sold to consumers, and variously describes manufacturers' responsibility as extending to "injury to health" and later to "injury to the consumer's life or property."[106] Although the broader descriptions of the material facts may blur legally relevant distinctions, these formulations should not determine the outcome of subsequent cases as judges in subsequent cases are not bound by the generality of any of Lord Atkin's formulations. For example, although there is no reason to suspect that a manufacturer of ginger beer has a different responsibility than a manufacturer of lemonade, this issue and issues like it are not directly determined in *Donoghue* because resolving these questions is not necessary to a decision in *Donoghue.* Judges in subsequent cases are expected to consider, in light of the material facts before them, the specific details of the earlier case. The *Donoghue* decision indirectly settles issues for subsequent cases, not because its stated *ratio* subsumes the facts of the subsequent cases, but because the situations can be shown to be relevantly similar. The level of generality of the formulated *ratio* is not as crucial as some have claimed.[107]

Inadequacies in Analogous Reasoning

A second challenge asserts that analogous reasoning is inherently inadequate in guiding judicial decision making in a rule-governed manner. For example, the author of a textbook on judicial reasoning describes the determination of factual similarities and differences as "unguided" and as a "mysterious activity, subject to little apparent governance by the analogical form or the rules of the common law."[108]

As a general response to this challenge, I refer to my earlier efforts in this chapter to explicate the nature of analogous reasoning and the standards that judges are expected to rely upon in reasoning from prior cases. I will consider here two specific arguments that have been offered as evidence of the inadequacy of analogous reasoning: (1) in determining relevant similarity or difference, judges appeal to open-ended and seemingly subjective criteria such as common sense, reasonableness, public policy, and justice; and (2) reasoning by analogy does not accommodate the common judicial practice of assessing the desirability of a precedent. Before I respond to these claims, it is important to acknowledge that judges will sometimes (or perhaps even often) defend their decisions by appealing to prior cases even though the evidence fails to substantiate their conclusions. There are many possible explanations for this failure to satisfy expectations (e.g., mistaken or inadvertent reasoning, bias). However, judicial failure to perform up to expectations is not a repudiation of the existence of legal standards. Most writers, including those who regard reasoning from analogy as law making, support the view that judges have an obligation to provide defensible reasons to justify the distinctions they draw.[109]

There is nothing inherently discretionary in judges relying on common sense, reasonableness, or justice when ascertaining whether relevant differences exist between cases. Consider, for example, the difference between duty of care cases involving manufacturers of lemonade and ginger beer. The modest differences between these two products suggests it is highly improbable that the law would have any reason to distinguish between them. Therefore an appeal to common sense is recognition of the futility of even attempting to find legal grounds for drawing this distinction. It need not imply that judges are authorized to appeal to extra-legal intuitions about the appropriateness of recognizing a difference.

A second source of skepticism about the extent to which reasoning from prior cases is rule governed arises because the case law sometimes appears to "run out." Critics correctly notice that judges move from considering relevant similarity between cases based on previously identified distinctions towards evaluating the desirability of recognizing certain distinctions. For a variety of reasons, prior cases do not provide a conclusive resolution of every case before the court. Often, existing case law provides some authority for reaching a conclusion but is not sufficiently persuasive to offset opposing arguments or conflicting precedents. Alternatively, it may be unclear whether or not the law recognizes a relevant distinction between earlier cases and the current case either because there are conflicting grounds for asserting a distinction or because there is very little evidence supporting or refuting the relevance of a distinction. In these situations, judges cannot decide the current case on the basis of what was previously established.

The shifts to judicial assessment of the *desirability* of treating cases similarly arise because in situations where reasoning from prior cases is inconclusive judges correctly resort to what I describe as reasoning from principle. I explore the difference between reasoning from prior cases and reasoning from principle more fully in the next chapter, but a few remarks are in order here. Although reasoning from principle often takes place in the context of discourse about prior cases, it is different from reasoning from prior cases. The latter form of reasoning focuses on establishing that there are no legal distinctions that warrant treating a current case differently from a prior case. However, in situations where analogous reasoning is insufficient to provide a clear resolution, judges may be forced to decide whether or not to follow a prior case on the basis of the *legal desirability* of treating the cases as relevantly similar. In other words, the grounds for accepting a precedent are not *settled* legal distinctions but *legally most defensible* distinctions. Unlike reasoning from prior cases, which involves establishing the parallelism between cases, reasoning from principle involves evaluating the legal implications and consequences of accepting a principle. Dennis Lloyd, author of a classic introductory book on law, discusses *Candler v. Crane, Christmas & Co.,* a case where reasoning from principle is used to assess the implications of adopting a common law principle. The issue in the case was whether or not the duty of care principle applied to a property evaluator whose negligently completed evaluation resulted in an investor losing money. There were no clearly conclusive reasons for distinguishing or following the duty of care cases; thus the argument turned to the effect of broadening the principle to protect against investor loss. It was thought that the consequences of this extension would be far reaching and legally undesirable. For example, it would imply that a cartographer who negligently made a mistake on a marine chart would be libel for the loss of an ocean liner whose navigator had relied on the chart. As Lloyd explains, the objective in raising the hypothetical situation about the ocean liner was "to show that if a certain analogy is accepted it will lead to unfortunate consequences in other cases not easily or rationally distinguished from the present case."[110] As I explain in the next chapter, assessing the consequences in other cases of setting a precedent is a form of reasoning from principle.

Whether, in every case, reasoning from principle provides sufficiently clear grounds to justify one alternative over the others and whether that justification is rule governed are questions to be addressed in the upcoming chapter. However, the fact that reasoning from prior cases does not provide an answer in every situation is neither a flaw in the mode of reasoning nor a conclusive indication of judicial discretion. It means simply that in some situations judges cannot legitimately justify their decisions solely on the basis of relevant similarity to prior cases.

Reasoning from Prior Cases as Law Making

A third general challenge to a rule-governed explanation of reasoning from prior cases stems from the apparently indisputable fact that case law is judge-made law. Many reviewers conclude that judges cannot simply be applying law, they must also be involved in law "reform," "adaption," or "renovation."[111] Although most proponents of this view recognize that the "law-making" authority of judges is not identical to the power possessed by legislators, it is held to be perpetuating a myth or engaging in judicial self-deception to deny some law-making capacity. Precedent-setting decisions are frequently cited as examples of the law-making function of judges. How can these cases set precedent if they do not involve the creation of new law? Although I will not engage very deeply in what Neil MacCormick characterizes as the "often hot but always arid controversy" over whether judges do and should make law, I will briefly discuss how judges "make" law in ways that do not imply the exercise of judicial discretion.[112]

To begin, it is important to see that it is not inconsistent to claim that, on the one hand, a judicial decision altered or created new law, and, on the other hand, the judge did so by correctly applying pre-existing legal standards. This view is reflected in former Chief Justice Dickson's remarks about a controversial case over which he was accused of engaging in judicial activism:

> Was I declaring the law as it has always existed or was I making law? Irrespective of the answer, my firm conviction is that I was fulfilling the duty of a judge to decide the case before him or her in a "reasoned way from principled decision and established concepts."[113]

In one respect, each declaration of a judicial decision is law making—it represents an initial, official formulation of a *ratio*. However, the judges may merely have *declared* law by adducing a correct decision from recognized legal standards that had not previously been applied to the given context. Setting a precedent may simply imply that a judicial decision is identified as having confirmed the authority of a rule and, as Dickson's remarks suggests, that the justification for the declared decision is consistent with pre-existing standards. Thus, it may be claimed without contradiction that *judicial reasoning* is a strictly law-applying activity and that *judicial pronouncements* have law-making force. This seemingly paradoxical observation is echoed by Gideon Gottlieb, another proponent of a rule-governed conception of judicial reasoning:

> Every inference made and every rule enunciated must be authorized or required by preexisting rules and principles, but precedent transforms that which is authorized or required into what authorizes or requires. There is, therefore, no contradiction between the two propositions that courts always apply pre-existing law and that courts create law.[114]

Not all those who claim that judges make law would accept my explanation that judicial law making may simply be the result of applying pre-existing standards. Critics may concede that judges may merely be applying existing legal standards when they fill in gaps in those areas where the law has been silent or is vaguely defined. However, in other cases—for instance, when judges overturn prior decisions or invalidate existing statutes—critics contend that existing legal standards have been altered, not merely affirmed in new situations.[115] This objection is not convincing: judicial overruling and invalidation of legislation need not imply judicial imposition of law; judges may merely have done what was required by the law, all things considered. This point can be illustrated by the *Big M Drug Mart* case, discussed initially in Chapter 3. In this 1985 case, the Supreme Court invalidated Sunday closing provisions in the *Lord's Day Act*, despite the fact that the original legislators and many court decisions upholding the *Act* had resolved that certain stores were to be closed on Sundays. Along comes *Big M Drug Mart,* and a majority of the judges who heard the case decide to change the law. How is this not an example of discretionary law making by judges? My reply to this challenge is to consider who really changed the law. It must be remembered that in 1982 the Canadian government promulgated the *Charter*, which holds that any law inconsistent with certain fundamental rights, including freedom of religion, is "to the extent of the inconsistency, of no force or effect." The Court's decision in 1985 was to strike from the law books those sections of the *Lord's Day Act* that, in the Court's view, had been rendered unconstitutional by the *Charter*. Seen in this light, the Court's invalidation of the Sunday closing legislation was, in effect, the official declaration of a change in legal standards that had occurred three years earlier.

Similar charges of judicial discretion occasioned by the overturning of settled common law can be explained in terms of a failure to recognize that changing conditions present legally relevant grounds for inconsistent results. Since the applicability of common law principles depends on relevant similarities, dramatic technical or social changes may produce unexpected but nevertheless correct decisions. Consider the 1959 Supreme Court of Canada decision in *Fleming v. Atkinson*, which was described by one noted legal scholar as "judicial innovation."[116] In holding a farmer responsible for damages resulting from cattle that had wandered onto the road, the Court rejected a principle of English common law, dating from medieval times, that expressly exempted farmers from damage caused by stray cattle. The principle arose at a time when it was not customary for farmers to fence in their pastures and the immunity was offered by the government to induce farmers to allow the building of roads throughout the countryside. Because users of the roads were likely travelling in slow-moving carts, it was not unreasonable *at the time* to put the onus on the traveller to avoid stray cattle. In a split decision, the Supreme Court ruled that developments in negligence law arising from the duty of care principle, and the drastically different conditions in twentieth-century Ontario, justified rejecting the "wandering cattle immunity" principle in *Fleming v. Atkinson*. For the reasons discussed earlier about the need, even in the case of repeatedly applied common law principles, to consider the possibility of relevant differences, the Court distinguished this case from previous applications of the "wandering cattle immunity" principle. It should not be claimed that just because the Court did not affirm the common law principle in this case that it was imposing new (discretionary) law. Justice Cardozo's often-quoted remarks are relevant in this regard: "precedents drawn from the days of travel by stagecoach do not fit the conditions of travel today. The principle that danger must be imminent does not change, but the things subject to the principle do change."[117]

I have argued that reasoning from prior cases requires analogous reasoning and that this mode of reasoning is rule governed. The evolution of case law as prior cases are distinguished and followed is consistent with judges regarding their decisions to be controlled by legal standards. Also, since reasoning from prior cases will not resolve all disputes which come before the courts, judges will appeal to reasoning from principle. (In the next chapter, I discuss this third mode of reasoning.) Finally, I have tried to illustrate how many so-called reversals in law attributed to judicial discretion can be explained in terms of controlled judgments in response to independent changes in conditions and legal standards.

6
Reasoning from Principle

In cases which cannot be decided solely on the basis of interpretation or precedent, judges rely upon a third mode of reasoning, called *reasoning from principle*. As one writer suggests, resorts to principled reasoning "seal the gaps and settle the conflicts among black-letter legal rules, converting a tattered and torn fabric of rules into a seamless web of principle."[118] Although this statement exaggerates the rigidity of rules, it usefully highlights the ability of principled reasoning to resolve legal anomalies and dilemmas. Reasoning from principle requires that judges resolve disputes which cannot be settled by pre-established rules by evaluating proposed principles in light of the broader constellation of legal standards. In this chapter I examine the nature of reasoning from principle, including its relationship to the other modes of reasoning. I describe four common "tests" that judges employ when determining the legal acceptability of proposed principles and I illustrate their application with examples drawn from Canadian, American, and British cases. As I hope will become apparent, these tests provide for more controlled decision making than is implied by the characterization cited in Chapter 1 of this mode of reasoning as a "rudimentary methodology" intended to disguise judicial imposition of political values. In defending against claims that reasoning from principle is not rule governed, I discuss how judges distinguish legally authorized standards from unauthorized, "extra-legal" standards. This is an important concern since many standards to which judges appeal when justifying acceptance of a principle are not always explicitly identified in law but, nevertheless, underlie or are *embedded* in legal rules, practices, and institutions. Finally, I critique a widely discussed, alternative account of principled reasoning put forward by Ronald Dworkin.

THE NATURE OF REASONING FROM PRINCIPLE

When the other two approaches to applying law have been exhausted and the issue remains unresolved (i.e., a decision is not controlled by these modes of reasoning), judges are not free either to refuse to decide the issue or to impose their personally preferred solution. Rather, they must decide what, legally speaking, is the just solution to the dispute. As philosopher Gregory Vlastos remarked, "An action is just if, and only if, it is prescribed exclusively by regard for the rights of all whom it affects substantially."[119] Thus, if judges are to resolve a case in a *legally* just manner, as I believe they are obliged to do, they must consider the legally sanctioned interests of all who may have some stake in the decision. This consideration is called reasoning from principle because, in effect, judges must decide the particular issue by adopting a principle that is most respectful of the range of interests and values embodied in law. To call something a principle is to imply that it is a generalizable norm or standard that should be considered across a range of situations, as opposed to regulating a singular event. Although the terms are sometimes used interchangeably, reasoning from principle is not identical with reaching a "policy decision." A policy decision may merely reflect judicial evaluation based on the desired results for a particular option in the immediate case. To reason from principle is to decide that the situation at hand and all other similar situations ought, legally speaking, to be decided in a like manner; that is, they ought to be governed by the same principle.

In a classic work on principled legal reasoning, Columbia University law professor Herbert Wechsler refers to this form of reasoning as a search for "neutral" principles— the term "neutral" emphasizes that judges are not to decide because of a preferred outcome or desired result in the case before them, but they are to decide by adopting a more general principle that would apply in the immediate case and in other cases:

> I put it to you that the main constituent of the judicial process is precisely that it must be genuinely principled, resting with respect to every step that is involved in reaching judgment on analysis and reasons quite transcending the immediate result that is achieved. To be sure, the courts decide, or should decide, only the case before them. But must they not decide on grounds of adequate neutrality and generality, tested not only by the instant application but by others that the principles imply? Is it not the very essence of judicial method to insist upon attending to such other cases, preferably those involving opposing interest, in evaluating any principle avowed?[120]

This general point was made many years earlier by Lord Truro in an 1852 House of Lords decision, *Egerton v. Earl Brownlow*, when he noted that in assessing the desirability of a particular action "the law looks not to the probability of public mischief occurring in the particular instance, but to the general tendency of the disposition."[121]

Judicial resort to reasoning from principle occurs whenever judges consider the implications of possible conclusions in the case before them and in other actual and hypothetical situations that might fall within the principle if it were to be adopted. Because the law protects many diverse interests and attaches differing relative importance to these interests, reasoning from principle requires a judgment, all things considered, about the most legally acceptable principle to adopt.[122]

Although principles are involved in reasoning from interpretive guidelines and prior cases, their role in these modes is different than in reasoning from principle. This difference is reflected in a distinction between *appealing to a principle* and *deciding as a matter of principle*. To appeal to a principle is to recognize an already-adopted principle as a reason for deciding how to act; to decide as a matter of principle is to determine what principle should be adopted as a guide to action. Consider the interpretive principle known as the presumption in favour of international law. This principle suggests that, in the absence of evidence to the contrary, judges should interpret legislation in a manner that is consistent with international law or treaties. That this is a recognized legal principle means that it is valid to appeal to this presumption when interpreting statutes. In reasoning from interpretive guidelines and reasoning from prior cases, existing legal principles are regularly appealed to as reasons for decisions—the purpose of these appeals to recognized precedents is to establish the meaning of words or the relevant similarity between cases. Reasoning from principle, on the other hand, requires that judges determine the acceptability of a principle—to establish whether or not a particular principle *warrants* being accepted as a reason for the decision. Suppose the presumption in favour of international law was not already recognized as a valid interpretive principle and that, in a given case, the only difference between two plausible interpretations of a statute was that only one was consistent with international law. If the interpretation that is more consistent with international law is to be accepted over the other interpretation, then the judge must decide, as a matter of principle, that the presumption *should* be accepted as a legal reason for deciding these types of situations. Justification for its adoption would be found by evaluating, for example, the compatibility or consistency of the proposed principle with other, more fundamental legal principles such as the rule of law and parliamentary supremacy. Since international treaties are typically ratified by parliament, judges are warranted in concluding that adopting this principle respects legislative wishes more than would a decision to reject the principle. The decision to adopt the principle could also be justified on the grounds that respecting public declarations of legal standards such as those embodied in international law promotes two recognized values of our legal system—certainty and predictability in law. In other words, in reasoning from principle the judge would evaluate the implications and consequences of adoption (or rejection) of the interpretive principle in light of other legal values and standards.

It is often difficult to distinguish when judges are *appealing to* principle (in the course of either reasoning from interpretive guidelines or reasoning from prior cases) and when they are *reasoning from* principle. One source of this difficulty is the frequent intertwining of the modes of reasoning. An example of reasoning from principle in connection with interpreting statutes was outlined in Chapter 4, when I discussed the introduction of legislative history as a principle of interpretation. To avoid the undesirable situation of having to contradict the clear intentions of the legislators, the U.S. Court accepted in *Holy Trinity Church v. United States* the use of legislators' remarks. A case discussed in Chapter 3, *Big M Drug Mart*, provides an example of reasoning from principle occurring in the context of reasoning from prior cases. As you may remember, several U.S. decisions upholding the constitutionality of Sunday closing legislation were offered as authority for a similar finding in connection with the *Lord's Day Act*. The American courts had concluded that because of repeated amendments and changing conditions, an initial Christian purpose for Sunday closing legislation had shifted, in effect, to a secular purpose. On the basis of this accepted shift in the purpose of the legislation, the U.S. courts upheld the constitutionality of American Sunday closing laws. Only if Canadian law recognized the "shifting purpose" approach would these American cases provide authority for the *Big M Drug Mart* case. Since there was no clear Canadian authority for the validity of this approach, the Supreme Court had to decide whether or not it was an acceptable principle. Reasoning from principle, the Court rejected the shifting purpose approach because if it were widely adopted in subsequent cases, it would undermine the doctrine of precedent and it was thus considered inconsistent with fundamental tenets of "Parliamentary intention." In effect, the Court interrupted its reasoning from prior cases to resolve uncertainty about the validity in Canadian law of the shifting purpose approach and decided this issue by considering the implications of accepting the approach as a principle of law.[123]

Understanding the difference between appealing to an accepted principle and deciding whether or not to adopt a principle is key to understanding how principled reasoning provides a mechanism for resolving disputes when the "rules" appear to run out. If principled reasoning consisted of application of a finite set of principles, situations would inevitably arise where the principles fail to control the decision. These gaps are unavoidable consequences of appealing to principles. No set of pre-determined principles will resolve all situations; problematic situations are bound to arise. As the British moral philosopher R.M. Hare explains:

> Suppose that we have a principle to act in a certain way in certain circumstances. Suppose then that we find ourselves in circumstances which fall under the principle, but have certain other peculiar features, not met before, which make us ask "Is this principle really intended to cover cases like this, or is it incompletely specified—is there here a case belonging to a class which should be treated as exceptional?" Our answer to this question will be a decision, but a decision of principle, as is shown by the use of the value-word "should." If we decide that this should be an exception, we thereby modify the principle by laying down an exception to it.[124]

Unlike appeals to principles, reasoning from principle provides a flexible mechanism by which unresolved conflicts and gaps can be considered. When confronted with a legal anomaly or dilemma that cannot be resolved by interpretation or precedent, judges evaluate which option best serves the broader legal values and standards that comprise a legal system. Although the conclusions frequently may be controversial because of the need to weigh conflicting considerations, there are abundant legally authorized standards upon which to determine the most acceptable resolution of a dispute.

RULES FOR REASONING FROM PRINCIPLE

Judges rely on reasoning from principle whenever reasoning from interpretive guidelines and from prior cases fail to produce a conclusive result. As I have explained, reasoning from principle requires that judges assess the broader acceptability of adopting a principle which decides the immediate issue before the court. In effect, judges "test" the acceptability of the principle they are asked to consider. University of British Columbia professor Jerrold Coombs has identified four ways by which principles are tested: (1) assessing a proposed principle for consistency with other fundamental principles; (2) assessing the consequences of adopting the principle for all parties who may be affected; (3) assessing the consequences of adopting the principle in other relevantly similar cases; and (4) assessing the cumulative consequences of adopting the principle in repeated instances.

In applying these tests, it will not always be immediately obvious whether or not a principle is legally acceptable. For example, a proposed principle may be consistent with some established legal principles and inconsistent with others. In these situations, judges must weigh the pros and cons in light of the relative importance of the legal values and standards involved. This need to weigh conflicting reasons is a similar form of conductive argumentation to that found in reasoning from interpretive guidelines and reasoning from prior cases. I will now discuss each of these ways of testing the acceptability of a principle.[125]

Consistency with Fundamental Principles

In cases where judges are faced with the need to decide whether or not to adopt a principle, they will consider if the proposed principle is consistent with already-recognized legal principles. It would be arbitrary for judges to ignore the extent to which a proposed principle advances the basic values of the legal system. In fact, this appeal to consistency with established legal principles is an extension of, and in some contexts difficult to distinguish from, judicial use of principles in interpretation and precedent. Consider the following three examples.

(1) In *R. v. Bryant*, the issue was the acceptability of a *Criminal Code of Canada* provision that denied accused persons the option of trial by jury if they failed to appear for trial at the scheduled time. The *Criminal Code* stipulated that individuals who failed to appear be tried by judge alone. The Crown argued that the failure to show up at the scheduled time should be seen as a waiver of the right, established under the *Charter,* to a jury trial. In rejecting this conclusion, Justice Blair reasoned that the principle implied by the argument was inconsistent with the very notion of constitutionally entrenched rights:

> I cannot fail to note the serious implications of the Crown's argument. If it prevailed, it might be possible to legislate the denial of *Charter* rights simply by providing that persons whose rights are taken away by statute are concurrently deemed to have waived them. *Charter* rights cannot be destroyed in this fashion.[126]

In other words, the judge rejected the *Criminal Code* provision as a reason for overriding a constitutionally protected right because the implied principle was inconsistent with the express purpose of constitutional rights—they are intended to protect citizens from governmental use of ordinary legislation to encroach on individual rights.

(2) In *Davis v. Johnson,* the English Court of Appeal considered whether an obviously incorrect decision by that Court in a prior case was binding in the present case. For Sir George Baker, the most compelling reason why an exception should be made to the doctrine of *stare decisis* was that to do otherwise would be inconsistent with his judicial oath. The judge averred that following a decision which he firmly believed to be based on an incorrect reading of a statute conflicted with his vow "to do right to all manner of people after the laws and usages of the Realm."[127]

(3) In *McCulloch v. Maryland,* the U.S. Supreme Court considered the legality of the State of Maryland's tax on federal bank notes issued by the Baltimore branch of the United States Bank. As the following report explains, one of Chief Justice Marshall's reasons for disallowing the tax was its inconsistency with the principle of no taxation without representation:

Counsel for the state asserted that, since the federal government may tax state-chartered banks, a corresponding power must be held to exist in the states. Marshall replied that the analogy was improper since the people of all the states, and the states themselves, were represented in Congress, while a state taxing the operations of the federal government would act upon institutions created by people over whom it had no control. In contrast to federal taxation, an exercise of such power by the states would constitute a form of taxation without representation, contrary to the basic intent of the Constitution.[128]

Consequences for All Parties

A second way in which judges evaluate the acceptability of a principle is by assessing the consequences of adopting the principle for all of the parties likely to be affected. This consideration extends beyond the litigants in a case to include third parties whose interests may be at stake. The consideration of other parties' interests is manifested in judges' willingness, especially in constitutional cases, to allow intervener status to individuals and groups with a legitimate stake in the outcome. One justification for the all parties test is the principle of equal treatment before the law. Implicit in the notion of equal treatment is the requirement that one's rights and legally sanctioned interests be respected as impartially as those of any other party who may be affected by a decision. Of course, not all consequences of a decision are legally relevant—only the consequences implied for the legal rights and sanctioned interests of each of the affected parties are to be considered. Consider the following three examples.

(1) In *M. v. Director of Child Welfare,* the Queen's Bench of Alberta decided that provincial welfare officials had the right to apprehend S., a premature baby, and authorize blood transfusions for her. As S.'s parents were Jehovah's Witnesses, it was against their sincerely held religious beliefs to allow their child to receive blood from another person. In deciding that the welfare officials' actions were warranted, the Court weighed the dire consequences for the baby of not overriding the parents' *Charter* rights to liberty and religious freedom:

> Even if one were to accept the view that one of the liberty interests to be protected by s[ection] 7 is the parental right to be free from state intervention as suggested in *T.T. v. C.C.A.S. of Metro Toronto* (1984) ... that case recognizes that the application of s.7 "requires in some cases an obvious balancing of protected but competing rights" (p. 358). In the circumstances of the case before me, S.'s right to life must take precedence over any competing right of the parents where to do otherwise would seriously endanger her chances for survival.
>
> In the case before me, it is true that the effect (although not the purpose) of the relevant sections of the *Child Welfare Act* is to impinge on the parents' rights to direct the medical treatment of their child in accordance with their religious beliefs. Nonetheless, if the exercise of the parents' right would result in the withholding of essential medical services to S., then the need to protect the health of S. and her right not to be deprived of life may result in her parents being required to act in a way contrary to their religion by giving up S. for the purpose of medical treatment including blood transfusions. ... It would overshoot the actual purpose of the *Charter* if religious freedom were allowed to be exercised in such a way as to deprive a baby of a realistic chance of life.[129]

(2) In *Express Newspapers v. McShane,* the English House of Lords considered rival arguments for interpreting labour relations legislation that provided union officials with immunity for acts done "in contemplation or furtherance" of labour disputes. It was not obvious whether the immunity applied as long as union officials believed that their acts would further the dispute or whether a more stringent condition was necessary; namely, that union officials have rational beliefs about the effects of their actions. According to the following report, two of the Lords argued for the more stringent interpretation because of the consequences for innocent people who might be affected if union leaders were allowed to invoke excessive measures:

> Lord Wilberforce thought that it would give no protection to innocent and powerless third parties against the actions of enthusiasts and extremists, who believed that their excessive action was necessary. Similarly, Lord Salmon argued that grievous harm could result to others, such as in the recent instance of pickets preventing oil deliveries to Charing Cross Hospital, which brought some cancer patients near to death.[130]

(3) In *Miranda v. Arizona,* the U.S. Supreme Court considered the protections due to accused persons in the criminal justice system. In arguing unsuccessfully against a requirement that accused persons be advised of their rights when detained by criminal justice officials—what eventually came to be known as the Miranda warnings—Justice White raised the need to consider the interests of society at large:

> The Court's duty to assess the consequences of its action is not satisfied by the utterance of the truth that a value of our legal system of criminal justice is "to respect the inviolability of the human personality" and to require government to produce the evidence against the accused by its own independent labor. ... More than the human dignity of the accused is involved; the human personality of others in the society must also be preserved. Thus the values reflected by the privilege are not the sole desideratum; society's interest in the general security is of equal weight.[131]

Consequences in New Cases

Another way of testing a principle involves considering the consequences should the decision in the present case establish a precedent. This test derives from the principle of formal justice that like cases be treated alike. If adopting the principle would have undesirable consequences when applied in a relevantly similar case, this is a reason for rejecting it in the present case. It has sometimes been thought that this consideration requires that judges "work out the full impact upon future cases" or have "fully elaborated theories" of an area of law, but this objection is based on a misunderstanding. The new cases test requires that judges consider the principles before them in light of other hypothetical cases that are *clearly* covered by the proposed principle and indistinguishable upon valid grounds from the current case. Consideration of the consequences for new cases does not presume a before-the-fact resolution of controversial future cases with uncertain results. Rather, it is a strategy for testing the broader acceptability of a principle. When a later court encounters a situation that an earlier court has explicitly cited as a hypothetical instance of a principle, the later court is not bound to regard the case in that way but may distinguish its case from the prior case that established the principle.[132]

The following three examples illustrate judicial testing of the acceptability of a principle by assessing the consequences in hypothetical cases considered to be relevantly similar to the one at issue.

(1) In *Morgentaler v. The Queen* (1988), one of the lawyers had urged jurors to find Dr. Morgentaler not guilty if they thought that the law restricting abortion was a "bad" law. The Supreme Court criticized this action because, among other things, it would set a precedent whereby lawyers could encourage juries to reject any law of which they did not approve. In arguing for the undesirability of this principle, former Chief Justice Dickson offered the following hypothetical case: "To give a harsh but I think telling example, a jury fueled by the passions of racism could be told that they need not apply the law against murder to a white man who had killed a black man." In other words, if the "bad law" principle was accepted in the *Morgentaler* case, it would sanction, in Chief Justice Dickson's opinion, the untenable use of the principle to encourage racist juries to reject the legal rights of others.[133]

(2) In *Donoghue v. Stevenson,* Lord Macmillan considered the desirability of adopting the duty of care principle by entertaining the following hypothetical situation:

Suppose that a baker, through carelessness, allows a large quantity of arsenic to be mixed with a batch of his bread, with the result that those who subsequently eat it are poisoned, could he be heard to say that he owed no duty to the consumers of his bread to take care that it was free from poison, and that, as he did not know that any poison had got into it, his only liability was for breach of warranty under his contract of sale to those who actually bought the poisoned bread from him?[134]

(3) In *Riggs v. Palmer,* Justice Earl offered a number of arguments why a teenager who murdered his grandfather should not be allowed to inherit under his grandfather's will. One argument appealed to the consequences arising in a variety of cases if a precedent was established allowing persons to gain their interest in property through crime.

If he had met the testator and taken his property by force, he would have had no title to it. Shall he acquire title by murdering him? If he had gone to the testator's house and by force compelled him, or by fraud or undue influence had induced him to will him his property, the law would not allow him to hold it. But can he give effect and operation to a will by murder, and yet take the property? To answer these questions in the affirmative, it seems to me, would be a reproach to the jurisprudence of our state, and an offense against public policy.[135]

Consequences for Repeated Instances

Another way in which judges test principles is by considering whether the desirability of deciding the case in a particular way would change if repeated instances of this type of case were to occur. There are two variations on this test. The first, known as the "floodgates" or "parade of horribles" or *in terrorem* argument, considers the consequences arising from the numerous cases that would immediately fall within the proposed principle. The second, commonly known as the "slippery slope" argument, looks to the consequences arising from the numerous cases that would gradually qualify within the law because of the inevitable direction in which adopting the proposed principle moves the law. Unlike considering the consequences in new cases, which is based on the desirability of results in any relevantly similar case, the repeated instance test considers whether the consequences of numerous occasions are acceptable. This test is derived from the principle of treating like cases alike. Even if the consequences arising from a single application of a principle may be acceptable, if the consequences of repeated applications are unacceptable, with no rational way to justify allowing only some instances of the act, then justice requires preventing everyone from acting in that way.[136] Consider the following examples.

(1) A second argument raised in *Morgentaler* against the lawyer's suggestion that jurors disregard "bad" law focused on the consequences of every jury acting on that advice. The cumulative effect would be to make it impossible to predict the law since the decision on every occasion would depend on how members of that jury happened to feel at the time. In presenting his opinion, Chief Justice Dickson cited an argument offered in an eighteenth-century English case involving criminal libel charges against a newspaper.

> In opposition to this, what is contended for?—That the law shall be, in every particular cause, what any twelve men who shall happen to be the jury, shall be inclined to think; liable to no review, and subject to no control, under all the prejudices of the popular cry of the day, and under all the bias of interest in this town, where thousands, more or less, are concerned in the publication of newspapers, paragraphs, and pamphlets. Under such an administration of law, no man could tell, no counsel could advise, whether a paper was or was not punishable.[137]

(2) In *London Street Tramways v. London County Council,* the House of Lords decided against reversing an earlier precedent even though the precedent had harsh consequences for individuals in the case before them. Their decision to adhere to the precedent relied heavily on the repeated instances test.

> I do not deny that cases of individual hardship arise, and there may be a current of opinion in the profession that such and such a judgment was erroneous; but what is that occasional interference with what is perhaps abstract justice compared with the inconvenience—the disastrous inconvenience—of having each question subject to being re-argued and the dealings of mankind rendered doubtful by reason of different decisions, so that in truth there can be no final court of appeal.[138]

(3) A second argument offered by Chief Justice Marshall in *McCulloch v. Maryland* against allowing the states to tax federal bank notes was the cumulative effects on the federal government's capacity to operate effectively should the constitutionality of the tax be upheld.

> If the states may tax one instrument, employed by the government in the execution of its powers, they may tax any and every other instrument. They may tax the mint; they may tax the mail; they may tax patent-rights; they may tax the papers of the custom house; they may tax judicial process; they may tax all the means employed by the government, to an excess which would defeat all ends of government.[139]

The discussion of reasoning from principle has focused thus far on the four ways by which judges test the legal acceptability of a principle. Although I have explained the form of these tests, I have said little about the standards to which these tests appeal, beyond the claim that these tests must be carried out in light of recognized legal standards. As I will now explain, a crucial issue in explicating this form of reasoning is distinguishing *bona fide* legal standards from what are often called "extra-legal" standards.

JUDICIAL DISCRETION AND REASONING FROM PRINCIPLE

The need to distinguish legal standards from other standards that might be appealed to in reasoning from principle arises because of the problem of judicial discretion. If there were no grounds for distinguishing legally valid arguments from "extra-legal" arguments, reasoning from principle would not control judicial decision making, as judges would be free to select their own criteria for deciding the issue. For example, in reasoning from principle on a case involving blood transfusions, judges might decide to evaluate the alternatives in light of their private religious convictions. This would not qualify as an appeal to *legally valid* standards because it is widely recognized that judges are not authorized to decide issues according to their personal views of what may be morally desirable. If reasoning from principle is rule guided, we should expect to find rules which establish the legal validity of the criteria to which judges are authorized to appeal when evaluating alternatives.

As indicated in the examples above, judges sometimes appeal to recognizable rules, such as the principle of no taxation without representation or a constitutional right to life, to provide the standards against which a proposed principle will be evaluated. However, in reasoning from principle judges often appeal to standards, such as "public policy," "social policy," "justice," and "community values," which are not self-evidently *bona fide* legal standards. These seemingly moral standards are regularly cited by judges as legal standards even though the specific principles have not been expressly and authoritatively stated beforehand. For example, in the *Miranda* opinion discussed above, Justice White confirmed that respect for the inviolability of the human personality was a value of the American legal system of criminal justice without there being any previous, expressly stated rule to that effect. Many moral and social values are relied upon by judges as reasons for deciding a case. How can these appeals be reconciled with the claim that judges are not authorized to appeal to "extra-legal" standards?

Legally Embedded Standards

The labels used to refer to standards can be arbitrary; it may be immaterial whether, for example, "justice" and "community values" are called "legal," "moral," or "social" values. The key issue is distinguishing, on the one hand, appeals to "moral" and other values that can legitimately be said to be recognized in law (i.e., those instantiated in laws, and implicit in the *bona fide* practices of legal officials and institutions) from, on the other hand, appeals to personal or political morality that are not legally sanctioned. Many so-called moral and social values are embodied in legal rules and practices: principles about keeping a certain range of promises underlie contract law; the principle of avoiding injury to others underlies the law of torts; and principles of fairness are reflected in our procedures for establishing the guilt of accused persons. It is permissible to appeal to these social and political values only because they are "the built-in values of the system"—embodied in accepted legal norms—and not because they are politically or morally attractive.[140]

The U.S. Supreme Court's reasoning in *Miranda* illustrates why references to "justice" and "community values" are not unauthorized appeals to "extra-legal" standards but valid appeals to standards grounded in law. In opening his majority opinion, Justice Warren remarked that the case raised "questions which go to the roots of our concepts of American criminal jurisprudence." Starting with the abusive treatment of prisoners in seventeenth-century England, he traced the rationale for protection of accused persons. Over time, the protection against such "iniquities" had become "firmly embedded in English, as well as in American jurisprudence." Although Justice White admitted that respect for the "inviolability of the human personality" was legal value, he added that it was also vitally important to protect other "community values" and in particular "society's interest in the general security." In justifying consideration of the latter value, he suggested that the most basic function of any government is to provide for the security of individuals and property. These aims of society are served by the criminal laws which, for the most part, seek to prevent crime. Significantly, in justifying reliance on these standards, the Court grounded these values in legal rules and institutions.[141]

Disputed Legal Standards

It is often not clear what values and standards are embedded in law. Judges may disagree about which values underlie a legal practice or constitute the purpose of a statute. It is sometimes suggested that judges bring their preferred values to the law rather than find them in the law. As I have explained previously, it is important to distinguish between situations where judges fail to live up to the impartial role they are expected to perform in carrying out their judicial duties and situations where the accepted forms of judicial reasoning fail to provide a rule-governed way of resolving disputes about legal standards. Only the latter kind of situation is a challenge to a rule-governed account of judicial reasoning.

The reasoning in *Law Society of Upper Canada v. Skapinker* indicates how disputes about embedded legal values are to be resolved in a rule-governed manner. Although the case involves reasoning from interpretive guidelines, it illustrates how judges justify, by appeal to secondary rules, their determinations of the purpose or implicit values in the constitution. In the *Skapinker* case, the Supreme Court was confronted with several "arguably applicable" interpretations of the *Charter*'s guarantee "to secure the gaining of a livelihood in any province." A key issue in deciding among rival interpretations was the underlying purpose of the provision. Was the point (or underlying value) to secure a right to work or to protect inter-provincial migration? The wording of the provision implied the former purpose, whereas the heading of the "mobility rights" section in which the provision fell implied the latter purpose. In the end, acceptance of the latter interpretation hinged on the validity of headings as indicators of implied purpose. The Court appealed to many interpretive guidelines, including Canadian interpretation acts, prior Canadian and foreign judicial decisions, and Canadian authorities on interpretation, as justification for deciding that headings were legitimate means for ascertaining the purpose of a specific provision.[142] On this basis, the Court determined that promoting inter-provincial mobility, and not guaranteed work, was the implicit value in this *Charter* provision. The important, more general, point is that judges are expected to rely on one or more of the three modes of reasoning when resolving disputes about embedded legal values and standards.

Before leaving our discussion of reasoning from principle, it will be useful to contrast the account I offer with the most widely discussed version of principled reasoning, an account offered by Ronald Dworkin. After presenting his version, I will explain its limitations.

DWORKIN'S ACCOUNT OF PRINCIPLED REASONING

Ronald Dworkin portrays law as a morally coherent practice. The implication for judicial reasoning is that judges must decide cases on the basis of the principles consistent with the best political justification for law as a coherent social practice.[143] In the context of principled reasoning, there are two important differences between Dworkin's conception and the one I offer. Under Dworkin's scheme, a judge would defend a principled decision by appealing to the underlying political justification for a particular area of law or, more generally, for the legal system as a whole; the position I put forward requires that judges defend a decision in light of specific, embedded legal standards. Also, for Dworkin, the justification of a decision must be, so far as is possible, in terms of a coherent theory of political morality; that is, it must reflect a single, uncompromising justification in light of the community's public standards of justice and fairness. According to the account I defend, judges are not required to assume that legal standards are part of a larger coherent scheme, nor must they construct a theory of political morality in order to decide which alternative to select. I will consider each of these differences.

Appeals to Extra-Legal Principles

Dworkin correctly notes that standards that have not been previously cited in textbooks or in prior judicial decisions are often used by judges in justifying their decisions. He recognizes that principles which are "embedded" or "implicit" in legal rules, practices, and institutions have "institutional support." Dworkin believes, however, that identifying embedded legal standards amounts to moral theorizing. He suggests that in most situations any number of values can qualify as the implicit legal standards. Dworkin's resolution of this predicament is to have judges select from among rival "embedded" principles or "implicit" values on the basis of the most flattering justification for the body of law in question. Thus, according to Dworkin, "the process of 'drawing' principles from institutional history is the process of judging justifications of that history."[144]

Dworkin's notion of what counts as an embedded principle is flawed because it collapses a crucial distinction between principles that *possibly* could be offered as justification and those that are *defensibly* attributed to a legal system. Dworkin's implicit definition of embedded is so loose that as long as a principle was a plausible justification for a rule it could be acceptable as the principle implied by the rule. According to the generally accepted notion of embedded legal values, judges are not at liberty to impute values merely because they *could* be a justification for a rule. For example, in *Quebec Association of Protestant School Boards v. Attorney-General,*

Quebec's Chief Justice distinguished the "philosophical foundation" of linguistic rights from the "legal attributes" and "judicial implementation" of linguistic rights. The latter and not the former were accepted as valid legal considerations.[145]

The importance of respecting a distinction between hypothetically and actually embedded legal values can be seen by considering the implications of admitting any possible reason for a rule as the principle or value implied by the rule. Imagine, for the sake of argument, that parents establish a rule limiting to one hour per day the amount of television their daughter may watch. Suppose the child realizes that on a given day she will not be able to watch television and so she requests permission to watch television for two hours on another day. The rule's proper application in this situation depends on what is taken to be the rule's purpose. If the point is to prevent possible damage to eyesight that is believed to occur when children watch sustained amounts of television in a short duration, then the rule would not allow accumulation of viewing time. However, if the point of the rule is to leave time for the child to develop other long-term interests, then, provided her total amount of viewing time is not increased, the rule's purpose would be met by allowing flexibility in allotting viewing time. Alternatively, if the point is to ensure that the daughter has ample time to complete her homework, then the proper application of the rule would be contingent on the amount of homework she had been assigned on the day in question. Without further information, we can be no more specific about the point of this rule beyond claiming that its purpose is to limit the amount of television that the child watches. If we know no more about the rule's purpose than is indicated above (i.e., we cannot determine which of these possible purposes underlies, or is embedded in, or could be taken to be implied by the rule), we cannot decide whether to allow the child to accumulate television time on the basis of the rule's purpose. Dworkin, on the other hand, invites us to select from the possible reasons for the parents' rule the one justification that would show the rule in its best light. It may turn out, however, that this justification is at odds with the parents' stated or generally agreed purpose for the rule.

Dworkin appeals to political morality because, in his opinion, it is the only defensible way for judges to reach a principled decision when faced with several alternatives. He recommends that judges appeal to the principles that (could) justify these alternatives. In other words, resolution of difficult cases pushes judges beyond the law to the political values that subsume the law. I have already discussed two reasons for rejecting this view: it is not inevitable that judges will be forced to decide between alternatives by appealing to political morality, and appeals of the sort Dworkin suggests are not representative of generally accepted judicial practice. I have argued that the modes of judicial reasoning provide for resolution of disputes about embedded legal values and standards in ways that do not require appeals to principles that are not clearly grounded in law. Furthermore, characterizing a principle as an embedded legal principle merely because it could possibly be offered as a desirable justification for a statute or legal practice is inconsistent with the recognized interpretation of this notion. Speculating about the politically most desirable justification for legislation or legal practices is considered beyond the judges' authority. In addition, cases like

Miranda suggest that embedded legal principles reflect legally sanctioned values such as the *recognized* purpose(s) of legislation and legal institutions and the interests clearly protected by individual laws and bodies of law. In other words, the established norms of the legal system, not the broader political community, supply the values that are to provide the criteria for judicial evaluation of the acceptability of proposed principles.[146]

Overall Coherence

A second discrepancy between Dworkin's conception of judicial reasoning and the one I propose involves the role of overall coherence. Overall coherence requires that judges assess the acceptability of an individual legal proposition by evaluating its fit with the most politically defensible conception of law. There are two reasons for dismissing Dworkin's claims about the coherence or "integrity" of law as a alternative to the account of judicial reasoning I propose: (1) Dworkin's proposal may, in fact, collapse into the account I offer, and (2) Dworkin does not appear to claim that judges actually regard appeals to overall coherence as authorized judicial practice.

In the final chapter of his book *Law's Empire*, Dworkin announces a significant compromise in his account of the role of overall coherence in judicial reasoning when he admits that his theory is an idealized picture of law. This admission is raised in the context of distinguishing two levels or kinds of integrity: inclusive integrity and pure integrity. Pure integrity is the ideal of a coherent justification of legal practice unsoiled by the constraints imposed by actual institutional practices. However, judicial implementation of this ideal is possible only if the legislation within a jurisdiction reflects a coherent theory of the political morality of the community. Dworkin admits that legislators often fail to live up to this ideal and that judges are left to implement inclusive integrity—"[t]he law we have, the actual concrete law for us, is fixed by inclusive integrity. This is law for the judge, the law he is obliged to declare and enforce."[147] Unlike pure integrity, which implies substantive coherence (the content of individual principles being consistent with the judge's perception of the overall justification of law), inclusive integrity is tied to formal criteria—a principle may be acceptable simply because it is embodied in legislation or implied by precedent. Consequently, judges are precluded from appealing to coherence theories of political morality (i.e., pure integrity) until the recognized legal standards protected by the principle of "fairness" are exhausted. It is significant that Dworkin refers to three types of second-order criteria for applying the law—precedent, interpretation, and local priority—as requirements of procedural due process.[148] If the modes of reasoning I offer are the accepted "procedural" standards of adjudication—part of what Dworkin calls "the legal standards of the day"—then inclusive integrity requires that judges adhere to them. Thus, Dworkin's notion of inclusive integrity may collapse into the modes of reasoning I articulate, and there may be few occasions, if any, where recognized legal standards fail to control judicial decisions.

Should Dworkin concede that the modes of judicial reasoning adequately characterize acceptable judicial practice, he must relegate his theory of adjudication to the most extreme cases, where the modes of reasoning I articulate fail to control judicial decisions. There is some attraction to the notion that, after exhausting the recognized standards of adjudication, judges would appeal to their view of the overall (idealized) point of law—to conceive of law in its best light—in attempting to decide the otherwise unresolved issue before them. Since Dworkin apparently holds a narrow and inflexible view of the "legal standards of the day" (viz., rules apply only to the extent of their explicit denotation), it is not surprising that he believes judges would need to resort to his adjudicative criteria in all "difficult" (i.e., most appeal) cases.[149] However, I have argued that a rule-guided model of judicial reasoning can account for standards that control judges' decisions in almost all cases. If I am right about the extent to which they control decisions in even difficult cases, then Dworkin's theory is largely superfluous.

Even if Dworkin's theory is not superfluous, there is good reason to suspect that Dworkin does not suppose that his theory faithfully represents judicial practice. Dworkin appears repeatedly to *urge* judicial adoption of his theory of integrity rather than to claim that it describes the reasoning that judges are currently expected to follow in applying law. Since my concern has been to explicate the authorized forms of reasoning, not to speculate about their improvements, Dworkin's theory is largely irrelevant to the central purpose of this book.[150]

Before moving to the final section, a few remarks are in order about what I have argued thus far. In this chapter and in the two previous chapters, I have outlined and documented three forms of reasoning that, I suggest, portray judicial application of law as it is supposed to be, and by and large is, practiced. My position is that judicial reasoning is rule governed; that is, judges are expected to resolve all questions of law on the basis of valid legal standards. I have entertained numerous challenges to this view and to the specifics of the modes of judicial reasoning I offer. I have suggested that objections to a rule-governed account of judicial reasoning are based, for the most part, on a lack of appreciation of how controversial disputes about the validity and application of primary rules *and* secondary rules can be controlled by legal standards. Critics have regarded the fact that judges seemingly establish new rules in the midst of deciding a case and the fact that, apparently, they have considerable latitude in selecting and applying those rules as refutations of rule-governed judicial reasoning. I have argued that judges are not free to adopt a particular version of a rule because they like the result it produces in a particular case; they are expected to judge sincerely and impartially what is the legally most defensible conclusion. If they are in doubt as to the validity of a rule or its proper interpretation in a given context, judges are expected to appeal to other legal criteria to resolve the issue. Although legal standards do not eliminate judicial disagreements, they explain how, even when the law is vague, ambiguous, or otherwise unsettled, judges can plausibly claim that their judgments are controlled by law. No doubt, some judges take advantage of the complexity of and lack of agreement about legal issues to impose their preferred values on the legal system. As I have tried to show, when they do this they are not fulfilling the expectations of their judicial role: *judicis est jus dicere non dare*—it is the province of a judge to declare the law, not to give it.

SECTION THREE:

JUDICIAL REASONING APPLIED

7
Case Study: *Riggs v. Palmer*

This chapter examines the majority and dissenting judges' reasoning in a celebrated 1889 American case, *Riggs v. Palmer*. The case involves a teenager who murdered his grandfather in order to safeguard and expedite his inheritance under his grandfather's will. In a split decision, the Court deprived the convicted murderer of any benefit under the will. The issue facing the Court was whether or not legislation on estate succession precluded persons convicted of murdering their potential benefactor from inheriting under the will. Since the legislation did not expressly deal with this kind of situation, the judges were faced with a difficult and controversial challenge. It is particularly appropriate to consider this case since Ronald Dworkin offers *Riggs* as a example that supports his theory of judicial reasoning. Two Canadian scholars, Sam Coval and Joseph Smith, have also used *Riggs* to support their theory of judicial reasoning. As I will argue, neither Dworkin nor Coval and Smith adequately account for the judges' reasoning. Before introducing and critiquing these rival explanations, I will summarize and discuss the arguments presented by the judges. In the process I reaffirm the capacity of a rule-guided conception to account for judges' reasoning. The actual opinions of the judges are found at the end of this chapter.

OVERVIEW OF THE ARGUMENTS

In a decision with two dissenting judges, a majority of judges decided that the statutes on succession should be interpreted so that the grandson would not inherit under his grandfather's will. The judges entertained many arguments for and against allowing the grandson to inherit under the will. As a way of illustrating the rule-governed nature of their reasoning, I have reconstructed each argument in terms of the reason advanced and the secondary rules which validate the reason or verify its conclusion. First, I summarize the majority-position arguments, put forward by Justice Earl, and then I consider the dissenting arguments, advanced by Justice Gray.

Majority Arguments

Six arguments were advanced by Justice Earl against allowing the grandson to inherit under the grandfather's will. The first four arguments involve reasoning from interpretive guidelines, the fifth argument involves reasoning from principle, and the last argument involves reasoning from prior cases.

(1) The exact words of the legislation cannot be presumed to determine that the murderer is allowed to benefit under the will.

Rules of application cited:

- The doctrine that interpretation of statutes must be guided by the legislators' intentions—the plain meaning of the words is not necessarily determinative of intention;

- The canon of construction that "a thing which is within the intention of the makers of the statute is as much within the statute as if it were within the letter; and a thing which is within the letter of the statute is not within the statute, unless it be within the intention of the makers."

(2) Since it is unreasonable to assume legislators intended to allow a murderer to collect from his victim's will, the legislation should be interpreted to exclude the grandson's claim.

Rules of application cited:

- Legal authorities confirm prior cases where "probable or rational" interpretation of statutes has been upheld;

- Statements that manifestly absurd consequences are to be avoided.

(3) The common law is against vesting oneself with title by crime (e.g., profiting from one's own fraud, or acquiring property by one's own crime).

Rules of application cited:

- Doctrine that the fundamental maxims of the common law control the scope of statutes;

- Prior cases held that wrongdoing voided expected benefits.

(4) The common law should be presumed to prohibit benefit accruing to the murderer of a benefactor since there are explicit civil law provisions to this effect in classic legal codes such as the *Civil Code of Lower Canada*, the *Napoleonic Code*, and Roman law.

Rule of application cited:

- A presumption that, in the absence of explicit legislation in the home country, well-accepted, long-standing law in other countries is to be reflected in existing common law.

(5) Denial of benefit under the will is not an additional punishment for crime, but merely prevents the teenager from acquiring property to which he is not entitled.

Rule of application implied:

- There is a general prohibition against punishing individuals more than once for the same crime (which would have been violated if the grandson had been entitled to the inheritance).

(6) A prior case upholding the accrual of benefit arising from a victim's death to an accessory to murder was wrongly decided since it failed to apply an established common law maxim.

Rule of application implied:

- Judges have authority to disapprove of cases that, in their view, are wrong in law.

Dissenting Arguments

Seven arguments were advanced in the dissenting opinion, by Justice Gray, in favour of the grandson inheriting under the grandfather's will. The first four arguments involve reasoning from interpretive guidelines, the fifth argument involves reasoning from prior cases, and the last two arguments involve reasoning from principle.

(1) The unconscionable behaviour of the grandson does not preclude his entitlement to benefit under the will.

Rule of application cited:

- The judicial obligation to decide a case by determining the relevant law.

(2) The explicit words and clear purpose of legislation regulate very closely the necessary and sufficient conditions for execution, alteration, and revocation of wills; in this area there is no room for liberal interpretation.

Rule of application implied:

- The doctrine that when words and purpose are clear, law must be applied in accordance with their plain meaning.

(3) The majority appeal to the civil law argument (i.e., majority argument #4 above) is invalid; those civil laws were remedial in that the loss of benefit under Roman law was a form of punishment imposed on the offender.

Rule of application cited:

- A presumption that in issues of remedial justice, there must be explicit legislation to effect a remedy; civil law provisions in other countries cannot be relied upon.

(4) The statutes expressly prohibit revoking wills except in explicitly mentioned ways.

Rule of application cited:

- Prior cases held that where intended alterations to wills were not executed in the prescribed manner, the wills were unchanged.

(5) The likelihood that the grandfather would have altered his will had he known of his grandson's plans is irrelevant to the will's validity.

Rule of application cited:

- Prior cases held that existing wills were valid despite the use of force or fraud to prevent individuals from altering their wills.

(6) The majority argument that since a criminal act vested the grandson's title to property under the will, he should forfeit entitlement under the will requires, in effect, that judges do what they have no authority to do, namely rewrite wills.

Rule of application implied:

- Judicial obligation to exercise authority within the limits of the law.

(7) The denial of benefit under the will would do what judges are prohibited from doing; namely, impose an additional punishment for the murder.

Rule of application cited:

- Prior case prohibited judges from enhancing punishments beyond those provided by law.

COMMENTARY

On first reading, it would seem that the opposing opinions in *Riggs* are based primarily on incompatible rules of interpretation. The principal argument put forward in the dissenting opinion is that the legislators' intention was adequately captured in the explicit language and the apparent purpose of the relevant legislation. The principal arguments for the majority position are predicated on the view that the legislators could not "reasonably" be presumed to have intended to allow named beneficiaries to vest in the estate under circumstances like those presented in *Riggs*. Is this not, as many critics have suggested, a clear example of the inadequacy of a rule-guided account of judicial reasoning? Before explaining how the reasoning in this case is consistent with the view of judicial reasoning I present in this book, it is important to draw attention to the difference between discretionary preference for one standard over another and legitimate judicial disagreement about the success of particular arguments. Despite their differences of opinion, if both sides can be shown to argue on the basis of valid legal standards that seemingly control their decision, then their reasoning is rule governed.

The dissenting opinion presented by Justice Gray regarded the wording of the statute—that no deviations of the will are allowable unless effected in a prescribed manner—to be a sufficiently explicit indication of the legislators' intentions to control the decision. In his view, the wording "has left no room" for resort to the legislative purpose or to common law principles. This approach is consistent with remarks made seven years before *Riggs*, when the plain meaning rule was cited in *Holy Trinity Church v. United States*.[151] As we saw earlier, the plain meaning rule states: "We are to adhere to the ordinary meaning of the words of a statute and to the grammatical construction unless that is at variance with the intention of the Legislature, to be collected from the statute itself, or leads to any manifest absurdity or repugnance."

Significantly, Justice Earl, in offering the majority opinion, relied on the same rule, except he disagreed that the literal meaning of the statute controlled the situation. He was moved for a variety of reasons, including inconsistency with the legislators' most likely intentions and with common law principles, to reject the inference that the statute's wording compelled the presumption that the legislators intended that persons like the grandson should inherit any part of the estate. As he wrote: "What could be more unreasonable than to suppose that it was the legislative intention in the general laws passed for the orderly, peaceable and just devolution of property, that they should have operation in favor of one who murdered his ancestor that he might speedily come into the possession of his estate?"[152]

Thus, the validity of both lines of argument stems from the same general interpretive rule; they differed only in their conclusions about how the details of the case satisfied the standards implied in the rule. Also, it is plausible to assume, given the conviction with which the opinions were offered, that each side felt that their conclusion was compelled by the relevant statutes and by the second-order rules controlling application of those statutes. Seen in this light, the arguments and judgment in *Riggs* support a rule-guided account of judicial reasoning.

RIVAL ACCOUNTS

As indicated earlier, this case has been the focus of much scholarly attention. I will consider two accounts of the reasoning in *Riggs* that are offered in support of rival conceptions of judicial reasoning—those by Dworkin and by Coval and Smith. This discussion illustrates the comparative ability, over rival accounts, of the conductive argument conception of judicial reasoning offered in this book to explain the reasoning that judges actually use to support their decisions.

Dworkin's Account

In *Law's Empire*, Dworkin casts the opposing judicial arguments in *Riggs* in light of his theory of judicial reasoning, which I examined in the previous chapter. According to Dworkin, the issue in *Riggs* is which interpretation is consistent with the more coherent account of the relevant area of law. Dworkin suggests that the judges, in effect, offered competing theories or explanations of the practice of statutory interpretation.[153] Supposedly, the dissenting judge argued for a literal theory of interpretation, whereas Justice Earl argued for a moral justice theory of interpretation—that judges should construct a statute so as to make it conform as closely as possible to principles of justice. Contrary to Dworkin's assertions, neither of the judges' opinions in the case can plausibly be interpreted as arguing for different theories of statutory interpretation. Judges are not authorized to choose a theory "in response to their own convictions and instincts" nor was *Riggs* argued from the judges' personal convictions regarding which approach to statutory interpretation would show judicial practice in its best light. There is no evidence of any attempt, as would be expected of judges arguing *for* a theory, to demonstrate that their interpretive theories were grounded in some "conviction about the 'point' of legal practice as a whole." Although the judges' arguments for their respective opinions necessarily presuppose a theory about proper interpretive practice, the judges in *Riggs* did not attempt to justify a theory nor is it apparent that they had different theories of interpretation. Rather, as was indicated above, both sides operated within the plain meaning rule.

We can more clearly see the inadequacy of this account by examining the specific arguments that Dworkin suggests are implied by Justice Earl's arguments. Dworkin suggests that the majority opinion was based on two theory-justifying arguments. He writes: "First, it is sensible to assume that legislators have a general and diffuse intention to respect traditional principles of justice unless they clearly indicate the contrary." Although this proposition may be true, it is not a reason that the judge offered. Rather, Justice Earl referred to the famous English jurist Lord Blackstone, who noted that deviations from the language of a law are permitted to avoid "absurd consequences manifestly contradictory to common reason." Justice Earl did not imply that the legislators' intentions were to promote justice when he appealed to the common law maxims loosely summarized as "no man may profit from his own wrong." Rather, he cited the (secondary) rule that "all laws as well as contracts may be controlled in their operation and effect by general, fundamental maxims of the common law." With support from two prior cases, Justice Earl noted that these maxims "frequently control the effect and nullify the language of wills."

The second of Dworkin's arguments is an appeal to overall coherence:

Second, since a statute forms part of a larger intellectual system, the law as a whole, it should be construed so as to make that larger system coherent in principle. Earl argued that the law elsewhere respects the principle that no one should profit from his own wrong, so the statute of wills should be read to deny inheritance to someone who has murdered to obtain it.

This second suggested reason is also without foundation. None of the judges offered reasons why judicial practice is best seen as requiring overall coherence. No attempt was made to justify why the proposition "no man may profit from his own wrong" belongs to a more defensible, coherent picture of existing law than the proposition, say, "sometimes a man may profit from his own wrong." Dworkin's suggestion that a dominant reason for the majority decision was a concern for justice is unwarranted.[154] The principle that no man should profit by his own wrong is not the main justification offered for the decision; in fact, the argument is introduced by the term "besides," suggesting that it is an additional, not a major, argument. Dworkin would have us believe that Justice Earl considered the principle because of its political desirability or because it is part of a coherent justification for law. The more plausible explanation is that Justice Earl correctly considered himself authorized to use common law maxims to limit application of legislation in certain circumstances. Clearly, Dworkin's account of the judges' reasoning in *Riggs* cannot be sustained in light of the actual opinions.[155]

Coval and Smith's Account

In *Law and Its Presuppositions*, Coval and Smith offer an account of judicial reasoning as a rule-governed practice. They suggest that, unlike in the conductive argument structure which I describe, disputes about law can be settled by "anomaly-resolving rules"—rules for resolving disputes which can be generated from the underlying purposes for law. Since Coval and Smith believe that law is primarily concerned with maximizing the ability of agents to act, they argue that it is defensible to decide disputes about the application of law in a manner that maximizes individual agency.

In discussing *Riggs*, Coval and Smith suggest that the relevant grounds for deciding whether or not to enforce the statute on wills stem from a default in agency known as inadvertence—if legislators could not have foreseen the consequences arising from their actions, they should not be held responsible for the consequences. This principle of excusing responsibility because of inadvertence is found in the criminal law—the law against killing, for example, is not enforced if individuals could not reasonably have foreseen that their actions would result in the death of others. Applied to *Riggs*, an anomaly-resolving rule based on this exception would be: "Since enforcing the rule (the statutes on inheritance) produces appropriate conduct (a duly executed will) and the desired goal (testamentary succession) but also something worse than the desired goal (the death of the testator at the hands of the beneficiary), the rule will not be enforced."[156] The difficult decision in *Riggs* arising from the legislators' failure to foresee the consequences of allowing people who murder to inherit property from their victim can be accommodated by this anomaly-resolving rule. Since the goals of criminal law (i.e., protecting bodily health and security) are more fundamental in promoting the ability of individuals to act than those of succession laws (i.e., allowing for the transfer of property), the law should not permit the grandson to inherit under the will.

Although this account provides a way to rationalize the decision, it bears little resemblance to how the judges actually argued and justified their judgment.[157] *Riggs* was argued and decided by the judges on several grounds, not on a single reason formulation, implied by the anomaly-resolving rule. In addition, the judges never implied, as the proposed formulation of the anomaly-resolving rule suggests, that the issue was whether or not to enforce the statutes on wills. On the contrary, they emphasized their responsibility to apply the law according to its intended purposes. Their principal disagreement was about the proper interpretation of that intention. Their arguments suggest that neither the dissenting nor majority judges believed that the case rested on a *weighing* of *competing* values. Rather, they wrote as though they faced questions of *identification* of legislators' intended values and *consistency* with prior decisions.

Even if we concede that some formulation of the anomaly-resolving rule can account for the majority argument in this case, Coval and Smith are open to a second line of criticism. If formal anomaly-resolving rules are guides to resolving disputes, as opposed to being mere after-the-fact summations of judicial reasoning, the rules must prescribe a decision in favour of one side or the other. For two reasons, it is not clear that the anomaly-resolving rule does this in *Riggs*: (1) it is possible to formulate a countervailing anomaly-resolving rule that would justify a finding in favour of the grandson and (2) the weighing of values presupposed by the anomaly-resolving rule is simplistic.

The first shortcoming of the notion of anomaly-resolving rules stems from the potential for the dissenting judges to counter with an equally compelling argument using the same anomaly-resolving rule relied upon by the majority. The counter-formulation of the anomaly-resolving argument might go as follows: "Applying succession rules according to a reasonable interpretation has the effect of promoting goals of criminal law (e.g., deterring murder) but it has worse consequences by punishing individuals twice for crimes (i.e., the grandson has already been sentenced for the murder) and by preventing the grandfather's apparent choice of beneficiary from inheriting." Which formulation should the Court adopt in deciding *Riggs*? The short response is that the Court has to decide the case before it can answer the question. Each formulation of the anomaly-resolving argument presupposes resolution of the key issues the judges faced. The dissenting opinion's formulation of the anomaly-resolving rule is acceptable only if one already agrees with the dissenting arguments. Since the majority rejected both the double punishment and the *bona fide* beneficiary arguments, they would deny the negative consequences presupposed by the counter-formulation. But they would not know to reject these arguments until they had already determined the acceptability of the reasonable interpretation argument. The double punishment argument evaporates *because* the majority judges, following a reasonable interpretation approach, believe that the grandson, by committing the murder, never became entitled to the estate.

Even if, in principle, the majority accepted the negative consequences cited in the counter-formulation, it is not clear that they would agree that these consequences were worse than, say, failing to discourage murder. This raises a second difficulty with Coval and Smith's account of anomaly-resolving rules. The problem of weighing consequences cannot be resolved simply by prioritizing goals. As we saw in our discussion on the weighing of arguments, the extent to which a particular action impairs a standard has an effect on the force of that argument. For example, although we might accept, in general, that respect for life takes precedence over rights to property, it is not obvious, in the *Riggs* case, that it is worse to decide on behalf of property interests. Since the loss of inheritance would only occur if a potential beneficiary had already been convicted of murder, the most significant deterrent might be the possibility of execution or life imprisonment, and not the financial loss. Put another way, if protection of life would be advanced only marginally by barring these beneficiaries from their inheritances, then the complete rejection of property interests might be regarded as a worse consequence.[158]

For all of these reasons, Coval and Smith's rival account of judicial reasoning fails to adequately explain the *Riggs* decision. More generally, my reconstruction of the multiple arguments and the criticisms of Dworkin's and of Coval and Smith's accounts help confirm the conductive argument structure of judicial reasoning—judges entertain many, often independent reasons for and against potential resolutions of a case, and these reasons and their relative weighting are grounded in secondary rules. To assist readers in assessing the relative merits of these competing explanations of the case, the opinions presented by Justices Earl and Gray are reproduced below.

THE ACTUAL OPINIONS

Riggs v. Palmer was an appeal by the estate's guardian (Mr. Riggs) of a Supreme Court of New York decision that had upheld the grandson's right to inherit under his grandfather's will. In the appeal, Justice Earl, speaking for the majority, decided to overturn the earlier decision and order that the grandson be disinherited. Justice Gray wrote a dissenting opinion on behalf of himself and one other judge. (Case and reference citations have been omitted; italicized notes appearing within brackets have been added for clarification.)

Justice Earl

The majority opinion by Justice Earl opens with a review of the facts of the case, noting that Elmer Palmer, the grandson of Francis Palmer, had been convicted of murdering his grandfather by poisoning him. The grandson had done this to prevent the grandfather from revoking his will, which involved a substantial bequest to the grandson.

> He [*the grandson*] now claims the property, and the sole question for our determination is, can he have it? The defendants [*the grandson and his family*] say that the testator [*the grandfather*] is dead; that his will was made in due form and has been admitted to probate, and that, therefore, it must have effect according to the letter of the law.

It is quite true that statutes regulating the making, proof and effect of wills, and the devolution of property, if literally construed, and if their force and effect can in no way and under no circumstances be controlled or modified, give this property to the murderer.

The purpose of those statutes was to enable testators to dispose of their estates to the objects of their bounty at death, and to carry into effect their final wishes legally expressed; and in considering and giving effect to them this purpose must be kept in view. It was the intention of the law-makers that the donees in a will should have the property given to them. But it never could have been their intention that a donee who murdered the testator to make the will operative should have any benefit under it. If such a case had been present to their minds, and it had been supposed necessary to make some provision of law to meet it, it cannot be doubted that they would have provided for it. It is a familiar canon of construction that a thing which is within the intention of the makers of a statute is as much within the statute as if it were within the letter; and a thing which is within the letter of the statute is not within the statute, unless it be within the intention of the makers. The writers of laws do not always express their intention perfectly, but either exceed it or fall short of it, so that judges are to collect it from probable or rational conjectures only, and this is called rational interpretation; and Rutherforth, in his *Institutes*, says: "When we make use of rational interpretation, sometimes we restrain the meaning of the writer so as to take in less, and sometimes we extend or enlarge his meaning so as to take in more than his words express."

Such a construction ought to be put upon a statute as will best answer the intention which the makers had in view, for *qui haeret in litera, haeret in cortice [he who considers merely the letter of an instrument goes but skin deep into its meaning]*. In Bacon's *Abridgement,* Puffendorf, Rutherforth, and in Smith's *Commentaries,* many cases are mentioned where it was held that matters embraced in the general words of statutes, nevertheless were not within the statutes, because it could not have been the intention of the law-makers that they should be included. They were taken out of the statutes by an equitable construction, and it is said in Bacon:

> By an equitable construction, a case not within the letter of the statute is sometimes holden to be within the meaning, because it is within the mischief for which a remedy is provided. The reason for such construction is that the law-makers could not set down every case in express terms. In order to form a right judgement whether a case be within the equity of a statute, it is a good way to suppose the law-maker present, and that you have asked him this question, did you intend to comprehend this case? Then you must give yourself such answer as you imagine he, being an upright and reasonable man, would have given. If this be that he did mean to comprehend it, you may safely hold the case to be within the equity of the statute; for while you do no more than he would have done, you do not act contrary to the statute, but in conformity thereto.

In some cases the letter of a legislative act is restrained by an equitable construction; in others it is enlarged; in others the construction is contrary to the letter. The equitable construction which restrains the letter of a statute is defined by Aristotle, as frequently quoted, in this manner: *Aequitas est correctio legis generaliter latae qua parti deficit [Equity is the correction of that wherein the law, by reason of its generality, is deficient]*. If the law-makers could, as to this case, be consulted, would they say that they intended by their general language that the property of a testator or of an ancestor should pass to one who had taken his life for the express purpose of getting his property? In Blackstone's *Commentaries* the learned author, speaking of the construction of statutes, says:

If there arise out of them any absurd consequences manifestly contradictory to common reason, they are, with regard to those collateral consequences, void. ... When some collateral matter arises out of the general words, and happen to be unreasonable, then the judges are in decency to conclude that the consequence was not foreseen by the parliament, and, therefore, they are at liberty to expound the statute by equity and only *quoad hoc [with respect to this]* disregard it;

and he gives as an illustration, if an act of parliament gives a man power to try all causes that arise within his manor of Dale, yet, if a cause should arise in which he himself is party, the act is construed not to extend to that because it is unreasonable that any man should determine his own quarrel.

There was a statute in Bologna that whoever drew blood in the streets should be severely punished, and yet it was held not to apply to the case of a barber who opened a vein in the street [*bleeding a patient was a medical treatment administered by a barber*]. It is commanded in the *Decalogue* that no work shall be done upon the Sabbath, and yet, giving the command a rational interpretation founded upon its design, the Infallible Judge held that it did not prohibit works of necessity, charity or benevolence on that day.

What could be more unreasonable than to suppose that it was the legislative intention in the general laws passed for the orderly, peaceable and just devolution of property, that they should have operation in favor of one who murdered his ancestor that he might speedily come into the possession of his estate? Such an intention is inconceivable. We need not, therefore, be much troubled by the general language contained in the laws.

Besides, all laws as well as all contracts may be controlled in their operation and effect by general, fundamental maxims of the common law. No one shall be permitted to profit by his own fraud, or to take advantage of his own wrong, or to found any claim upon his own iniquity, or to acquire property by his crime. These maxims are dictated by public policy, have their foundation in universal law administered in all civilized countries, and have nowhere been superseded by statutes. They were applied in the decision of the case of *New York Mutual Life Insurance Company v. Armstrong.* There it was held that the person who procured a policy upon the life of another, payable at his death, and then murdered the assured to make the policy payable, could not recover thereon. Mr. Justice Field, writing the opinion, said:

Independently of any proof of the motives of Hunter in obtaining the policy, and even assuming that they were just and proper, he forfeited all rights under it when, to secure its immediate payment, he murdered the assured. It would be a reproach to the jurisprudence of the country if one could recover insurance money payable on the death of a party whose life he had feloniously taken. As well might he recover insurance money upon a building that he had willfully fired.

These maxims, without any statute giving them force or operation, frequently control the effect and nullify the language of wills. A will procured by fraud and deception, like any other instrument, may be decreed void and set aside, and so a particular portion of a will may be excluded from probate or held inoperative if induced by the fraud or undue influence of the person in whose favor it is. (*Allen v. M'Pherson; Harrison's Appeal.*) So a will may contain provisions which are immoral, irreligious or against public policy, and they will be held void.

Here there was no certainty that this murderer would survive the testator, or that the testator would not change his will, and there was no certainty that he would get this property if nature was allowed to take its course. He, therefore, murdered the testator expressly to vest himself with an estate. Under such circumstances, what law, human or divine, will allow him to take the estate and enjoy the fruits of his crime? The will spoke and became operative at the death of the testator. He caused that death, and thus by his crime made it speak and have operation. Shall it speak and operate in his favor? If he had met the testator and taken his property by force, he would have had no title to it. Shall he acquire title by murdering him? If he had gone to the testator's house and by force compelled him, or by fraud or undue influence had induced him to will him his property, the law would not allow him to hold it. But can he give effect and operation to a will by murder, and yet take the property? To answer these questions in the affirmative, it seems to me, would be a reproach to the jurisprudence of our state, and an offense against public policy.

Under the civil law evolved from the general principles of natural law and justice by many generations of jurisconsults, philosophers and statesmen, one cannot take property by inheritance or will from an ancestor or benefactor whom he has murdered. (Domat; *Code Napoleon*; Mackeldy's *Roman Law.*) In the *Civil Code of Lower Canada* the provisions on the subject in the *Code Napoleon* have been substantially copied. But, so far as I can find, in no country where the common law prevails has it been deemed important to enact a law to provide for such a case. Our revisers and law-makers were familiar with the civil law, and they did not deem it important to incorporate into our statutes its provisions upon this subject. This is not a *casus omissus* [*an omitted case*]. It was evidently supposed that the maxims of the common law were sufficient to regulate such a case and that a specific enactment for that purpose was not needed.

For the same reasons the defendant Palmer cannot take any of this property as heir. Just before the murder he was not an heir, and it was not certain that he ever would be. He might have died before his grandfather, or might have been disinherited by him. He made himself an heir by the murder, and he seeks to take property as the fruit of his crime. What has before been said to him as legatee applies to him with equal force as an heir. He cannot vest himself with title by crime.

My view of this case does not inflict upon Elmer any greater or other punishment for his crime than the law specifies. It takes from him no property, but simply holds that he shall not acquire property by his crime, and thus be rewarded for its commission.

Our attention is called to *Owens v. Owens*, as a case quite like this. There a wife had been convicted of being an accessory before the fact to the murder of her husband, and it was held that she was, nevertheless, entitled to dower. I am unwilling to assent to the doctrine of that case. The statutes provide dower for a wife who has the misfortune to survive her husband and thus lose his support and protection. It is clear beyond their purpose to make provision for a wife who by her own crime makes herself a widow and willfully and intentionally deprives herself of the support and protection of her husband. As she might have died before him, and thus never have been his widow, she cannot by her crime vest herself with an estate. The principle which lies at the bottom of the maxim, *volenti non fit injuria* [*those who knowingly expose themselves to danger are deemed to assume the risk, and are precluded from recovery for injury*], should be applied to such a case, and a widow should not, for the purpose of acquiring, as such, property rights, be permitted to allege a widowhood which she has wickedly and intentionally created.

The judge concludes by declaring that because he murdered his grandfather, Elmer Palmer was to be deprived of any interest in his grandfather's estate.

Justice Gray

In opening the dissenting opinion, Justice Gray observes that the appeal presents "an extraordinary state of facts" and that the case is "without precedent in this state." He briefly summarizes the facts before considering the arguments presented by Mr. Riggs' lawyers for excluding the grandson from the will.

To sustain their position the appellants' counsel [*Mr. Riggs' lawyers*] has submitted an able and elaborate brief, and if I believed that the decision of the question could be affected by considerations of an equitable nature, I should not hesitate to assent to views which commend themselves to the conscience. But the matter does not lie within the domain of conscience. We are bound by the rigid rules of law, which have been established by the legislature, and within the limits of which the determination of this question is confined. The question we are dealing with is, whether a testamentary disposition can be altered, or a will revoked, after the testator's death, through an appeal to the courts, when the legislature has, by its enactments, prescribed exactly when and how wills may be made, altered and revoked, and, apparently, as it seems to me, when they have been fully complied with, has left no room for the exercise of an equitable jurisdiction by courts over such matters. Modern jurisprudence, in recognizing the right of the individual, under more or less restrictions, to dispose of his property after his death, subjects it to legislative control, both as to extent and as to mode of exercise. Complete freedom of testamentary disposition of one's property has not been and is not the universal rule; as we see from the provisions of the *Napoleonic Code*, from those systems of jurisprudence in other countries which are modeled upon the Roman law, and from the statutes of many of our states. To the statutory restraints, which are imposed upon the disposition of one's property by will, are added strict and systematic statutory rules for the execution, alteration and revocation of the will; which must be, at least, substantially, if not exactly, followed to insure validity and performance. The reason for the establishment of such rules, we may naturally assume, consists in the purpose to create those safeguards about these grave and important acts, which experience has demonstrated to be the wisest and surest. That freedom, which is permitted to be exercised in the testamentary disposition of one's estate by the laws of the state, is subject to its being exercised in conformity with the regulations of the statutes. The capacity and the power of the individual to dispose of his property after death, and the mode by which that power can be exercised, are matters of which the legislature has assumed the entire control, and has undertaken to regulate with comprehensive particularity.

The appellants' argument is not helped by reference to those rules of the civil law, or to those laws of other governments, by which the heir or legatee is excluded from benefit under the testament, if he has been convicted of killing, or attempting to kill, the testator. In the absence of such legislation here, the courts are not empowered to institute such a system of remedial justice. The deprivation of the heir of his testamentary succession by the Roman law, when guilty of such a crime, plainly, was intended to be in the nature of a punishment imposed upon him. The succession, in such a case of guilt, escheated to the exchequer. (See Domat's *Civil Law*.)

I concede that rules of law, which annul testamentary provision made for the benefit of those who have become unworthy of them, may be based on principles of equity and of natural justice. It is quite reasonable to suppose that a testator would revoke or alter his will, where his mind has been so angered and changed as to make him unwilling to have his will executed as it stood. But these principles only suggest sufficient reasons for the enactment of laws to such cases.

The statutes of this state have prescribed various ways in which a will may be altered or revoked; but the very provision, defining the modes of alteration and revocation, implies a prohibition of alteration or revocation in any other way. The words of the section of the statute are: "No writing, except in the cases hereafter mentioned, nor any part thereof, shall be revoked or altered otherwise," etc. Where, therefore, none of the cases mentioned are met by the facts, and the revocation is not in the way described in the section, the will of the testator is unalterable. I think that a valid will must continue as a will always, unless revoked in the manner provided by the statutes. Mere intention to revoke a will does not have the effect of revocation. The intention to revoke is necessary to constitute the effective revocation of a will; but it must be demonstrated by one of the acts contemplated by the statute. As Woodworth, J. [*Justice*], said in *Dan v. Brown*: "Revocation is an act of the mind, which must be demonstrated by some outward and visible sign of revocation." The same learned judge said in that case: "The rule is that if the testator lets the will stand until he dies, it is his will; if he does not suffer it to do so, it is not his will." (*Goodright v. Glasier, Pemberton v. Pemberton.*)

The finding of fact of the referee, that, presumably, the testator would have altered his will, had he known of his grandson's murderous intent, cannot affect the question. We may concede it to the fullest extent; but still the cardinal objection is undisposed of, that the making and the revocation of a will are purely matters of statutory regulation, by which the court is bound in the determination of questions relating to these acts. Two cases in this state and in Kentucky, at an early day, seem to me to be much in point. *Gains v. Gains* was decided by the Kentucky Court of Appeals in 1820. It was there urged that the testator intended to have destroyed his will, and that he was forcibly prevented from doing so by the defendant in error or devisee, and it was insisted that the will, though not expressly, was thereby virtually revoked. The court held, as the act concerning wills prescribed the manner in which a will might be revoked, that as none of the acts evidencing revocation were done, the intention could not be substituted for the act. In that case the will was snatched away and forcibly retained. In 1854, Surrogate Bradford, whose opinions are entitled to the highest consideration, decided the case of *Leaycraft v. Simmons*. In that case the testator, a man of eighty-nine years of age, desired to make a codicil [*a supplement or addition*] to his will, in order to enlarge the provisions for his daughter. His son having the custody of the instrument, and the one to be prejudiced by the change, refused to produce the will, at testator's request, for the purpose of alteration. The learned surrogate refers to the provisions of the civil law for such and other cases of unworthy conduct in the heir or legatee, and says,

> our statute has undertaken to prescribe the mode in which wills can be revoked (citing the statutory provision). This is the law by which I am governed in passing upon questions touching the revocation of wills. The whole of this subject is now regulated by statute, and a mere intention to revoke, however well authenticated, or however defeated, is not sufficient.

And he held that the will must be admitted to probate. I may refer also to the case in the Pennsylvania courts. In that state the statute prescribed the mode for repealing or altering a will, and in *Clingan v. Mitcheltree* the Supreme Court of the state held, where a will was kept from destruction by the fraud and misrepresentation of the devisee, that to declare it cancelled as against the fraudulent party would be to enlarge the statute.

I cannot find any support for the argument that the respondent's succession to the property should be avoided because of his criminal act, when the laws are silent. Public policy does not demand it, for the demands of public policy are satisfied by the proper execution of the laws and punishment of the crime. There has been no convention between the testator and his legatee, nor is there any such contractual element in such a disposition of property by a testator, as to impose or imply conditions in the legatee. The appellants' argument practically amounts to this: That as the legatee has been guilty of a crime, by the commission of which he is placed in a position to sooner receive the benefits of the testamentary provision, his rights to the property should be divested of his estate. To allow their argument to prevail would involve the diversion by the court of the testator's estate into the hands of persons, whom, possibly enough, for all we know, the testator might not have chosen or desired as its recipients. Practically the court is asked to make another will for the testator. The laws do not warrant this judicial action, and mere presumption would not be strong enough to sustain it.

But more than this, to concede appellants' views would involve the imposition of an additional punishment or penalty upon the respondent. What power or warrant have the courts to add to the respondent's penalties by depriving him of property? The law has punished him for his crime, and we may not say that it was all insufficient punishment. In the trial and punishment of the respondent the law has vindicated itself for the outrage which he committed, and further judicial utterance upon the subject of punishment or deprivation of rights is barred. We may not, in the language of the court in *People v. Thornton*, "enhance the pains, penalties and forfeitures provided by law for the punishment of crime."

Justice Gray concludes by supporting the lower court decision to allow the grandson to inherit under the will.

8
Case Study: *Davis v. Johnson*

The capacity of reasoning from principle to provide a rule-guided explanation of disputed secondary rules of application is discussed in the context of *Davis v. Johnson*. In this 1977 case, the English Court of Appeal considered whether or not the doctrine of precedent bound the Court to follow an incorrectly decided prior case. A majority of the judges hearing this appeal rejected the traditional rule of precedent which held that, with few exceptions, courts were bound to follow earlier decisions of the same court. *Davis* is a particularly appropriate case to examine since the Court's rejection of the traditional doctrine of precedent is regarded by at least one theorist as a clear instance of judges *bringing* differing principles to the law.[159]

I begin the discussion with some background to the decision and proceed by reviewing the arguments offered by the five judges who heard *Davis* at the Court of Appeal level. Finally, by drawing upon subsequent comments offered by the House of Lords on the appeal of this decision, I explain how these conflicting and somewhat controversial opinions can be reconciled with a rule-governed account of judicial reasoning. The chapter closes with extended excerpts from the Court of Appeal and House of Lords opinions.

BACKGROUND

The case involved the *Domestic Violence and Matrimonial Proceedings Act 1976* and two nearly identical Court of Appeal cases that were decided several months before *Davis*. There was some confusion about the protection that this *Act* offered to women who were living with, but not married to, men who abused them. Despite what appeared to be explicit language to the contrary, in two earlier cases the Court of Appeal had decided that, in the event of family violence, a married woman, but not an unmarried woman, could retain possession of the family home. When *Davis* reached the Court of Appeal, five judges who were not party to the earlier cases were confronted with a dilemma: the majority of them considered the two earlier decisions to be clearly incorrect, and yet the doctrine of precedent seemed to require that they adhere to those rulings. The "received view" of the doctrine of precedent for the Court of Appeal had been set out earlier in *Young v. Bristol Aeroplane Co.*[160] It specified that the Court of Appeal was bound to follow its own prior decisions with three exceptions: (1) if there were conflicting decisions; (2) if a prior decision was clearly inconsistent with a House of Lords decision; or (3) if a prior decision was reached *per incuriam*—

without consideration of an important statutory provision or other binding authority. Complicating the question of binding authority was a 1966 "practice statement"—a statement of judicial policy not issued in connection with a specific case but as an formal announcement of general practice—by the House of Lords (the court of final appeal for most legal matters) indicating that it was no longer absolutely bound by its prior decisions.

In a split decision in the *Davis* case, the Court of Appeal deviated from the doctrine of precedent and rejected the earlier cases, thereby allowing unmarried women who were battered by their mates to retain possession of the family home. On subsequent appeal, the House of Lords rejected the Court of Appeal's conclusion that the lower court was warranted in deviating from its earlier decisions in this instance, although they confirmed that the earlier cases had been wrongly decided.[161] My primary interest in raising this case is with the arguments relied upon by the Court of Appeal judges in rejecting or modifying the supposedly established doctrine of precedent. More particularly, I want to explore how a rule-guided conception of judicial reasoning can account for the varied and conflicting arguments about the validity of the doctrine of precedent.

OVERVIEW OF THE ARGUMENTS

The five Court of Appeal judges in *Davis* responded to the received view of precedent in various ways. Lord Denning challenged outright the validity of the doctrine established by *Young*. Two judges, Sir George Baker and Lord Justice Shaw, accepted the basic doctrine but argued for additional exceptions to the rule. The remaining two judges, Lord Justices Goff and Cumming-Bruce, accepted the doctrine of precedent without alteration. Let us examine more closely the arguments offered in support of these contradictory positions.

The Rejection Position

Lord Denning was insistent that the Court not follow the incorrectly decided prior cases. He offered the following arguments for rejecting the supposedly established doctrine of precedent:

(1) Reasoning from principle, Lord Denning argued that since the two prior decisions were clearly wrongly decided, it would be unjust to the injured parties to wait for the House of Lords to overrule the earlier decisions.

(2) He argued that, eighty years earlier, *Seward v. The Vera Cruz* had established that precedent was a matter of *judicial comity*—a matter of respect and deference but not an obligation. Thus, precedent was not a rule, in the strict sense, but merely a principle of practice.[162]

(3) Lord Denning cited eleven cases heard between 1852 and 1941 in which the Court of Appeal had reconsidered prior decisions and, when necessary, had reversed them.

(4) Lord Denning suggested that the House of Lords' shift in its view of precedent from its 1898 position that the Court considered itself bound by its own

prior decisions, to its 1966 position that it was no longer absolutely bound by precedent, was evidence that precedent was not binding.

(5) Finally, he suggested that the exceptions that already had been added to the doctrine of precedent as formulated in *Young*, combined with other exceptions that ought to be made, had the effect of "eating up the rule." Consequently, it would be better to adopt the position on precedent that the House of Lords had recently taken, which was not to be *absolutely* bound by previous decisions.

The Modification Position

Lord Justice Shaw and Sir George Baker argued that the *Young* formulation of the doctrine of precedent did not exhaust the exceptions that a proper understanding would allow. Given the circumstances in *Davis*, a modification, not a rejection, of the rule underlying *Young* was warranted. Lord Justice Shaw offered a very specific exemption which he thought deserved to be added to the exemptions cited in *Young*; Sir George Baker's suggested exemption was somewhat broader.[163] Most of their arguments for modifying the doctrine were based on reasoning from principle, although one of Lord Justice Shaw's argument was based on prior cases:

(1) Lord Justice Shaw suggested that the *Young* decision itself recognized that some exceptions to application of the doctrine of *stare decisis* are warranted. The *Young* formulation need not be accepted as exhausting those exceptions, especially since that Court admitted some authority for a power to overrule incorrect decisions.

(2) Both Lord Justice Shaw and Sir George Baker argued that requiring courts to follow an obviously incorrect decision is inconsistent with promoting respect for the administration of justice.

(3) Sir George Baker suggested that failing to allow the exception would give preference to an incorrect judicial decision at the expense of the seemingly obvious legislative will. This would be inconsistent with both the principle of the supremacy of Parliament and, more importantly, the judicial oath to uphold the laws of the Realm. In a conflict between a judicial decision and a statute, Sir George Baker consider the latter to be a proper indication of the law.

(4) Lord Justice Shaw considered the consequences for the parties in this case and in similar cases. Not allowing the exception would perpetrate an irreversible injustice on the women who were entitled under the statute to protection from violence. There was concern that unless the Court of Appeal took immediate steps, protection would, at best, be delayed until the House of Lords could reverse the earlier decisions and, at worst, could be denied indefinitely in the event that the appeal did not reach the House of Lords.

The Received Position

Two judges, Lord Justices Goff and Cumming-Bruce, accepted the doctrine of precedent as formulated in *Young*. As the principal voice in support of this position, Lord Justice Goff offered three reasons for the received view:

(1) Reasoning from principle, he suggested that the consequences of repeated rejection of earlier decisions would impair a fundamental legal value, that of the need for certainty in law.

(2) Based on consistency with fundamental principles, he suggested that judicial attempts to correct perceived injustices by ignoring the law undermine the rule of law. This is captured in the adage that "hard decisions make bad law."

(3) For the most part, he referred to the numerous cases re-affirming the doctrine that the Court was bound by precedent.

Lord Justice Cumming-Bruce endorsed Lord Justice Goff's position, and offered his own arguments in support of the first and third reasons put forward by his fellow justice. Lord Justice Cumming-Bruce suggested, hypothetically, that the two earlier decisions could be ignored on the grounds that a clearly incorrect interpretation of a statute qualifies as a decision reached *per incuriam*.[164]

COMMENTARY

What sense can be made of these conflicting arguments? Is the reasoning in this case incompatible with a rule-guided account of judicial reasoning? I will consider each judge's position in light of the capacity of the rule-guided conception to account for their respective arguments. However, in doing this we should again keep in mind the difference between judicial behaviour that repudiates the existence of accepted standards of reasoning and judicial behaviour that fails to perform well in light of them. As Owen Fiss remarked, "Not every mistake in adjudication is an example of lawlessness." The fact that, on occasion, judges reason poorly or prejudicially is a separate, albeit important, issue from the question of the existence of valid rules of judicial reasoning.[165]

There would appear to be little need to question Lord Justices Goff and Cumming-Bruce's position on the received doctrine of precedent. In fact, Lord Justice Goff's arguments from precedent and principle were echoed unanimously by the five-member bench that delivered the House of Lords decision. With regard to Lord Cumming-Bruce's suggestion that the two prior cases could be judged *per incuriam*, he is mistaken in his understanding of this exception. A proper reading of the *per incuriam* exception requires that the error be attributable to "ignorance or forgetfulness of some inconsistent statutory provision." There is no evidence that the admittedly incorrect prior decisions were attributable to either of these conditions.[166]

The principled arguments presented by Lord Justice Shaw and Sir George Baker suggested that the limited amount of uncertainty and inconsistency likely to result from their exceptions would be offset by the benefits of reversing the injustice caused by the incorrect interpretation of the *Act*. Because of the expense of further appeal,

Lord Justice Shaw was concerned that *Davis* might not reach the House of Lords. The judges plausibly concluded that, unless allowed to occupy the matrimonial home, many women would be forced to return to the abusing mate or live without their children in whatever accommodation they could secure. The House of Lords had considerable sympathy for Lord Justice Shaw's arguments based on the irreversible injustice of the individual case before the court.[167] His formulation was referred to as a "one-off" exception (i.e., an exception that is unlikely to apply to any other than the present case). As such, it was not regarded as undermining the doctrine of precedent by establishing a new class of exceptions. The House of Lords rejected Sir George Baker's exception, even though he regarded it as a "carefully limited" one, because they regarded it as "wide enough to cover any previous decision on the construction of a statute which the majority of the court thought was wrong." The effect, they argued, would be to seriously undermine the doctrine of precedent. Thus, the difference between Sir George Baker's position and the House of Lords' position may depend on differences of opinion as to the likely incidence of exceptions that would be allowed under his reformulation of the doctrine of precedent.

Lord Denning's reasoning was rejected by the House of Lords (and also by Lord Justice Goff) on the grounds that the view expressed in *Seward v. The Vera Cruz* had been considered and rejected by the Court of Appeal in *Young*, which decision was expressly approved of in the House of Lords. Moreover, the House of Lords dismissed Lord Denning's comparisons between their shifting position on precedent and the Court of Appeal's right to do the same on the grounds that there are obvious, relevant differences between the two courts.[168] Although members of the House of Lords had sympathy for Lord Denning's principled argument, they considered the injustice caused by delays in reversing a few clearly incorrect decisions to be overshadowed by the injustice caused by the inconsistency and uncertainty arising from an abandonment of the doctrine of precedent:

> There are now as many as 17 Lords Justices in the Court of Appeal, and I fear that if *stare decisis* disappears from that court there is a real risk that there might be a plethora of conflicting decisions which would create a state of irremediable confusion and uncertainty in the law. This would do far more harm than the occasional unjust result which *stare decisis* sometimes produces but which can be remedied by an appeal to your Lordships' House.[169]

In general, the House of Lords was very critical of Lord Denning's attempts to undermine the doctrine of precedent and expressed surprise that the validity of the doctrine was "even arguable." Their dominant response was criticism of his "heterodox" view—in the face of clear and repeatedly affirmed decisions to the contrary, Lord Denning's "one-man crusade" was considered inconsistent with the rules of acceptable practice. These rebukes suggest either that Lord Denning was grossly mistaken about the law or that he had hoped to alter what was considered by the judicial community to be the acceptable standard. Either way, Lord Denning's reasoning does not threaten the existence of rules of judicial reasoning any more than a person who is confused about, or refuses to adhere to, the rules of a game challenges the proper rules of the game. The fact that an individual is criticized for failing to conform to the proper rules is evidence that the rules exist.

In summary, the broad disagreements in *Davis* are explicable in terms of human error or bias and the inevitable judgment that must be exercised when dealing with complex issues. My explanations of the reasoning in this contentious case are consistent with the view that judges are expected to adhere to, and in fact their decisions should be controlled by, the primary and secondary rules that form the law.

In the final sections of this chapter I present excerpts from the actual judicial opinions in both the Court of Appeal (decided November 1977) and House of Lords (decided March 1978) decisions in *Davis v. Johnson*. (Footnotes indicating case and statute citations have been omitted; italicized notes appearing within brackets have been added for clarification.)

COURT OF APPEAL OPINIONS

Two issues preoccupied the English Court of Appeal in *Davis v. Johnson*: (1) possible grounds for distinguishing two prior cases—*B v. B* and *Cantliff v. Jenkins*—dealing with the then newly enacted *Domestic Violence and Matrimonial Proceedings Act 1976*, and (2) the authority of the Court of Appeal to ignore previous decisions which it now considered to be clearly in error. Since the interesting controversy raised by *Davis* centres on the second issue, only those parts of the opinions that pertain to the authority of the Court of Appeal to overturn its own prior decisions will be cited. For varying reasons, three of the five judges decided that they had some authority to depart from *stare decisis* in civil matters.

Master of the Rolls Lord Denning

Lord Denning takes the strongest position against being bound to follow the two seemingly incorrectly decided cases.

> I turn to the second important point: can we depart from those two cases? Although convinced that they are wrong, are we at liberty to depart from them? What is the correct practice for this court to follow?

> On principle, it seems to me that, whilst this court should regard itself as normally bound by a previous decision of the court, nevertheless it should be at liberty to depart from it if it is convinced that the previous decision was wrong. What is the argument to the contrary? It is said that, if an error has been made, this court has no option but to continue the error and leave it to be corrected by the House of Lords. The answer is this: the House of Lords may never have an opportunity to correct the error; and thus it may be perpetuated indefinitely, perhaps forever. That often happened in the old days when there was no legal aid. A poor person had to accept the decision of this court because he had not the means to take it to the House of Lords. It took 60 years before the erroneous decision in *Carlisle and Cumberland Banking Co. v. Bragg* (1911) was overruled by the House of Lords in *Saunders (Executrix of Estate of Gallie) v. Anglia Building Society* (1971). Even today a person of moderate means may be outside the legal aid scheme, and not be able to take his case higher, especially with the risk of failure attaching to it. That looked as if it would have been the fate of Mrs. Farrell when the case was decided in this court; but she afterwards did manage to collect enough money together, and by means of it to get the decision of this court reversed by the House of Lords. Apart from monetary considerations, there have been many instances where cases have been settled pending an appeal to the House of Lords; or, for one reason or another, not taken

there, especially with claims against insurance companies or big employers. When such a body has obtained a decision of this court in its favour, it will buy off an appeal to the House of Lords by paying ample compensation to the appellant. By so doing, it will have a legal precedent on its side which it can use with effect in later cases. I fancy that such may have happened in cases following *Oliver v. Ashman* (1962). By such means an erroneous decision on a point of law can again be perpetuated forever. Even if all those objections are put on one side and there is an appeal to the House of Lords, it usually takes 12 months or more for the House to reach its decision. What then is the position of the lower courts meanwhile? They are in a dilemma. Either they have to apply the erroneous decision of the Court of Appeal, or they have to adjourn all fresh cases to await the decision of the House of Lords. That has often happened. So justice is delayed and often denied, by the lapse of time before the error is corrected. The present case is a crying instance. If it took the ordinary course of appeals to the House, it would take some months before it was decided. Meanwhile many women would be denied the protection which Parliament intended they should have. They would be subjected to violence without redress; because the county court judges would have to say to them: "We are sorry but the Court of Appeal says we have no jurisdiction to help you." We were told that, in this very case, because of the urgency, the House might take special measures to hear it before Christmas. But, even so, I doubt whether they would be able to give their decision until well on in the New Year. In order to avoid all the delay, and the injustice consequent on it, it seems to me that this court, being convinced that the two previous decisions were wrong, should have the power to correct them and give these women the protection which Parliament intended they should have. It was suggested that, if we did this, the county court judges would be in a dilemma. They would not know whether to follow the two previous decisions or the later decision of this court. There would be no such dilemma. They should follow this later decision. Such a position always arises whenever the House of Lords corrects an error made by a previous decision. The lower courts, of course, follow the latest decision. The general rule is that, where there are conflicting decisions of courts of co-ordinate jurisdiction, the later decision is to be preferred, if it is reached after full consideration of the earlier decision: see *Minister of Pensions v. Higham* (1948).

So much for principle. But what about our precedents? What about *Young v. Bristol Aeroplane Co. Ltd.*? [*the 1944 case reaffirming the court's duty to follow prior decisions*]

Lord Denning draws from numerous cases—heard between 1873, when the Court of Appeal first became a final appeal court, and 1941—to support the view that the Court of Appeal was not, during this period, absolutely bound by earlier decisions. Illustrative of these references is the House of Lords decision in *Hutton v. Bright* (1852), which notes the following:

... you are not bound by any rule of law which you may lay down, if upon a subsequent occasion, you should find reason to differ from that rule; that is, that this *House, like every Court of Justice,* possesses an inherent power to correct an error into which it may have fallen.

In a similar vein, Lord Denning cites the Court of Appeal decision in *Mills v. Jennings* (1880):

As a rule, this Court ought to treat the decisions of the Court of Appeal in Chancery as binding authorities, but we are at liberty not to do so when there is a sufficient reason for overruling them. As the decision in *Tassell v. Smith* (1858) may lead to consequences so serious, we think that we are at liberty to reconsider and review the decision in that case as if it were being re-heard in the old Court of Appeal in Chancery, as was not uncommon.

Lord Denning suggests that the Court of Appeal position on precedent changed in 1944:

In *Young v. Bristol Aeroplane Co. Ltd.* the court overruled the practice of a century. Lord Greene M.R. [*Master of the Rolls*], sitting with a court of five, laid down that this court is bound to follow its previous decision as well as those of co-ordinate jurisdiction, subject to only three exceptions: (i) where there are two conflicting decisions, (ii) where a previous decision cannot stand with a decision of the House of Lords, (iii) if a previous decision was given *per incuriam.*

It is to be noticed that the court laid down that proposition as a rule of law. That was quite the contrary of what Brett M.R. had declared in *The Vera Cruz (No. 2)* in 1884. He said it [*the binding authority of prior cases*] arose only as a matter of judicial comity [*out of respect for other courts, not as an obligation*]. Events have proved that in this respect that Brett M.R. was right and Lord Greene M.R. was wrong. I say this because the House of Lords in 1898 had held itself bound by its own previous decisions as a rule of law: see *London Street Tramways Co. Ltd. v. London County Council.* But yet in 1966 it discarded that rule. In a statement it was said:

Their Lordships nevertheless recognise that too rigid adherence to precedent may lead to injustice in a particular case and also unduly restrict the proper development of the law. They propose, therefore, to modify their present practice, and while treating former decisions of this House as normally binding, to depart from a previous decision when it appears right to do so.

That shows conclusively that a rule as to precedent (which any court lays down for itself) is not a rule of law at all. It is simply a practice or usage laid down by the court itself for its own guidance; and as such, the successors of that court can alter that practice or amend it or set up other guidelines, just as the House of Lords did in 1966. Even as the judges in *Young v. Bristol Aeroplane Co. Ltd.* thought fit to discard the practice of a century and declare a new practice or usage, so we in 1977 can discard the guidelines of 1944 and set up new guidelines of our own or revert to the old practice laid down by Brett M.R. Nothing said in the House of Lords, before or since, can stop us from doing so. Anything said about it must needs be *obiter dicta* [*comments that are not necessary to the decision reached in the case*]. This was emphasized by Salmon L.J. [*Lord Justice*] in this court in *Gallie v. Lee* (1969):

The point about the authority of this court has never been decided by the House of Lords. In the nature of things it is not a point that could ever come before the House for decision. Nor does it depend on any statutory or common law rule. This practice of ours apparently rests solely on a concept of judicial comity laid down many years ago and automatically followed ever since. ... Surely today judicial comity would be amply satisfied if we were to adopt the same principle in relation to our own decisions as the House of Lords has recently laid down for itself by pronouncement of the whole House.

So I suggest that we are entitled to lay down new guidelines. To my mind, the court should apply similar guidelines to those adopted by the House of Lords in 1966. Whenever it appears to this court that a previous decision was wrong, we should be at liberty to depart from it if we think it right to do so. Normally, in nearly every case of course, we would adhere to it. But in an exceptional case we are at liberty to depart from it.

Alternatively, in my opinion, we should extend the exceptions in *Young v. Bristol Aeroplane Co. Ltd.* when it appears to be a proper case to do so. I realise that comes virtually to the same thing, but such new exceptions have been created since *Young v. Bristol Aeroplane Co. Ltd.* For instance, this court can depart from a previous decision of its own when sitting on a criminal cause or matter: see the recent cases of *R. v. Gould* (1968) and *R. v. Newsome, R. v. Browne* (1970). Likewise by analogy it can depart from a previous decision in regard to contempt of court. Similarly in the numerous cases when this court is sitting as a court of last resort. There are many statutes which make this court the final court of appeal. In every jurisdiction throughout the world a court of last resort has, and always has had, jurisdiction to correct the errors of a previous decision ... [*lists ten cases that are exceptions to the notion of absolutely binding precedent*].

The truth is that the list of exceptions from *Young v. Bristol Aeroplane Co. Ltd.* is now getting so large that they are in process of eating up the rule itself; and we would do well simply to follow the same practice as the House of Lords.

Sir George Baker

In his opinion, Sir Baker supports the non-binding position on precedent in two ways: by suggesting grounds for distinguishing the present case, and by posing what he regards as a modest additional exception to those outlined in *Young*.

The second and very important question is whether this court can and should refuse to follow *B v. B*, an earlier decision of its own, which it is satisfied is not only wrong but clearly contrary to the plain terms and intent of a recent Act of Parliament which it refused to apply, or whether this court is bound by what was said in *Young v. Bristol Aeroplane Co. Ltd.*, in this court and in the House of Lords, about this court being bound to follow its own previous decisions.

Sir Baker explains why on "somewhat narrow grounds" he thinks that *B v. B* can be distinguished from the present case. But he admits that this approach to the problem "is not entirely satisfactory, because it leaves *B v. B* as an authority despite my opinion that it was wrongly decided." Sir Baker then proceeds to consider why the Court of Appeal is not bound to follow previous decisions that are wrong decided.

Certainty is an important and indeed vital factor on our legal system, though not perhaps so vital in the sphere of family law, where circumstances are so various as in commercial law and the law of contract. Coke C.J. [*Chief Justice*] said centuries ago: "It is better that the law should be certain than that every Judge should speculate improvements in it." Great weight is given, and rightly given, by every puisine judge to the decisions of his brethren, but in the last resort they do not bind him. The House of Lords is no longer irrevocably bound by its previous decisions ... [*cites the 1966 announcement, previously quoted by Lord Denning, on the House of Lord's authority to depart from prior decisions*].

I do not think that it is possible to bring this case within any of the existing exceptions which were spelled out in *Young v. Bristol Aeroplane Co. Ltd.* or came later in criminal cases. As to the first, that the court is entitled and bound to decide which of two conflicting decisions of its own it will follow, counsel for the applicant has pointed out that as the court is bound to follow its previous decision, it is difficult to envisage two conflicting decisions.

If however I am right in my view that *B v. B* can be distinguished, a later court could decide which case it should follow. This again is unsatisfactory.

It is not possible to say that *B v. B* was decided *per incuriam* and is therefore within the third exception to the rule. In *Huddersfield Police Authority v. Watson* (1947). Lord Goddard C.J. defined *per incuriam* as—

> giving a decision when a case or a statute has not been brought to the attention of the court and they have given the decision in ignorance or forgetfulness of the existence of that case or that statute.

He powerfully supported what had been said three years before in *Young's* case, saying that the Divisional Court should follow its own decisions even where it was a final court of appeal. He was, however, not satisfied that their earlier decision *Garvin v. City of London Police Authority* (1948) was wrongly decided, so what he said was *obiter*.

I have listened with care to counsel for the applicant's careful argument that *Young's* case does not bind this court. I cannot agree with that, but I am prepared to accept that there should be, and must be, a further carefully limited exception which is in part founded on an extension of, or gloss on, the second exception in *Young's* case: that the court is bound to refuse to follow a decision of its own which though not expressly overruled cannot in its opinion stand with a decision of the House of Lords.

I would attempt to define the exception thus: "The court is not bound to follow a previous decision of its own if satisfied that that decision was clearly wrong and cannot stand in the face of the will and intention of Parliament expressed in simple language in a recent Act passed to remedy a serious mischief or abuse, and further adherence to the previous decision must lead to injustice in the particular case and unduly restrict proper development of the law with injustice to others." My reasons, briefly, are (1) the practice statement in the House of Lords which recognises the danger of injustice, (2) that there is a conflict between a statutory provision and a decision which has completely misinterpreted the recent statute and failed to understand its purpose, (3) and to me the most compelling, by his judicial oath a judge binds himself to do "right to all manner of people after the laws and usages of this Realm." Here, by refusing the injunction, I would be doing a great wrong to the applicant, her child, and many others by following a decision which I firmly believe is not the law. The statute is the law, the final authority.

It is said that the proper course for this court is to be bound by the precedent of *B v. B*, whatever we may think of it, give leave to appeal and grant an injunction until the hearing which can be expedited. If one learns anything in the Family Division it is that the unexpected always happens in family affairs. There is no certainty that this case will ever reach the House of Lords. The respondent may end his tenancy. The applicant may decide to go and stay elsewhere. There are many possibilities which could lead to the withdrawal of legal aid which is not normally given in order that an important point of law may be decided where the decision will not benefit the immediate parties.

Lord Justice Shaw

In his opinion, Lord Justice Shaw argues for the addition of a very limited exception to the binding authority of prior decisions.

> It is not inapt to observe that whatever inhibition may be engendered by the powerful factors which justify and support the principle that this court should follow its own decisions (subject only to the possible exceptions stated in the judgment in *Young's* case), there is no provision under any statute which precludes a departure from earlier decisions. Indeed, had there been, Lord Greene M.R.'s exegesis 70 years after the *Supreme Court of Judicature Act 1873* would have been both unnecessary

and superfluous. It is incontrovertible that certainty in the law is a factor of high importance in the proper administration of justice, but it is not of itself the ultimate ideal. One has to ask in a particular case whether a rigid adherence to what appears to be plainly wrong conduces to the purity of justice or respect for its administration. In almost all cases it may do so but the principle of *stare decisis* cannot be absolutely universal in its application, as the judgment delivered by Lord Greene M.R. in *Young v. Bristol Aeroplane Co. Ltd.* shows. Why should that judgment have shut the door on the emergence of other, albeit very special, cases wherein this court should feel that there are considerations so strong against preserving the authority of an erroneous occasion as to compel it to depart from that decision and to correct the error? Otherwise a wrong view of the law will continue to operate until the House of Lords is provided with the opportunity to correct it, an opportunity which arises fortuitously only if and when some dissatisfied litigant resolves and is able to carry his cause there.

By and large it is probably the case that the general public interest will suffer no mortal blow during the period that a fallacious decision by the Court of Appeal prevails as a statement of the law relating to a particular topic such as finance or commerce or other materialistic subject-matter. Anyone who has a sufficient interest to challenge such a decision may do so when the occasion arises for him to assert his right in the courts. When ultimately the House of Lords determines the matter that litigant will obtain his redress retrospectively. Others before him might have done the same. *Stare decisis* in the long run does not inexorably make such litigants the hapless and helpless victims of judicial error.

That sort of situation bears no relationship to a case like the present arising as it does out of the enactment of a statute which in the judgment of this court was plainly intended to protect the victims of domestic violence from being thereby driven from the matrimonial home. In less than five months after the coming into force of the relevant provisions of the Act its teeth were effectively drawn by a decision of the Court of Appeal. The result has been not merely to deprive the present appellant of the protection which Parliament intended; it has disfranchised all those who have the misfortune to be in like case, and there are no doubt very many.

If, when the House of Lords has had the opportunity of considering the meaning of s 1, their Lordships should come to the conclusion that *B v. B* was wrongly decided the reversal by them of that decision will afford no retrospective relief at all and not even the coldest comfort to anyone who in the meanwhile has been refused the remedies which this court now considers were intended to be and were made available by the statute. Because of a legalistic attitude, such persons will have had to make a choice between submitting to the risk of suffering the infliction of further violence or being rendered homeless. Such an outcome of insisting on the inflexibly binding force of an earlier decision would in the minds of reasonable citizens cast a greater slur on the administration of justice than would some limited relaxation of the doctrine of *stare decisis*. If, however, the House of Lords should uphold the view taken by the court in *B v. B* the harm done by its temporary eclipse will be very much less comparatively. For my part I venture to think that if in 1944 a situation like the present had been in contemplation a further exception might have found a place in the judgment in *Young v. Bristol Aeroplane Co. Ltd.* It would be in some such terms as that the principle of *stare decisis* should be relaxed where its application would have the effect of depriving actual and potential victims of violence of a vital protection which an Act of Parliament was plainly designed to afford to them, especially where, as in the context of domestic violence, that deprivation must inevitably give rise to an irremediable detriment to such victims and create in regard to them an injustice irreversible by a later decision of the House of Lords.

Lord Justice Shaw quotes from a case that is taken to recognize that the court has power to overrule its previous decisions. He concludes his judgment with the following comments:

> After anxious consideration and without, I trust, any abandonment of appropriate judicial restraint I have come to the clear view that, when one has regard to the nature of the proceedings with which this appeal is concerned and when one bears in mind that their outcome must have an immediate and direct impact not only on the position of the applicant but on that of many others who are now become the victims of domestic violence, it is right and proper and indeed imperative that this court should not only decide how s 1 is to be construed and how it is to operate but, having so decided, that it should also act decisively in pursuance of that view. I thus agree with the result of the judgments of Lord Denning M.R. and Sir George Baker P. for the reasons I have stated.

Lord Justice Goff

Despite his regret at not being able to distinguish the present case from the earlier decisions, Lord Justice Goff cannot justify departing from established precedent. He begins by considering the reasons for dismissing these earlier cases.

> It is said that the principles laid down by Lord Greene M.R. in *Young v. Bristol Aeroplane Co. Ltd.* were *obiter* only and do not bind the Court of Appeal, which should now find either that, albeit to be rarely exercised, the court has power to go behind its own previous decisions, in the same way as the House of Lords now has, or at least that the class of exceptions to the general rule laid down in that case is not closed and the present case should be regarded as an exception. Counsel for the applicant in his able and persuasive argument adumbrated four categories which he submitted either separately or collectively fall outside the general rule, and embrace the present case. They were: (1) a case in which the well-being of a person or a child is a central issue; (2) where a recent important statute has in the view of the court been misinterpreted; (3) where a decision is plainly wrong and the consequence of following it would be far reaching; and (4) where in the interests of the administration of justice generally it is urgently necessary to correct an error. I think, though in different words, that formulation of the proposition accords with what has found favour with Lord Denning M.R. and Sir George Baker P. Alternatively, it has been suggested that the present court, being five in number and not three, has power not possessed by three to disregard previous decisions, at least when in those cases the court consisted of not more than three members. For reasons which I will develop later, I cannot accept any of these submissions.
>
> It was further argued that even if the rule in *Young's* case is binding on this court, and that, notwithstanding it is constituted as it is with five members, still the present case falls within one of the recognised exceptions, namely, where in the earlier decision the court has acted in ignorance of, and contrary to, some statute or statutory provision; but, with respect, in my judgment, that cannot apply to this case. In *B v. B* and *Cantliff v. Jenkins* the court did not act in ignorance of the *Domestic Violence Act* or in any way *per incuriam*. On the contrary, it construed it. If they will forgive me saying so, the learned Lords Justices who decided those cases may have got it wrong, but that does not make it *per incuriam* or take it out of the general role, as Lord Greene M.R. himself pointed out in *Young's* case.
>
> In my judgment, with the greatest respect to those who think otherwise, this court when exercising its civil jurisdiction is bound by the general rule in *Young's* case, save possibly where it is the final court of appeal, and further the class of exceptions

is closed. My reasons for this conclusion are the necessity for preserving certainty in our law, which has great value in enabling persons to obtain definite advice on which they can order their affairs, the care which should always be taken to see that hard cases do not make bad law and the oft repeated occasions on which *Young's* case has been approved on the highest authority.

Lord Justice Goff devotes much of his opinion to countering the suggestion that "there is no statutory or common law obligation on the Court of Appeal to follow its own decisions." He begins by quoting what he regards as the decisive statement on this point made by Master of the Rolls Lord Greene in *Young's* case:

Lord Greene M.R. laid down the position as follows:

On a careful examination of the whole matter we have come to the clear conclusion that this court is bound to follow previous decisions of its own as well as those of courts of co-ordinate jurisdiction. The only exceptions to this rule ... are those already mentioned which for convenience we here summarise: (i) The court is entitled and bound to decide which of two conflicting decisions of its own it will follow. (ii) The court is bound to refuse to follow a decision of its own which, though not expressly overruled, cannot in its opinion stand with a decision of the House of Lords. (iii) The court is not bound to follow a decision of its own if it is satisfied that the decision was given *per incuriam*.

Lord Justice Goff explains that this statement was approved by Viscount Simon when the case came to the House of Lords, but that Lord Denning took a less strict position in a subsequent case, *Gallie v. Lee*, on the duty to abide by prior decisions:

... We are, or course, bound by the decisions of the House [*of Lords*], but I do not think we are bound by prior decisions of our own, or at any rate, not absolutely bound. We are not fettered as it was once thought. It was a self-imposed limitation; and we who imposed it can also remove it. The House of Lords have done it. So why should not we do likewise? We should be just as free, no more and no less, to depart from a prior precedent of our own, as in like case is the House of Lords or a judge of first instance. It is very, very rare that we will go against a previous decision of our own, but if it is clearly shown to be erroneous, we should be able to put it right.

However, Lord Denning's view was not shared by the other two members of the court that decided *Gallie v. Lee*. In fact, Lord Justice Russell "clearly disagreed" with Lord Denning:

I add that I do not support the suggestion that this court is free to override its own decisions, now that the House of Lords has given itself ability to override its own decisions. I am a firm believer in a system by which citizens and these advisers can have as much certainty as possible in the ordering of their affairs. Litigation is an activity that does not markedly contribute to the happiness of mankind, though it is sometimes unavoidable. An abandonment of the principle that this court follows its own decisions on the law would I think lead to greater uncertainty and tend to produce more litigation. In the case of decisions of the House of Lords' error, or what is later considered to be error, could only previously be corrected by statute; and the other demands on parliamentary time made this possibility so remote that the decision of the House of Lords not necessarily to be bound by a previous decision was justifiable at the expense of some loss of certainty. But the availability of the House of Lords to correct error in the Court of Appeal makes it in my view unnecessary for this court to depart from its existing discipline.

Lord Justice Salmon, the other member of the court that decided *Gallie v. Lee*, also disagreed with Lord Denning:

> ... I am, however, convinced that so long as this court considers itself absolutely bound by its own decisions I have no power to adopt Lord Denning M.R.'s conclusion; I must accept the law as stated in the authorities to which I have referred in spite of the fact that it results too often in inconsistency, injustice, and an affront to common sense. The *dicta* to the effect that this court is absolutely bound by its own decisions are very strong (see, for example, *Young v. Bristol Aeroplane Co. Ltd.,* and *Bonsor v. Musicians' Union* (1956)), but no stronger than those by virtue of which the House of Lords until recently treated itself as similarly bound by its own decisions. The point about the authority of this court has never been decided by the House of Lords. In the nature of things it is not a point that could ever come before the House for decision. Nor does it depend on any statutory or law rule. This practice of ours apparently rests solely on a concept of judicial comity laid down many years ago and automatically followed ever since, see *The Vera Cruz (No. 2)* ... Surely today judicial comity would be satisfied if we were to adopt the same principles in relation to our own as the House of Lords has recently laid down for itself by a pronouncement of the whole House. It may be that one day we shall make a similar pronouncement. I can see no valid reasons why we should not do so and many why we should. But that day is not yet. It is, I think, only by a pronouncement of the whole court that we could effectively alter a practice which is so deeply rooted. In the meantime I find myself reluctantly obliged to accept the old authorities, however much I disagree with them ... [*continues with this quotation*].

Lord Justice Goff cites extensively from a line of cases that dispute Lord Denning's view of the Court of Appeal's authority to overturn decisions. These include the following quote from the judgment of Lord Scarman in *Tiverton Estates Ltd. v. Wearwell Ltd.* (1975):

> ... The Court of Appeal occupies a central, but, save for a few exceptions, an intermediate position in our legal system. To a large extent the consistency and certainty of the law depend on it. It sits almost always in divisions of three: more judges can sit to hear a case, but their decision enjoys no greater authority than a court composed of three. If, therefore, throwing aside the restraints of *Young v. Bristol Aeroplane Co. Ltd.*, one division of the court should refuse to follow another because it believed the other's decision to be wrong, there would be a risk of confusion and doubt arising where there should be consistency and certainty. The appropriate forum for the correction of the Court of Appeal's errors is the House of Lords, where the decision will at least have the merit of being final and binding—subject only to the House's power to review its own decisions. The House of Lords, as the court of last resort, needs this power of review: it does not follow that an intermediate appellate court needs it: and, for the reasons I have given, I believe the Court of Appeal is better without it, save in the exceptional circumstances specified in *Young v. Bristol Aeroplane Co. Ltd.*

Lord Justice Goff concludes his "long line of citation from authority" with the following House of Lords decision by Lord Simon of Glaisdale in *Farrell v. Alexander* (1977):

> The relevant law on this point has been laid down beyond all question by two of the most eminent judges who have ever held the great office of Master of the Rolls— Lord Greene (in *Young v. Bristol Aeroplane Co. Ltd.*) and Lord Denning (in *Miliangos v. George Frank (Textiles) Ltd.* (1975)). I content myself with citing the latter:

We have further considered this case and we consider we are bound by the earlier decision [of the Court of Appeal in *Schorsch Meier GmbH v. Hennin* (1975)] ... The law on this subject has been authoritatively stated in *Young v. Aeroplane Co.* and *Morelle Ltd. v. Wakeling* (1955). This court is bound to follow its own decisions—including majority decisions—except in closely defined circumstances ... I have myself often said that this court is not actually bound by its own decisions and may depart from them just as the House of Lords from theirs: but my colleagues have not gone so far. So that I am in duty bound to defer to their view.

Lord Denning M.R. explained the relevant defined circumstances in which the Court of Appeal could depart from a previous decision of that court. They did not, of course, extend to a case where the court conceived that the result of an appeal to your Lordships' House was "a foregone conclusion."

In closing Lord Justice Goff offers the following remarks:

Such being the state of the authorities, I cannot for my part doubt but that we are bound by *B v. B* and *Cantliff v. Jenkins* and, therefore, I would dismiss this appeal on that short ground; but with great reluctance, since, and with humble respect to the members of the two powerful divisions who decided those cases and with no small trepidation in the presence of so great a cloud of witnesses, I venture to say that I do not agree with their conclusions, although in many respects I feel the force of their careful reasoning.

Lord Justice Cumming-Bruce

Lord Justice Cumming-Bruce joins with Lord Justice Goff in arguing that the Court of Appeal is not free to depart from the earlier decided cases. He opens by considering an argument against his position.

Counsel for the applicant submits that this court is and that its jurisdiction and statutory duty is to be collected from the words of s 24(7) of the *Supreme Court of Judicature Act 1873*, wherein it was enacted that the Court of Appeal "shall have the power to grant all such remedies as any of the parties may be entitled to." He submits that, if this court holds that the construction of the state preferred in *B v. B* and followed in *Cantliff v. Jenkins* was clearly wrong, no decided case or previous practice can preclude us from doing right and granting to the applicant any remedy to which she is entitled.

It appears to be clear that the practice of this court has been consistent at least since 1944. It is explained in 1884 as based on comity; it was affirmed in *Young v. Bristol Aeroplane Co. Ltd.* in 1944 when the court stated the exceptional situations in which it would not regard itself as bound by its previous decisions. It was affirmed again by a court of five in *Morelle Ltd. v. Wakeling,* where Evershed M.R. said:

... [cites the main issue in the case] ... In our judgment acceptance of the Attorney-General's argument [to ignore a prior decision considered to be incorrectly decided] would necessarily involve the proposition that it is open to this court to disregard an earlier decision of its own or of a court of co-ordinate jurisdiction (at least in any case of significance or complexity) whenever it is made to appear that the court had not, on the earliest occasion, had the benefit of the best argument that the researches and industry of counsel could provide. Such a proposition would, as it seems to us, open the way to numerous and costly attempts to re-open questions now held to be authoritatively decided. Although, as was pointed out in *Young v. Bristol Aeroplane Co. Ltd.*, a "full court" of five judges of the Court of Appeal has no greater jurisdiction or higher authority than a normal division of the court consisting of three judges, we cannot help thinking that, if the Attorney-General's argument were accepted, there would be a strong tendency in cases of public interest and importance, to invite a "full court" in effect to usurp the function of the House of Lords and to reverse a previous decision of the Court of Appeal. Such a result would plainly be inconsistent with the maintenance of the principle of *stare decisis* in our courts.

Lord Justice Cumming-Bruce refers to the previous disagreements between Lord Denning and the majority of the court on the question of binding authority.

Scrutiny of these cases and respectful consideration of the dissenting views expressed by Lord Denning M.R. in this court lead me to the conclusion that the practice is based on an appreciation of the policy which is most likely to afford the Crown and its subjects a judicial system in which the conflicting claims of certainty and justice in individual cases are reconciled. It seems to me that in any system of law the undoubted public advantages of certainty in civil proceedings must be purchased at the price of the risk of injustice in difficult individual situations. I would think that the present practice holds the balance just about right. The temptation to depart from it would be much less seductive if there could be readier access to the House of Lords. The highest tribunal is within the reach of those whose modest means enable them to qualify for legal aid, and of the extremely rich. Its doors are closed, for practical purposes, to everyone else. The injustice which today is liable to flow from the fact that unsatisfactory old cases are so seldom capable of review in the House of Lords would be mitigated or removed if Parliament decided to give this court and the House of Lords power to order that costs in the House of Lords should be paid by the Exchequer in those cases in which this court or the House of Lords on an application for leave to appeal certified that an appeal to the House of Lords was desirable in order to enable that House to review a decision regarded as mistaken but binding on the Court of Appeal. The expense to the public and any resulting inconvenience could be infinitely less than that which would flow from a relaxation of the present practice in respect of stare decisis as declared in *Young's* case. I consider that we are bound to act in accordance with the practice as stated in *Young's* case and the *Morelle Ltd.* case. This is because I consider that the constitutional functions of their Lordships sitting in their judicial capacity include the function of declaring with authority the extent to which the Court of Appeal is bound by its previous decisions, and the function of defining with authority the exceptional situations in which it is open to this court to depart from a previous decision. So I hold that this court is bound by the declaration made by Viscount Dilhorne, Lord Simon of Glaisdale and Lord Russell of Killowen in *Farrell v. Alexander* that this court is bound by precedent exactly as stated by Scarman L.J. in his judgment in the Court of Appeal in that case affirming the declaration made by Lord Hailsham of St Marylebone L.C. [*Lord Chancellor*] in *Cassell & Co. Ltd. v. Broome* (1972), a declaration again which commanded the express assent of a majority of their Lordships' House.

HOUSE OF LORD OPINIONS

Since the House of Lords was not bound by the two earlier decisions which had originated from the Court of Appeal, they considered afresh in this appeal of *Davis v. Johnson* what interpretation to give the *Domestic Violence and Matrimonial Protection Act.* As well, the House of Lords considered whether the Court of Appeal was bound by its prior decisions. Only those parts of the opinion that address the *stare decisis* question are reproduced here. The judges were unanimous in their support for a policy of binding authority. Lord Diplock's opinion was the most extensive on this issue; Lord Salmon offered a few comments on the matter. The remaining opinions, which are not reproduced here, added little: Lord Kilbrandon and Lord Scarman simply supported the comments by the others, Viscount Dilhorne did likewise, although he added an observation about the difference between the House of Lords' and lower courts' right to overturn prior decisions.

Lord Diplock

After a brief review of the facts and history of the case, Lord Diplock turns to the question of the Court of Appeal's duty to follow its own previous decisions. He notes that "the law on this question is now clear and unassailable. It has been so for more than 30 years." He explains that the Court of Appeal's position on the doctrine of *stare decisis* was the subject of "close examination" by the Court of Appeal in *Young v. Bristol Aeroplane Co. Ltd.* He then lays out this position, with the three exceptions, as summarized by Master of the Rolls Lord Greene (see Lord Goff's opinion).

> The rule as expounded in the *Bristol Aeroplane* case was not new in 1944. It had been acted on on numerous occasions and had, as recently as the previous year, received the express confirmation in this House of Viscount Simon L.C. with whose speech Lord Atkin agreed: see *Perrin v. Morgan* (1943). Although prior to 1944 there had been an occasional deviation from the rule, which was why a court of six was brought together to consider it, there has been none since. It has been uniformly acted on by the Court of Appeal and re-affirmed, notably in a judgment of a Court of Appeal of five, of which Lord Denning M.R. as Denning L.J. was a member, in *Morelle Ltd. v. Wakeling* (1955). This judgment emphasised the limited scope of the *per incuriam* exception to the general rule that the Court of Appeal is bound by its own previous decisions. The rule has also been uniformly accepted by this House as being correct. Because until recently it has never been questioned the acceptance of the rule has generally been tacit in the course of recounting the circumstances which have rendered necessary an appeal to your Lordships' House; but occasionally the rule has been expressly referred to, as by Viscount Simon in the *Bristol Aeroplane* case itself and by Lord Morton of Henryton and Lord Porter in *Bonsor v. Musicians' Union* (1956).

> Furthermore, the provisions of the *Administration of Justice Act 1969* which authorise "leap frog" appeals in civil cases direct from the High Court to this House [*which by-pass the Court of Appeal*] are based on the tacit assumption that the rule as stated in the *Bristol Aeroplane* case is correct. One of the two grounds on which a High Court judge may authorise a "leap frog" appeal is if he is satisfied that a point of law of general importance involved in his decision—

>> is one in respect of which the judge is bound by a decision of the Court of Appeal or of the House of Lords in previous proceedings, and was fully considered in the judgments given by the Court of Appeal or the House of Lords (as the case may be) in those previous proceedings.

> The justification for by-passing the Court of Appeal when the decision by which the judge is bound is one given by the Court of Appeal itself in previous proceedings is because that court also is bound by the decision, if the point of law was fully considered and not passed over *per incuriam*.

So the rule as it had been laid down in the *Bristol Aeroplane* case had never been questioned thereafter until, following on the announcement by Lord Gardiner L.C. in 1966 that the House of Lords would feel free in exceptional cases to depart from a previous decision of its own, Lord Denning M.R. conducted what may be described, I hope without offence, as a one-man crusade with the object of freeing the Court of Appeal from the shackles which the doctrine of *stare decisis* imposed on its liberty of decision by the application of the rule laid down in the *Bristol Aeroplane* case to its previous decisions; or, for that matter, by any decisions of this House itself of which the Court of Appeal disapproved: see *Broome v. Cassell Co. Ltd.* (1971); *Schorsch Meier GmbH v. Hennin* (1975). In his judgment in the instant appeal, Lord Denning M.R. refers to a number of cases after 1966 in which he suggests that the Court of Appeal has either refused to apply the rule as laid down in the *Bristol Aeroplane* case or has added so many other exceptions to the three that were stated by Lord Greene M.R. that it no longer operates as a curb on the power of the Court of Appeal to disregard any previous decision of its own which the majority of those members who happen to be selected to sit on a particular appeal think is wrong. Such, however, has not been the view of the other two members of the Court of Appeal who were sitting with Lord Denning M.R. in any of those cases to which he refers. Where they felt able to disregard a previous decision of the Court of Appeal this was only because, in their opinion, it fell within the first or second exception stated in the *Bristol Aeroplane* case. When *Miliangos v. George Frank (Textiles) Ltd.* (1975) was before the Court of Appeal Lord Denning M.R. appears to have reluctantly recanted ... [*provides a brief context for the following remarks by Lord Denning*].

> I have myself often said that this court is not absolutely bound by its own decisions and may depart from them just as the House of Lords from theirs: but my colleagues have not gone so far. So that I am in duty bound to defer to their view.

The reasons why his colleagues had not agreed to follow him are plain enough. In an appellate court of last resort a balance must be struck between the need on the one side for the legal certainty resulting from the binding effect of previous decisions and on the other side the avoidance of undue restriction on the proper development of the law. In the case of an intermediate appellate court, however, the second desideratum can be taken care of by appeal to a superior appellate court, if reasonable means of access to it are available; while the risk to the first desideratum, legal certainty, if the court is not bound by its own previous decisions grows ever greater with increasing membership and the number of three-judge divisions in which it sits, as the arithmetic which I have earlier mentioned shows. So the balance does not lie in the same place as in the case of a court of last resort. That is why Lord Gardiner L.C.'s announcement about the future attitude towards precedent of the House of Lords in its judicial capacity concluded with the words: "This announcement is not intended to affect the use of precedent elsewhere than in this House."

Much has been said in the instant case about the delay and expense which would have been involved if the Court of Appeal had treated itself as bound by its previous decisions in *B v. B* (1978) and *Cantliff v. Jenkins* (1978), so as to make it necessary for the respondent to come to this House to argue that those decisions should be overruled. But a similar reasoning could also be used to justify any High Court or county court judge in refusing to follow a decision of the Court of Appeal which he thought was wrong. It is true that since the appeal in the instant case was from the county court, not the High Court, the "leap-frog" procedure was not available, but since it was conceded that the instant case was indistinguishable from *Cantliff v. Jenkins,* there was no need for anything but the hearings in the Court of Appeal. The appeal to this House could in that event have been heard before Christmas instead of in January; and at less cost. The decision could have been announced at once and the reasons given later. Of the various ways in which Lord Denning M.R.'s colleagues had expressed the reasons for continuing to regard the rule laid down in the *Bristol Aeroplane* case as salutary in the interest of the administration of justice, I select those given by Scarman L.J., in *Tiverton Estates Ltd. v. Wearwell Ltd.* ... [*cites the passage, previously quoted in Lord Justice Goff's opinion, about the confusion arising if intermediate-level courts were allowed to ignore their earlier decisions.*]

My own reason for selecting this passage out of many is because in the following year in *Farrell v. Alexander* (1977) Scarman L.J. again referred to it in dissociating himself from the view, to which Lord Denning M.R. had by then once again reverted, that the Court of Appeal was not bound by any previous decision of its own which it was satisfied was wrong. What Scarman L.J. there said was:

> ... I have immense sympathy with the approach of Lord Denning M.R. I decline to accept his lead only because I think it damaging to the law in the long term— though it would undoubtedly do justice in the present case. To some it will appear that justice is being denied by a timid, conservative adherence to judicial precedent. They would be wrong. Consistency is necessary to certainty—one of the great objectives of law. The Court of Appeal—at the very centre of our legal system—is responsible for its stability, its consistency, and its predictability [*cites case reference*]. The task of law reform, which calls for wide-ranging techniques of consultation and discussion that cannot be compressed into the forensic medium, is for others. The courts are not to be blamed in a case such as this. If there be blame, it rests elsewhere.

When *Farrell v. Alexander* reached this House Scarman L.J.'s way of putting it was expressly approved by my noble and learned friends, Viscount Dilhorne and Lord Simon of Glaisdale, while the other member of this House who adverted to the question of *stare decisis*, Lord Russell of Killowen, expressed his "unreserved disapproval" of that part of Lord Denning M.R.'s judgment in which he persisted in his heterodox views on the subject.

Having dealt with Lord Denning's arguments, Lord Diplock then considers and rejects the exceptions put forth by Sir George Baker and Lord Justice Shaw:

> My Lords, the exception as stated by Sir George Baker P. would seem wide enough to cover any previous decision on the construction of a statute which the majority of the court thought was wrong and would have consequences that were regrettable, at any rate if they felt sufficiently strongly about it. As stated by Shaw L.J. the exception would appear to be what might be termed a "one-off" exception. It is difficult to think of any other statute to which it would apply. In my opinion, this House should take this occasion to re-affirm expressly, unequivocally and unanimously that the rule laid down in the *Bristol Aeroplane* case as to *stare decisis* is still binding on the Court of Appeal.

The remaining arguments in Lord Diplock's opinion deal with the correct interpretation to be given the *Domestic Violence and Matrimonial Proceedings Act.*

Lord Salmon

In his opinion, Lord Salmon offers the follows remarks on the matter of binding precedent.

> I entirely agree with your Lordships that in appeal in civil cases, the Court of Appeal is bound by its own previous decisions subject to the three exceptions laid down in *Young v. Bristol Aeroplane Co. Ltd.* Although the balance of authority prior to 1944 supported that rule, there had been a number of *dicta* and decisions of the Court of Appeal (alluded to by Lord Denning M.R.) which had rejected it. That is why the appeal in the *Bristol Aeroplane* case was heard by Lord Greene M.R. and five out of the eight Lords Justices who then sat regularly in that court.
>
> Ever since 1944 this rule has been applied by the Court of Appeal except in the instant case. Your Lordships' House on a number of occasions (once before and three times after 1944) has confirmed the application of the rule to decisions of the Court of Appeal, and has thereby greatly strengthened the rule. In the nature of things, however, the point could never come before your Lordships' House for decision or form part of its *ratio decidendi.* This House decides every case that comes before it according to the law. If, as in the instant case, the Court of Appeal decides an appeal contrary to one of its previous decisions, this House, much as it may deprecate the Court of Appeal's departure from the rule, will nevertheless dismiss the appeal if it comes to the conclusion that the decision appealed against was right in law.
>
> I am afraid that I disagree with Lord Denning M.R. when he says that the Court of Appeal is not absolutely bound by its own decisions and may depart from them just as your Lordships may depart from yours. As my noble and learned friend, Lord Diplock, has pointed out, the announcement made in 1966 by Lord Gardiner L.C. about the future attitudes of this House towards precedents ended with words: "This announcement is not intended to affect the use of precedents elsewhere than in this House." I would also point out that announcement was made with the unanimous approval of all the Law Lords, and that, by contrast, the overwhelming majority of the present Lords Justices have expressed the view that the principle of *stare decisis* still prevails and should continue to prevail in the Court of Appeal. I do not understand how, in these circumstances, it is even arguable that it does not.
>
> I sympathise with the views expressed on this topic by Lord Denning M.R., but until such time, if ever, as all his colleagues in the Court of Appeal agree with those views, *stare decisis* must still hold the field. I think that this may be no bad thing. There are now as many as 17 Lords Justices in the Court of Appeal, and I fear that if *stare decisis* disappears from that court there is a real risk that there might be a plethora of conflicting decisions which would create a state of irremediable confusion and uncertainty in the law. This would do far more harm than the occasional unjust result which *stare decisis* sometimes produces but which can be remedied by an appeal to your Lordships' House. I recognise, as Cumming-Bruce L.J. points out, that only those who qualify for legal aid or the very rich can afford to bring such an appeal. This difficulty could however be surmounted if when the Court gave leave to appeal from a decision it has felt bound to make by an authority with which it disagreed, it had a power conferred on it by Parliament to order the appellants' and/or the respondents' costs of the appeal to be paid out of public funds. This would be a very rare occurrence and the consequent expenditure of public funds would be minimal.
>
> I do not agree with the reasons given by Sir George Baker P. for departing from the rule in the *Bristol Aeroplane* case. A high proportion of the decisions of the Court of Appeal turn on the construction of statutes. The fact that the decision concerns a

recent statute is, to my mind, irrelevant. Shaw L.J.'s decision however is based on the ground that the most exceptional and appalling facts of the present case were never in the contemplation of the Court of Appeal in the *Bristol Aeroplane* case, and I confess that I find the reasons on which he founded his decision very persuasive. I need not however express any opinion on that judgment for I agree with my noble and learned friend, Lord Diplock, that the exception formulated by Shaw L.J. is what may be termed a "one-off" exception and that it is difficult to think of any other statute to which it could apply. I therefore entirely agree with your Lordships that the rule laid down in the *Bristol Aeroplane* case binds the Court of Appeal.

9
Selected Judicial Opinions

Any serious assessment of the account of judicial reasoning presented in this book requires that we look to judges' written opinions for formal justification of their decisions in individual cases. Given our concern to explain authorized judicial practice, this approach is more appropriate than interviewing judges privately. Judges' publicly stated reasons are reliable indicators of the "rules" of judicial reasoning in the same way that we can learn about proper driving behaviour by studying motorists in some formal situation, say while being observed by a police officer or by a driving instructor. As we know, motorists do not always drive as they are expected to when they believe that no one is looking. The rules of the road, like the rules of judicial reasoning, are often broken (both inadvertently and intentionally). Like all human institutions, the judiciary is prone to error and prejudice—and a biased or mistaken decision, unless overruled in some way, will carry with it the full force of law. However, the fact that, in practice, these rules are ignored or are poorly applied does not extinguish the judicial obligation to abide by them. For this reason, formal expressions of judicial reasoning, rather than private declarations, provide the ultimate test of any account of how judges are *authorized* to apply law.[170]

This final chapter contains excerpts from 13 judicial opinions originating from three cases—*Royal College of Nursing v. Department of Health and Social Security*, *Donoghue v. Stevenson*, and *Morgentaler v. The Queen* (1988). The opinions are classified according to which mode of reasoning dominates the decision (although the other two modes often appear in the opinions). For all three cases, majority and dissenting opinions are presented. The focus on controversial decisions involving multiple opinions is to illustrate how opposing positions can be grounded in legal standards and to emphasize the difficult decisions that judges face. For simplicity of reading, case and statute citations have been removed from the opinions. Italicized notes appearing within brackets have been added for clarification.

REASONING FROM INTERPRETIVE GUIDELINES

In this part are found excerpts from the opinions of the Court of Appeal and the House of Lords decisions in *Royal College of Nursing v. Department of Health and Social Security*. This controversial 1980 English case, discussed in Chapter 3, focuses on the interpretation of the *Abortion Act 1967* which allows that pregnancies may be "terminated by a registered medical practitioner." Both levels of judgments were decided predominantly on the basis of reasoning from interpretive guidelines.

Royal College of Nursing: Court of Appeal Decision

In *Royal College of Nursing v. Department of Health and Social Security* the issue before the Appeal Court, and subsequently appealed to the House of Lords, was whether or not a recently introduced "medical induction" method of abortion which is administered for the most part by nurses could be considered to be "terminated by a registered medical practitioner." All three justices of the Court of Appeal concluded that it did not meet this required standard. The opinions of Lord Denning and Sir George Baker are reproduced here.

Master of the Rolls Lord Denning

Lord Denning begins his opinion by introducing the question the Court is asked to decide; namely, "when a pregnancy is terminated by medical induction, who should do the actual act of termination? Should it be done by a doctor? Or can he leave it to the nurses?" Lord Denning summarizes the legislative history of abortion, noting that before the current legislation the *Offences Against the Person Act 1861* made the termination of pregnancies a felony. Subsequently, the *Abortion Act 1967* legalized abortions provided the pregnancy was "terminated by a registered medical practitioner." Lord Denning explains that for approximately five years after the 1967 legislation there was no difficulty interpreting the Act since abortions employed surgical methods carried out by doctors—i.e., by registered medical practitioners. Since 1972, however, a new method, called medical induction, had been introduced. This process, which induces abortions by a chemical fluid pumped into the mother's womb, has two distinct stages. The first stage, done by a doctor, simply involves inserting a catheter. The second stage, which takes between 18 and 30 hours, is done by nurses. It involves pumping the fluid through the catheter into the womb. Lord Denning emphasizes and documents that it is the second stage—the injection of the fluid—that induces labour and causes the foetus to abort. He characterizes the insertion of the catheter "as only a preparatory act." The second stage, done by the nurses, is the act that "terminates the pregnancy." Lord Denning then comments on the reluctance of many nurses to take part in this "heart-rending task."

> It is against this background that the Royal College of Nursing ask the question: is it lawful for nurses to be called upon to terminate pregnancy in this way? The Royal College says [sic] "No. It is not lawful. It is not a nurse's job to terminate a pregnancy." The Department of Health say "Yes. It is lawful." They have issued a circular [*a written directive*] in which they presume to lay down the law for the whole of the medical profession. They say that it is no offence if the pregnancy is terminated by a suitably qualified person in accordance with the written instructions of a registered medical practitioner. This is the wording of the circular:
>
> > However, the Secretary of State is advised that the termination can properly be said to have been termination by the registered medical practitioner provided it is decided upon by him, initiated by him, and that he remains throughout responsible for its overall conduct and control in the sense that any actions

> needed to bring it to conclusion are done by appropriately skilled staff acting on his specific instructions but *not necessarily in his presence.*

Note those words "not necessarily in his presence." They are crucial.

Before considering whether this Department of Health directive satisfies the requirements of the statute, Lord Denning comments on the highly charged nature of the subject of abortion. He suggests that "Emotions run so high on both sides that I feel that we as judges must go by the very words of the statute—without stretching it one way or the other—and writing nothing in which is not there." Lord Denning then explores an ordinary-meaning interpretation of the Act.

> If there should ever be a case in the courts, the decision would ultimately be that of a jury. Suppose that during the process the mother died or became seriously ill—owing to the nurse's negligence in administering the wrong chemical fluid—and the nurse was prosecuted under the *Offences against the Person Act 1861* for unlawfully administering her a noxious thing or using other means with intent to procure her miscarriage. The nurse would have no defence unless the pregnancy was "terminated by a registered medical practitioner." Those are simple English words which should be left to a jury to apply—without the judge attempting to put his own gloss upon them: see *Cozens v. Brutus* (1973). I should expect the jury to say that the pregnancy was not terminated by a registered medical practitioner, but by a nurse.
>
> If in such a case there were a claim for damages, the nurse might not be covered by insurance because she would not be engaged in "nursing professional services accepted by the Royal College of Nursing."
>
> Statutes can be divided into two categories. In the first category Parliament has expressly said "by a registered practitioner or by a person acting accordance with the directions of any such practitioner," or words to that effect: see the *Radioactive Substances Act 1948*; *Therapeutic Substances Act 1956*; *Medicines Act 1968*; *Tattooing of Minors Act 1969*. In the second category Parliament has deliberately confined it, by "by a full registered medical practitioner," omitting any such words as "or by his direction"; see the *Human Tissues Act 1961*. This statute is in the second category.

Lord Denning refers in passing to an argument put forward by a lower court judge who heard the case. He then examines the argument for deviating from a plain-meaning interpretation.

> The Solicitor-General emphasised the word "treatment" in sections 1 (3), 3 (1) (a) and (c) and 4 (1). He suggested that section 1 (1) should be read as if it said that a person should not be guilty of an offence "when the treatment (for termination of a pregnancy) is by a registered medical practitioner." He submitted that whenever the registered medical practitioner did what the Department of Health advised it satisfied the statute, because the treatment, being initiated by him and done under his instructions, was "by" him.
>
> I cannot accept this interpretation. I think the word "treatment" in those sections means "the actual act of terminating the pregnancy." When the medical induction method is used, this means the continuous act of administering prostaglandin [*the fluid that induces labour*] from the moment it is started until the unborn child is expelled from the mother's body. This continuous act must be done by the doctor personally. It is not sufficient that it is done by a nurse when he is not present.
>
> Stress was laid by the Solicitor-General on the effect of this ruling. The process of medical induction can take from 18 to 30 hours. No doctor can be expected to be

present all that time. He must leave it to the nurses; or not use the method at all. If he is not allowed to leave it to the nurse, the result will be either that there will be fewer abortions or that the doctor will have to use the surgical method with its extra hazards. This may be so. But I do not think this warrants us departing from the statute. The Royal College of Nursing have advised their nurses that under the statute they should not themselves terminate a pregnancy. If the doctor advises it, he should do it himself, and not call upon the nurses to do it.

I think that the Royal College are quite right. If the Department of Health want the nurses to terminate a pregnancy, the Minister should go to Parliament and get the statute altered. He should ask them to amend it by adding the words "or by a suitably qualified person in accordance with the written instructions of a registered medical practitioner." I doubt whether Parliament would accept the amendment. It is too controversial. At any rate, that is the way to amend the law; and not by means of a departmental circular.

Sir George Baker

After briefly setting the context, Sir Baker identifies the crux of the case: whether or not the medical induction approach satisfied the provisions of the *Abortion Act 1967* which require that a pregnancy be "terminated by a registered medical practitioner."

... The words "terminated by a registered medical practitioner" are by themselves clear and unambiguous. The operative act or acts which have or are intended to have an abortifacient effect must be done by or performed or carried out by a registered medical practitioner. But the department say that the words should not be read literally for that would "defeat the obvious intention of the legislation and ... produce a wholly unreasonable result ..." [*cites case reference*]. They should on the contrary be read as meaning that if the treatment for the termination of a pregnancy is by a registered medical practitioner then no offence is committed by the nurse (or person) who administers abortifacient or does any other act with intent to procure the miscarriage.

Sir Baker discusses the Department of Health directive on medical induction and the Department's interpretation of the Act. He concludes: "this direction or guidance and, indeed the basic argument of the department, seems to me to be that not only doctors' acts but also doctors' orders will satisfy section 1 (1) of the *Abortion Act 1967*."

Much has been said about the apparent anomalies of the strict or literal interpretation of section 1 (1), that there is no defence for doctors or any person if (a) there is no pregnancy, or (b) the pregnancy is not terminated, but with the wider "doctors' orders" interpretation the nurse would apparently be committing an offence under section 58 if she failed to follow or misinterpreted the instructions of the doctor or, indeed, if, possibly unknown to her, the prerequisite opinions of the two registered medical practitioners had not been formed in good faith.

The department's case necessitates section 1 (1) being read as meaning:

If two registered medical practitioners are of opinion, formed in good faith etc., then provided that the treatment for termination of the pregnancy is carried out in a hospital vested in the Minister ... or in a place approved for the time being etc., a person *participating or assisting in that treatment* and who would otherwise be guilty of an offence under the law relating to abortion as defined in this Act shall not be guilty of such an offence when *the treatment is* by a registered medical practitioner.

Sir Baker closely reviews three relevant subsections of the *Abortion Act* and two other regulations to see if the Department's interpretation is supported in the actual legal documents. He concludes this review as follows:

In my opinion there is nothing in the Act or Regulations to indicate that the intention of Parliament was other than that clearly expressed in the simple words "when a pregnancy is terminated by a registered medical practitioner." They are words which have to be understood by ordinary mortals in legislation on a topic which can arouse great emotions: see *Paton v. British Pregnancy Advisory Services Trustees* (1978). Maybe Parliament never had in mind abortions by medical induction which, as the Ministry letter indicates, has been employed in the past ten years; maybe a decision that it can be done only by a registered medical practitioner and not by a nurse on doctor's orders in any causative respect will result in a safe and easy method being less used with consequent hardship or even greater danger to pregnant women. I do not know. Even if so, it is not for judges "to read words into an Act of Parliament unless clear reason for it is to be found within the four corners of the Act itself" [*cites two cases*]. Nor is a judge entitled to read an Act differently from what it says simply because he thinks Parliament would have so provided had the situation been envisaged at that time. In the words of Lord Simon of Glaisdale [*cites case reference*]:

... in a society living under the rule of law citizens are entitled to regulate their conduct according to what a statute has said, rather than by what it was meant to say or by what it would have otherwise said if a newly considered situation had been envisaged; ...

There is no manifest absurdity; on the contrary the provision is clear and understandable. If the intention had been to make lawful the acts of persons participating in or carrying out the termination of a pregnancy on doctors' orders that could have been expressly stated either as the department suggest the section should be read, or by some other appropriate words ... [*cites example*].

Sir Baker concludes: "*The Abortion Act 1967* requires the termination to be by the operative acts of the registered medical practitioner himself; his orders are not enough."

Royal College of Nursing: House of Lords Decision

Within one month of the Court of Appeal's decision in *Royal College of Nursing v. Department of Health and Social Security*, the House of Lords heard the appeal, and two months later delivered its judgment. As we saw in the Court of Appeal opinions, the issue was whether or not a new "medical induction" method of abortion, administered for the most part by nurses, could be considered to be "terminated by a registered medical practitioner." In a three-to-two decision, the House of Lords overturned the earlier judgment and accepted that nurse-administered induction was consistent with the statute requiring that a medical practitioner terminate pregnancy. Excerpts from all three majority opinions are presented; the only dissenting opinion included is that of Lord Wilberforce.

Lord Wilberforce

Lord Wilberforce is one of two judges who dissented (the other is Lord Edmund-Davis). He opens with a review of the relevant legislative history and a description of the medical induction approach. He then explains that at the time of the legislation in 1967 legislators would not have been aware of any abortion procedures administered by nurses, since this approach was first reported in 1972. Accordingly, "Parliament's concern must have been to prevent existing methods being carried out by unqualified persons and to insist that they should be carried out by doctors." In Lord Wilberforce's view this is why Parliament required that a pregnancy be terminated by a "registered medical practitioner."

> In interpreting an Act of Parliament it is proper, and indeed necessary, to have regard to the state of affairs existing, and known by Parliament to be existing, at the time. It is a fair presumption that Parliament's policy or intention is directed to that state of affairs. Leaving aside cases of omission by inadvertence, this being not such a case, when a new state of affairs, or a fresh set of facts bearing on policy, comes into existence, the courts have to consider whether they fall within the Parliamentary intention. They may be held to do so if they fall within the same genus of facts as those to which the expressed policy has been formulated. They may also be held to do so if there can be detected a clear purpose in the legislation which can only be fulfilled if the extension is made. How liberally these principles may be applied must depend upon the nature of the enactment, and the strictness or otherwise of the words in which it has been expressed. The courts should be less willing to extend expressed meanings if it is clear that the Act in question was designed to be restrictive or circumscribed in its operation rather than liberal or permissive. They will be much less willing to do so where the subject matter is different in kind or dimension from that for which the legislation was passed. In any event there is one course which the courts cannot take under the law of this country; they cannot fill gaps; they cannot by asking the question "What would Parliament have done in this current case—not being one in contemplation—if the facts had been before it?" attempt themselves to supply the answer, if the answer is not to be found in the terms of the Act itself.

> In my opinion this Act should be construed with caution. It is dealing with a controversial subject involving moral and social judgments on which opinions strongly differ. It is, if ever an Act was, one for interpreting in the spirit that only that which Parliament has authorised on a fair reading of the relevant sections should be held to be within it. The new (post-1967) method of medical induction is clearly not just a fresh species or example of something already authorised. The Act is not for "purposive" or "liberal" or "equitable" construction. This is a case where the courts must hold that anything beyond the legislature's fairly expressed authority should be left for Parliament's fresh consideration.

Lord Wilberforce observes that on the basis of the legislative history and the state of affairs prior to the passage of the law he cannot find justification to read the words "pregnancy terminated by a registered medical practitioner" to cover cases where nurses, midwives, or even lay persons play a significant part in the process of termination. Although he admits that the induction method may be an improvement on prior practice, it clearly introduces a new dimension to the law which "should not be sanctioned by judicial decision, but only by Parliament after proper consideration of the implications and necessary safeguards." Lord Wilberforce then turns to the argument that the Act is framed in sufficiently wide terms to authorise nurse-administered abortions. He rejects the claim that the words "pregnancy is terminated by a registered medical practitioner" can defensibly be interpreted to mean "pregnancy is terminated by treatment of a registered medical practitioner in accordance with recognised medical practice."

> But, with all respect, this is not construction: it is rewriting. And, moreover, it does not achieve its objective. I could perhaps agree that a reference to treatment could fairly be held to be implied: no doubt treatment is necessary. But I do not see that this alone carries the matter any further: it must still be treatment by the registered medical practitioner. The additional words, on the other hand, greatly extend the enactment, and it is they which are supposed to introduce nurse participation. But I cannot see that they do this. For a nurse to engage in abortifacient acts cannot, when first undertaken, be in accordance with recognised practice, when it is the legality of the practice that is in question. Nor can the recognised practice (if such there is, though the agreed statements do not say so), by which nurses connect up drips to supply glucose or other life-giving or preserving substances cover connecting up drips, etc., giving substances designed to destroy life—for that is what they are. The added words may well cover the provision of swabs, bandages, or the handing up of instruments—that would only be common sense: they cannot be used as cover for a dimensional extension of the Act.

> The argument for the department is carried even further than this, for it is said that the words "when a pregnancy is terminated by a registered medical practitioner" mean "when treatment for the termination of pregnancy is carried out by a registered medical practitioner." This is said to be necessary in order to cover the supposed cases where the treatment is unsuccessful, or where there is no pregnancy at all. The latter hypothesis I regard as fanciful: the former, if it was Parliament's contemplation at all in 1967 (for failures under post-1967 methods are not in point) cannot be covered by any reasonable reading of the words. Termination is one thing: attempted and unsuccessful termination wholly another. I cannot be persuaded to embark upon a radical reconstruction of the Act by reference to a fanciful hypothesis or an improbable *casus omissus* [*an option that was overlooked by Parliament*].

> It is significant, as Lord Denning M.R. has pointed out, that recognised language exists and has been used, when it is desired that something shall be done by doctors with nurse participation. This takes the form "by a registered medical practitioner or by a person acting in accordance with the directions of any such practitioner." This language has been used in four Acts of Parliament (listed by Lord Denning M.R.), three of them prior to the Act of 1967, all concerned with the administration of substances, drugs or medicines which may have an impact upon the human body. It has not been used, surely deliberately, in the present Act. We ought to assume that Parliament knew what it was doing when it omitted to use them.

> In conclusion, I am of [the] opinion that the development of prostaglandin induction methods invites, and indeed merits, the attention of Parliament. It has justly given rise to perplexity in the nursing profession. I doubt whether this will be allayed when it is seen that a majority of the judges who have considered the problem share their views. On this appeal I agree with the judgments in the Court of Appeal that an extension of the Act of 1967 so as to include all persons, including nurses, involved in the administration of prostaglandin is not something which ought to, or can, be effected by judicial decision. I would dismiss the appeal.

Lord Diplock

Lord Diplock offers one of the three opinions in support of interpreting the law to permit medical induction. After providing a brief background, he turns to discuss the Act itself. He notes the Act "started its parliamentary life as a private member's bill and, maybe for that reason, it lacks that style and consistency of draftsmanship both internal to the Act itself and in relation to other statutes which one would expect to find in legislation that had its origin in the office of parliamentary counsel." He explains, regardless of "the technical imperfections of its draftsmanship," its purpose "becomes clear if one starts by considering what was the state of the law relating to abortion before the passing of the Act, what was the mischief that required amendment, and in what respect was the existing law unclear." Lord Diplock then details what he see as the "unsatisfactory and uncertain state of the law that the *Abortion Act 1967* was intended to amend and clarify":

> What the Act sets out to do is to provide an exhaustive statement of the circumstances in which treatment for the termination of a pregnancy may be carried out lawfully. That the statement, which is contained in section 1, is intended to be exhaustive, appears from section 5 (2):
>
>> For the purposes of the law relating to abortion, anything done with intent to procure the miscarriage of a woman is unlawfully done unless authorised by section 1 of this Act.

Lord Diplock offers a few other remarks, including quoting, in full, section 1 of the Act.

> My Lords, the wording and structure of the section are far from elegant, but the policy of the Act, it seems to me, is clear. There are two aspects to it: the first is to broaden the grounds upon which abortion may be lawfully obtained; the second is to ensure that the abortion is carried out with all proper skill and in hygienic conditions ... [*Lord Diplock explains these observations*].

> I have spoken of the requirements of the Act as to the way in which "treatment for the termination of the pregnancy" is to be carried out rather than using the word "termination" or "terminated" by itself, for the draftsman appears to use the longer and the shorter expressions indiscriminately, as is shown by a comparison between subsections (I) and (3) of section 1, and by the reference in the conscience clause to "treatment authorised by this Act." Furthermore if "termination" or "terminated" meant only the event of miscarriage and not the whole treatment undertaken with that object in mind, lack of success, which apparently occurs in one to two per cent of cases, would make all who had taken part in the unsuccessful treatment guilty of an offence under section 58 or 59 of the *Offences against the Person Act 1861.* This cannot have been the intention of Parliament.

> The requirement of the Act as to the way in which the treatment is to be carried out, which in my view throws most light upon the second aspect of its policy and the true construction of the phrase in subsection (1) of section 1 which lies at the root of the dispute between the parties to this appeal, is the requirement in subsection (3) that, except in cases of dire emergency, the treatment must be carried out in a National Health Service hospital (or private clinic specially approved for that purpose by the minister). It is in my view evident that in providing that treatment for termination of pregnancies should take place in ordinary hospitals, Parliament contemplated that (conscientious objections apart) like other hospital treatment, it would be undertaken

as a team effort in which, acting on the instructions of the doctor in charge of the treatment, junior doctors, nurses, para-medical and other members of the hospital staff would each do those things forming part of the whole treatment, which it would be in accordance with accepted medical practice to entrust to a member of the staff possessed of their respective qualifications and experience.

Subsection (1) although it is expressed to apply only "when a pregnancy is terminated by a registered medical practitioner" (the subordinate clause that although introduced by "when" is another protasis [*an introductory clause in a sentence*] and has caused the differences of judicial opinion in the instant case) also appears to contemplate treatment that is in the nature of a team effort and to extend its protection to all those who play a part in it. The exoneration from guilt is not confined to the registered medical practitioner by whom a pregnancy is terminated, it extends to any person who takes part in the treatment for its termination.

What limitation on this exoneration is imposed by the qualifying phrase: "when a pregnancy is terminated by a registered medical practitioner"? In my opinion in the context of the Act, what it requires is that a registered medical practitioner, whom I will refer to as a doctor, should accept responsibility for all stages of the treatment for the termination of the pregnancy. The particular method to be used should be decided by the doctor in charge of the treatment for termination of the pregnancy; he should carry out any physical acts, forming part of the treatment, that in accordance with accepted medical practice are done only by qualified medical practitioners, and should give specific instructions as to the carrying out of such parts of the treatment as in accordance with accepted medical practice are carried out by nurses or other members of the hospital staff without medical qualifications. To each of them, the doctor, or his substitute, should be available to be consulted or called on for assistance from beginning to end of the treatment. In other words, the doctor need not do everything with his own hands; the requirements of the subsection are satisfied when the treatment for termination of a pregnancy is one prescribed by a registered medical practitioner carried out in accordance with his direction and of which a registered medical practitioner remains in charge throughout.

Lord Diplock concludes with a summary comment on his support for the appeal.

Lord Keith of Kinkel

In opening his opinion in support of the appeal, Lord Keith reviews the medical induction procedure and identifies the issue before the Court. He then considers the main argument against the appeal:

The argument for the respondents is, in essence, that the words of the subsection do not apply because the pregnancy has not been terminated by any registered medical practitioner, but by the nurse who did the act or acts which directly resulted in the administration to the pregnant woman of the abortifacient drugs.

In my opinion this argument involves placing an unduly restricted and unintended meaning on the words "when a pregnancy is terminated." It seems to me that these words, in their context, are not referring to the mere physical occurrence of termination. The sidenote to section 1 is "Medical termination of pregnancy." "Termination of pregnancy" is an expression commonly used, perhaps rather more by medical people than by laymen, to describe in neutral and unemotive terms the bringing about of an abortion. So used, it is capable of covering the whole process designed to lead to that result, and in my view it does so in the present context. Other provisions of the Act make it clear that termination of pregnancy is envisaged as being a process of treatment. Section 1(3) provides that, subject to an exception for cases of emergency, "treatment for the termination of pregnancy" must be carried out in a National Health Service hospital or a place for the time being approved by the minister. There are similar references to treatment for the termination of pregnancy in section 3, which governs the application of the Act to visiting forces. Then by section 4(1) it is provided that no person shall be under any duty "to participate in any treatment authorised by this Act to which he has a conscientious objection." This appears clearly to recognise that what is authorised by section 1(1) in relation to the termination of pregnancy is a process of treatment leading to that result. Section 5(2) is also of some importance. It provides that: "For the purposes of the law relating to abortion, anything done with intent to procure the miscarriage of a woman is unlawfully done unless authorised by section 1 of this Act." This indicates a contemplation that a wide range of acts done when a pregnancy is terminated under the given conditions are authorised by section 1, and leads to the inference that, since all that section 1 in terms authorises is the termination of pregnancy by a registered medical practitioner, all such acts must be embraced in the termination.

Given that the termination of pregnancy under contemplation in section 1(1) includes the whole process of treatment involved therein, it remains to consider whether, on the facts of this case, the termination can properly be regarded as being "by a registered medical practitioner." In my opinion this question is to be answered affirmatively. The doctor has responsibility for the whole process and is in charge of it throughout. It is he who decides that it is to be carried out. He personally performs essential parts of it which are such as to necessitate the application of his particular skill. The nurse's actions are done under his direct written instructions. In the circumstances I find it impossible to hold that the doctor's role is other than that of a principal, and I think he would be very surprised to hear that the nurse was the principal and he himself only an accessory. It is true that it is the nurse's action which leads directly to the introduction of abortifacient drugs into the system of the patient, but that action is done in a ministerial capacity and on the doctor's orders. Even if it were right to regard the nurse as a principal, it seems to me inevitable that the doctor should also be so regarded. If both the doctor and the nurse were principals, the provisions of the subsection would be still satisfied, because the pregnancy would have been terminated by the doctor notwithstanding that it had also been terminated by the nurse.

I therefore conclude that termination of pregnancy by means of the procedures under consideration is authorised by the terms of section 1(1). This conclusion is the more satisfactory as it appears to me to be fully in accordance with that part of the policy and purpose of the Act which was directed to securing that socially acceptable abortions should be carried out under the safest conditions attainable ... [*offers a few additional closing remarks*].

Lord Roskill

The final opinion, in support of the appeal, opens with a review of relevant facts and a summary of the competing arguments. Lord Roskill then describes his struggle to make sense of the legislation:

My Lords, I have read and re-read the Act of 1967 to see if I can discern in its provisions any consistent pattern in the use of the phrase "a pregnancy is terminated" or "termination of a pregnancy" on the one hand and "treatment for the termination of a pregnancy" on the other hand. One finds the former phrase in section 1(1) and (1)(a), the latter in section 1(3), the former in section 1(4), the latter in section 2(1)(b), and again in section 3(1) (a) and (c). Most important to my mind is section 4 which is the conscientious objection section. This section in two places refers to "participate in treatment" in the context of conscientious objection. If one construes section 4 in conjunction with section 1(1), as surely one should do in order to determine to what it is that conscientious objection is permitted, it seems to me that section 4 strongly supports the wider construction of section 1(1). It was suggested that acceptance of the appellants' submission involved re-writing that subsection so as to add words which are not to be found in the language of the subsection. My Lords, with great respect to that submission, I do not agree. If one construes the words "when a pregnancy is terminated by a registered medical practitioner" in section 1(1) as embracing the case where the "treatment for the termination of a pregnancy is carried out under the control of a doctor in accordance with ordinary current medical practice" I think one is reading "termination of pregnancy" and "treatment for termination of pregnancy" as virtually synonymous and as I think Parliament must have intended they should be read. Such a construction avoids a number of anomalies as, for example, where there is no pregnancy or where the extra-amniotic process fails to achieve its objective within the normal limits of time set for its operation ... [comments on a technical point, before offering his concluding remarks]. ... My Lords, I have reached this conclusion simply as a matter of the construction of the Act of 1967.

Lord Roskill closes by indicating his support for the appeal.

REASONING FROM PRIOR CASES

Donoghue v. Stevenson

In one of the most famous of cases, *Donoghue v. Stevenson*, the English House of Lords in 1932 considered whether Mr. Stevenson, a manufacturer of ginger beer, was liable for damages to Mrs. Donoghue, who had suffered shock and stomach pains as a result of drinking from a bottle of ginger beer that contained a partially decomposed snail. The case, discussed in Chapter 5, focuses on what is called the duty of care principle: Does a supplier or producer have a duty to take proper measures to secure the safety of its product? The settled common law up to this point indicated that a duty existed if there was a breach of an explicit contract, if there was knowing misrepresentation, or if the product was inherently dangerous. In a controversial 3-2 decision, a majority of Lords found that a duty also existed if a manufacturer failed to exercise sufficient care in safeguarding its products. This judgment, reached by reasoning from prior cases, reflects five judges' efforts to determine the conclusions to be drawn from a extensive body of intricately related, seemingly conflicting cases. Below are excerpts from four of these opinions; Lord Tomlin's brief comments against a duty of care are omitted, since he agrees "in every respect" with Lord Buckmaster.

Lord Buckmaster

Lord Buckmaster opens his dissenting opinion with a review of the facts of the case. He explains that the alleged duty stems from negligence (i.e., a failure to exercise due care), not from fraud (i.e., not because of intentional misrepresentation). In other words, if the manufacturer has a duty of care it is because of negligence in providing a pure product. As well, Lord Buckmaster emphasizes the need to decide the case on the basis of established law:

> The law applicable is the common law, and, though its principles are capable of application to meet new conditions not contemplated when the law was laid down, these principles cannot be changed nor can additions be made to them because any particular meritorious case seems outside their ambit.

Lord Buckmaster then begins his review of the relevant cases.

> I turn, therefore, to the decided cases to see if they can be construed so as to support the appellant's [*Mrs. Donoghue's*] case. One of the earliest is the case of *Langridge v. Levy* (1838). It is a case often quoted and variously explained. There a man sold a gun which he knew was dangerous for the use of the purchaser's son. The gun exploded in the son's hands, and he was held to have a right of action in tort against the gunmaker. How far it is from the present case can be seen from the judgment of Parke B. [*Baron*], who, in delivering the judgment of the Court, used these words: "We should pause before we make a precedent by our decision which would be an authority for an action against the vendors, even of such instruments and articles as are dangerous in themselves, at the suit of any person whomsoever into whose hands they might happen to pass, and who should be injured thereby"; and in *Longmeid v. Holliday* (1851) the same eminent judge points out that the earlier case was based on a fraudulent statement, and he expressly repudiates the view that it has any wider application. The case of *Langridge v. Levy*, therefore, can be dismissed from consideration with the comment that it is rather surprising it has so often been cited for a proposition it cannot support.

> The case of *Winterbottom v. Wright* (1842) is, on the other hand, an authority that is closely applicable. Owing to negligence in the construction of a carriage it broke down, and a stranger to the manufacture and sale sought to recover damages for injuries which he alleged were due to negligence in the work, and it was held that he had no cause of action either in tort or arising out of contract. This case seems to me to show that the manufacturer of any article is not liable to a third party injured by negligent construction, for there can be nothing in the character of a coach to place it in a special category. It may be noted, also, that in this case Alderson B. said: "The only safe rule is to confine the right to recover to those who enter into the contract; if we go one step beyond that, there is no reason why we should not go fifty."

> *Longmeid v. Holliday* was the case of a defective lamp sold to a man whose wife was injured by its explosion. The vendor of the lamp, against whom the action was brought, was not the manufacturer, so that the case is not exactly parallel to the present, but the statement of Parke B. in his judgment covers the case of manufacturer, for he said:

> > It would be going much too far to say, that so much care is required in the ordinary intercourse of life between one individual and another, that, if a machine not in its nature dangerous, ... but which might become so by a latent defect entirely unknown, although discoverable by the exercise of ordinary care, should be lent or given by one person, even by the person who manufactured it, to another, the former should be answerable to the latter for a subsequent damage accruing by the use of it.

> It is true that he uses the words "lent or given" and omits the word "sold," but if the duty be entirely independent of contract and is a duty owed to a third person, it seems to me to be the same whether the article be originally given or sold. The fact in the present case that the ginger-beer originally left the premises of the

manufacturer on a purchase, as was probably the case, cannot add to his duty, if such existed, to take care in its preparation.

It has been suggested that the statement of Parke B. does not cover the case of negligent construction, but the omission to exercise reasonable care in the discovery of a defect in the manufacture of an article where the duty of examination exists is just as negligent as the negligent construction itself.

Lord Buckmaster offers his interpretation of the law arising from these three cases: there is no general duty to potential users of a product unless (1) the products are inherently dangerous or (2) although not inherently dangerous, if the products are dangerous because of a defect that is known to the manufacturer. In the first instance— if products are "dangerous in themselves"—there is a "peculiar duty to take precautions." In the second instance, an obligation exists to warn potential users of the defect, otherwise the manufacturer is guilty of fraud. Lord Buckmaster continues with his survey of the relevant case law:

Of the remaining cases, *George v. Skivington* (1869) is the one nearest to the present, and without that case, and the statement of Cleasby B. in *Francis v. Cockrell* (1870) and the *dicta* of Brett M.R. [*Master of the Rolls*] in *Heaven v. Pender* (1883), the appellant would be destitute of authority. *George v. Skivington* related to the sale of a noxious hairwash, and a claim made by a person who had not bought it but who had suffered from its use, based on its having been negligently compounded, was allowed. It is remarkable that *Langridge v. Levy* was used in support of the claim and influenced the judgment of all the parties to the decision. Both Kelly C.B. [*Chief Baron*] and Pigott B. stressed the fact that the article had been purchased to the knowledge of the defendant for the use of the plaintiff, as in *Langridge v. Levy*, and Cleasby B., who, realizing that *Langridge v. Levy* was decided on the ground of fraud, said: "Substitute the word 'negligence' for 'fraud,' and the analogy between *Langridge v. Levy* and this case is complete." It is unnecessary to point out too emphatically that such a substitution cannot possibly be made. No action based on fraud can be supported by mere proof of negligence.

I do not propose to follow the fortunes of *George v. Skivington*; few cases can have lived so dangerously and lived so long. Lord Sumner, in the case of *Blacker v. Lake & Elliot, Ld.* (1912), closely examines its history, and I agree with his analysis. He said that he could not presume to say that it was wrong, but he declined to follow it on the ground which is, I think, firm, that it was in conflict with *Winterbottom v. Wright.*

In *Francis v. Cockrell* the plaintiff had been injured by the fall of a stand on a racecourse, for a seat in which he had paid. The defendant was part proprietor of the stand and acted as receiver of the money. The stand had been negligently erected by a contractor, though the defendant was not aware of the defect. The plaintiff succeeded. The case has no bearing upon the present, but in the course of his judgment Cleasby B. made the following observation:

The point that Mr. Matthews referred to last was raised in the case of *George v. Skivington*, where there was an injury to one person, the wife, and a contract of sale with another person, the husband. The wife was considered to have a good cause of action, and I would adopt the view which the Lord Chief Baron took in that case. He said there was a duty in the vendor to use ordinary care in compounding the article sold, and that this extended to the person for whose use he knew it was purchased, and this duty having been violated, and he, having failed to use reasonable care, was liable in an action at the suit of the third person.

It is difficult to appreciate what is the importance of the fact that the vendor knew who was the person for whom the article was purchased, unless it be that the case was treated as one of fraud, and that without this element of knowledge it could not be brought within the principle of *Langridge v. Levy.* Indeed, this is the only view of the matter which adequately explains the references in the judgments in *George v. Skivington* to *Langridge v. Levy* and the observations of Cleasby B. upon *George v. Skivington.*

The *dicta* of Brett M.R. in *Heaven v. Pender* are rightly relied on by the appellant. The material passage is as follows:

> The proposition which these recognized cases suggest, and which is, therefore, to be deduced from them, is that whenever one person is by circumstances placed in such a position with regard to another that every one of ordinary sense who did think would at once recognize that if he did not use ordinary care and skill in his own conduct with regard to those circumstances he would cause danger of injury to the person or property of the other, a duty arises to use ordinary care and skill to avoid such danger. ... Let us apply this proposition to the case of one person supplying goods or machinery, or instruments or utensils, or the like, for the purpose of their being used by another person, but with whom there is no contract as to the supply. The proposition will stand thus: whenever one person supplies goods, or machinery or the like, for the purpose of their being used by another person under such circumstances that everyone of ordinary sense would, if he thought, recognize at once that unless he used ordinary care and skill with regard to the condition of the thing supplied or the mode of supplying it, there will be danger of injury to the person or property of him for whose use the thing is supplied, and who is to use it, a duty arises to use ordinary care and skill as to the condition or manner of supplying such thing. And for a neglect of such ordinary care or skill whereby injury happens a legal liability arises to be enforced by an action for negligence. This includes the case of goods, etc., supplied to be used immediately by a particular person or persons, or one of a class of persons, where it would be obvious to the person supplying, if he thought, that the goods would in all probability be used at once by such persons before a reasonable opportunity for discovering any defect which might exist, and where the thing supplied would be of such a nature that a neglect of ordinary care or skill as to its condition or the manner of supplying it would probably cause danger to the person or property of the person for whose use it was supplied, and who was about to use it. It would exclude a case in which the goods are supplied under circumstances in which it would be a chance by whom they would be used or whether they would be used or not, or whether they would be used before there would probably be means of observing any defect, or where the goods would be of such a nature that a want of care or skill as to their condition or the manner of supplying them would not probably produce danger of injury to person or property. The cases of vendor and purchaser and lender and hirer under contract need not be considered, as the liability arises under the contract, and not merely as a duty imposed by law, though it may not be useless to observe that it seems difficult to import the implied obligation into the contract except in cases in which if there were no contract between the parties the law would according to the rule above stated imply the duty.

"The recognized cases" to which the Master of the Rolls refers are not definitely quoted, but they appear to refer to cases of collision and carriage and the cases of visitation to premises on which there is some hidden danger—cases far removed from the doctrine he enunciates. None the less this passage has been used as a *tabula in naufragio* [*literally, a plank in a shipwreck*] for many litigants struggling in the seas of adverse authority. It cannot, however, be divorced from the fact that the case had nothing whatever to do with the question of manufacture and sale. An unsound staging had been erected on premises to which there had been an invitation to the plaintiffs to enter, and the case really depended on the duty of the owner of the premises to persons so invited. None the less it is clear that Brett M.R. considered the cases of manufactured articles, for he examined *Langridge v. Levy*, and says that it does not negative the proposition that the case might have been supported on the ground of negligence.

In the same case, however, Cotton L.J. [*Lord Justice*], in whose judgment Bowen L.J. concurred, said that he was unwilling to concur with the Master of the Rolls in laying down unnecessarily the larger principle which he entertained, inasmuch as there were many cases in which the principle was impliedly negatived. He then referred to *Langridge v. Levy*, and stated that it was based upon fraudulent misrepresentation, and had been so treated by Coleridge J. in *Blackmore v. Bristol and Exeter Ry. Co.* (1858), and that in *Collis v. Selden* (1868) Willes J. had said that the judgment in *Langridge v. Levy* was based on the fraud of the defendant. The Lord Justice then proceeded as follows:

> This impliedly negatives the existence of the larger general principle which is relied on, and the decisions in *Collis v. Selden* and in *Longmeid v. Holliday* (in case of which the plaintiff failed), are in my opinion at variance with the principle contended for. The case of *George v. Skivington*, and especially what is said by Cleasby B., in giving judgment in that case, seems to support the existence of the general principle. But it is not in terms laid down that any such principle exists, and that case was decided by Cleasby B. on the ground that the negligence of the defendant, which was his own personal negligence, was equivalent, for the purposes of that action, to fraud, on which (as he said) the decision in *Langridge v. Levy* was based. In declining to concur in laying down the principle enunciated by the Master of the Rolls, I in no way intimate any doubt as to the principle that anyone who leaves a dangerous instrument, as a gun, in such a way as to cause danger, or who without due warning supplies to others for use an instrument or thing which to his knowledge, from its construction or otherwise, is in such a condition as to cause danger, not necessarily incident to the use of such an instrument or thing, is liable for injury caused to others by reason of his negligent act.

With the views expressed by Cotton L.J. I agree.

In *Le Lievre v. Gould* (1893) the mortgagees of the interest of a builder under a building agreement advanced money to him from time to time on the faith of certificates given by a surveyor that certain specified stages in the progress of the buildings had been reached. The surveyor was not appointed by the mortgagees and there was no contractual relationship between him and them. In consequence of the negligence of the surveyor the certificates contained untrue statements as to the progress of the buildings, but there was no fraud on his part. It was held that the surveyor owed no duty to the mortgagees to exercise care in giving his certificates, and they could not maintain an action against him by reason of his negligence. In this case Lord Esher seems to have qualified to some extent what he said in *Heaven v. Pender*, for he says this:

> But can the plaintiffs rely upon negligence in the absence of fraud? The question of liability for negligence cannot arise at all until it is established that the man who has been negligent owed some duty to the person who seeks to make him liable for his negligence. What duty is there when there is no relation

between the parties by contract? A man is entitled to be as negligent as he pleases towards the whole world if he owes no duty to them. The case of *Heaven v. Pender* has no bearing upon the present question. That case established that, under certain circumstances, one man may owe a duty to another even though there is no contract between them. If one man is near to another, or is near to the property of another, a duty lies upon him not to do that which may cause a personal injury to that other, or may injure his property.

In that same case A. L. Smith L.J. said:

> The decision of *Heaven v. Pender* was founded upon the principle, that a duty to take due care did arise when the person or property of one was in such proximity to the person or property of another that, if due care was not taken, damage might be done by the one to the other. *Heaven v. Pender* goes no further than this, though it is often cited to support all kinds of untenable propositions.

In *Earl v. Lubbock* (1905) the plaintiff had been injured by a wheel coming off a van which he was driving for his employer and which it was the duty of the defendant under contract with the employer to keep in repair. The county court judge and the Divisional Court both held that, even if negligence was proved, the action would not lie. It was held by the Appeal Court that the defendant was under no duty to the plaintiff and that there was no cause of action. In his judgment Sir Richard Henn Collins M.R. said the case was concluded by the authority of *Winterbottom v. Wright*, and he pointed out that the *dictum* of Lord Esher in *Heaven v. Pender* was not a decision of the Court, and that it was subsequently qualified and explained by Lord Esher himself in *Le Lievre v. Gould*. Stifling L.J. said that in order to succeed in the action the plaintiff must bring his case within the proposition enunciated by Cotton L.J. and agreed to by Bowen L.J. in *Heaven v. Pender*, while Mathew L.J. made the following observation:

> The argument of counsel for the plaintiff was that the defendant's servants had been negligent in the performance of the contract with the owners of the van, and that it followed as a matter of law that anyone in their employment, or, indeed, anyone else who sustained an injury traceable to that negligence, had a cause of action against the defendant. It is impossible to accept such a wide proposition, and, indeed, it is difficult to see how, if it were the law, trade could be carried on. No prudent man would contract to make or repair what the employer intended to permit others to use in the way of his trade.

In *Bates v. Batey & Co., Ld.* (1913), the defendants, ginger-beer manufacturers, were held not liable to a consumer (who had purchased from a retailer one of their bottles) for injury occasioned by the bottle bursting as the result of a defect of which the defendants did not know, but which by the exercise of reasonable care they could have discovered. In reaching this conclusion Horridge J. stated that he thought the judgments of Parke B. in *Longmeid v. Holliday*, of Cotton and Bowen L.JJ. in *Heaven v. Pender*, of Stirling L.J. in *Earl v. Lubbock*, and of Hamilton J. in *Blacker v. Lake & Elliot, Ld.*, made it clear that the plaintiff was not entitled to recover, and that he had not felt himself bound by *George v. Skivington*.

So far, therefore, as the ease of *George v. Skivington* and the *dicta* in *Heaven v. Pender* are concerned, it is in my opinion better that they should be buried so securely that their perturbed spirits shall no longer vex the law.

Before concluding his opinion, Lord Buckmaster briefly considers and dismisses a few American cases that were said to support the duty of care principle.

In my view, therefore, the authorities are against the appellant's contention, and, apart from authority, it is difficult to see how any common law proposition can be formulated to support her claim.

The principle contended for must be this: that the manufacturer, or indeed the repairer, of any article, apart entirely from contract, owes a duty to any person by whom the article is lawfully used to see that it has been carefully constructed. All rights in contract must be excluded from consideration of this principle; such contractual rights as may exist in successive steps from the original manufacturer down to the ultimate purchaser are *ex hypothesi* [*given the theory advanced*] immaterial. Nor can the doctrine be confined to cases where inspection is difficult or impossible to introduce. This conception is simply to misapply to tort doctrine applicable to sale and purchase.

The principle of tort [*a right to recover for injury other than that caused by a breach of contract*] lies completely outside the region where such considerations apply, and the duty, if it exists, must extend to every person who, in lawful circumstances, uses the article made. There can be no special duty attaching to the manufacture of food apart from that implied by contract or imposed by statute. If such a duty exists, it seems to me it must cover the construction of every article, and I cannot see any reason why it should not apply to the construction of a house. If one step, why not fifty? Yet if a house be, as it sometimes is, negligently built, and in consequence of that negligence the ceiling falls and injures the occupier or any one else, no action against the builder exists according to the English law, although I believe such a right did exist according to the laws of Babylon. Were such a principle known and recognized, it seems to me impossible, having regard to the numerous cases that must have arisen to persons injured by its disregard, that, with the exception of *George v. Skivington*, no case directly involving the principle has ever succeeded in the Courts, and, were it well known and accepted, much of the discussion of the earlier cases would have been waste of time, and the distinction as to articles dangerous in themselves or known to be dangerous to the vendor would be meaningless.

In *Mullen v. Barr & Co.* (1929), a case indistinguishable from the present excepting upon the ground that a mouse is not a snail, and necessarily adopted by the Second Division in their judgment, Lord Anderson says this:

> In a case like the present, where the goods of the defenders are widely distributed throughout Scotland, it would seem little short of outrageous to make them responsible to members of the public for the condition of the contents of every bottle which issues from their works. It is obvious that, if such responsibility attached to the defenders, they might be called on to meet claims of damages which they could not possibly investigate or answer.

In agreeing, as I do, with the judgment of Lord Anderson, I desire to add that I find it hard to dissent from the emphatic nature of the language with which his judgment is clothed. I am of opinion that this appeal should be dismissed, and I beg to move your Lordships accordingly.

Lord Atkin

Lord Atkin opens his opinion in support of a duty of care principle by stating the crucial issue before the court: "in order to support an action for damages for negligence the complainant has to show that he has been injured by the breach of a duty owed to him in the circumstances by the defendant to take reasonable care to avoid such injury. ... We are solely concerned with the question whether, as a matter of law in the circumstances alleged, the defender owed any duty to the pursuer to take care."

It is remarkable how difficult it is to find in the English authorities statements of general application defining the relations between parties that give rise to the duty. The Courts are concerned with the particular relations which come before them in actual litigation, and it is sufficient to say whether the duty exists in those circumstances. The result is that the Courts have been engaged upon an elaborate classification of duties as they exist in respect of property, whether real or personal, with further divisions as to ownership, occupation or control, and distinctions based on the particular relations of the one side or the other, whether manufacturer, salesman or landlord, customer, tenant, stranger, and so on. In this way it can be ascertained at any time whether the law recognizes a duty, but only where the case can be referred to some particular species which has been examined and classified. And yet the duty which is common to all the cases where liability is established must logically be based upon some element common to the cases where it is found to exist. To seek a complete logical definition of the general principle is probably to go beyond the function of the judge, for the more general the definition the more likely it is to omit essentials or to introduce non-essentials. The attempt was made by Brett M.R. in *Heaven v. Pender*, in a definition to which I will later refer. As framed, it was demonstrably too wide, though it appears to me, if properly limited, to be capable of affording a valuable practical guide.

At present I content myself with pointing out that in English law there must be, and is, some general conception of relations giving rise to a duty of care, of which the particular cases found in the books are but instances. The liability for negligence, whether you style it such or treat it as in other systems as a species of *culpa [fault or negligence]*, is no doubt based upon a general public sentiment of moral wrongdoing for which the offender must pay. But acts or omissions which any moral code would censure cannot in a practical world be treated so as to give a right to every person injured by them to demand relief. In this way rules of law arise which limit the range of complainants and the extent of their remedy. The rule that you are to love your neighbour becomes in law, you must not injure your neighbour; and the lawyer's question, Who's is my neighbour? receives a restricted reply. You must take reasonable care to avoid acts or omissions which you can reasonably foresee would be likely to injure your neighbour. Who, then, in law is my neighbour? The answer seems to be—persons who are so closely and directly affected by my act that I ought reasonably to have them in contemplation as being so affected when I am directing my mind to the acts or omissions which are called in question. This appears to me to be the doctrine of *Heaven v. Pender*, as laid down by Lord Esher (then Brett M.R.) when it is limited by the notion of proximity introduced by Lord Esher himself and A. L. Smith L.J. in *Le Lievre v. Gould*. Lord Esher says:

> That case established that, under certain circumstances, one man may owe a duty to another, even though there is no contract between them. If one man is near to another, or is near to the property of another, a duty lies upon him not to do that which may cause a personal injury to that other, or may injure his property.

So A. L. Smith L.J.:

> The decision of *Heaven v. Pender* was found upon the principle, that a duty to take due care did arise when the person or property of one was in such proximity to the person or property of another that, if due care was not taken, damage might be done by the one to the other.

I think that this sufficiently states the truth if proximity be not confined to mere physical proximity, but be used, as I think it was intended, to extend to such close and direct relations that the act complained of directly affects a person whom the person alleged to be bound to take care would know would be directly affected by his careless act. That this is the sense in which nearness of "proximity" was intended by Lord Esher is obvious from his own illustration in *Heaven v. Pender* of the application of his doctrine to the sale of goods.

Lord Atkin quotes directly from Lord Esher's (at the time he was called Master of Rolls Brett) *dicta,* which was previously cited by Lord Buckmaster.

I draw particular attention to the fact that Lord Esher emphasizes the necessity of goods having to be "used immediately" and "used at once before a reasonable opportunity of inspection." This is obviously to exclude the possibility of goods having their condition altered by lapse of time, and to call attention to the proximate relationship, which may be too remote where inspection even of the person using, certainly of an intermediate person, may reasonably be interposed. With this necessary qualification of proximate relationship as explained in *Le Lievre v. Gould*, I think the judgment of Lord Esher expresses the law of England; without the qualification, I think the majority of the Court in *Heaven v. Pender* were justified in thinking the principle was expressed in too general terms. There will no doubt arise cases where it will be difficult to determine whether the contemplated relationship is so close that the duty arises. But in the class of case now before the Court I cannot conceive any difficulty to arise. A manufacturer puts up an article of food in a container which he knows will be opened by the actual consumer. There can be no inspection by any purchaser and no reasonable preliminary inspection by the consumer. Negligently, in the course of preparation, he allows the contents to be mixed with poison. It is said that the law of England and Scotland is that the poisoned consumer has no remedy against the negligent manufacturer. If this were the result of the authorities, I should consider the result a grave defect in the law, and so contrary to principle that I should hesitate long before following any decision to that effect which had not the authority of this House. I would point out that, in the assumed state of the authorities, not only would the consumer have no remedy against the manufacturer, he would have none against any one else, for in the circumstances alleged there would be no evidence of negligence against any one other than the manufacturer; and, except in the case of a consumer who was also a purchaser, no contract and no warranty of fitness, and in the case of the purchase of a single article under its patent or trade name, which might well be the case in the purchase of some articles of food or drink, no warranty protecting even the purchaser consumer. There are other instances than of articles of food and drink where goods are sold intended to be used immediately by the consumer, such as many forms of goods sold for cleaning purposes, where the same liability must exist. The doctrine supported by the decision below would not only deny a remedy to the consumer who was injured by consuming bottled beer or chocolates poisoned by the negligence of the manufacturer, but also to the user of what should be a harmless proprietary medicine, an ointment, a soap, a cleaning fluid or cleaning powder. I confine myself to articles of common household use, where every one, including the manufacturer, knows that the articles will be used by other persons than the actual ultimate purchaser—namely, by members of his family and his servants, and in some cases his guests. I do not think so ill of our jurisprudence as to suppose that its principles are so remote from the ordinary needs of civilized society and the ordinary claims it makes upon its members as to deny a legal remedy where there is so obviously a social wrong.

It will be found, I think, on examination that there is no case in which the circumstances have been such as I have just suggested where the liability has been negatived. There are numerous cases, where the relations were much more remote, where the duty has been held not to exist. There are also *dicta* in such cases which go further than was necessary for the determination of the particular issues, which have caused the difficulty experienced by the Courts below. I venture to say that in the branch of the law which deals with civil wrongs, dependent in England at any rate entirely upon the application by judges of general principles also formulated by judges, it is of particular importance to guard against the danger of stating propositions of law in wider terms than is necessary, lest essential factors be omitted in the wider survey and the inherent adaptability of English law be unduly restricted. For this reason it is very necessary in considering reported cases in the law of torts that the actual decision alone should carry authority, proper weight, of course, being given to the *dicta* of the judges.

In my opinion several decided cases support the view that in such a case as the present the manufacturer owes a duty to the consumer to be careful. A direct authority is *George v. Skivington.* That was a decision on a demurrer [*admitting the facts as alleged, but insisting that they are insufficient to justify proceeding further*] to a declaration which averred that the defendant professed to sell a hairwash made by himself, and that the plaintiff Joseph George bought a bottle, to be used by his wife, the plaintiff Emma George, as the defendant then knew, and that the defendant had so negligently conducted himself in preparing and selling the hairwash that it was unfit for use, whereby the female plaintiff was injured. Kelly C.B. said that there was no question of warranty, but whether the chemist was liable in an action on the case for unskillfulness and negligence in the manufacture of it. "Unquestionably there was such a duty towards the purchaser, and it extends, in my judgment, to the person for whose use the vendor knew the compound was purchased." Pigott and Cleasby BB. put their judgments on the same ground. I venture to think that Cotton L.J., in *Heaven v. Pender*, misinterprets Cleasby B.'s judgment in the reference to *Langridge v. Levy.* Cleasby B. appears to me to make it plain that in his opinion the duty to take reasonable care can be substituted for the duty which existed in *Langridge v. Levy* not to defraud. It is worth noticing that *George v. Skivington* was referred to by Cleasby B. himself, sitting as a member of the Court of Exchequer Chamber in *Francis v. Cockrell*, and was recognized by him as based on an ordinary duty to take care. It was also affirmed by Brett M.R. in *Cunnington v. Great Northern Ry. Co.* (1883), decided July 2 at a date between the argument and the judgment in *Heaven v. Pender*, though, as in that case the Court negatived any breach of duty, the expression of opinion is not authoritative. The existence of the duty contended for is also supported by *Hawkins v. Smith* (1896), where a dock labourer in the employ of the dock company was injured by a defective sack which had been hired by the consignees from the defendant, who knew the use to which it was to be put, and had been provided by the consignees for the use of the dock company, who had been employed by them to unload the ship on the dock company's premises.

Lord Atkin discusses three other cases, not mentioned by Lord Buckmaster, to support his contention that there is an implicit duty to care where potential users have no opportunity to inspect the goods for themselves. He then begins a review of those cases that have been offered as evidence against a duty to take care.

In *Dixon v. Bell* (1816), the defendant had left a loaded gun at his lodgings and sent his servant, a mulatto girl aged about thirteen or fourteen, for the gun, asking the landlord to remove the priming and give it her. The landlord did remove the priming and gave it to the girl, who later levelled it at the plaintiff's small son, drew the trigger and injured the boy. The action was in case for negligently entrusting the young servant with the gun. The jury at the trial before Lord Ellenborough had returned a verdict for the plaintiff. A motion by Sir William Gatrow (Attorney-General) for a new trial was dismissed by the Court, Lord Ellenborough and Bayley J., the former remarking that it was incumbent on the defendant, who by charging the gun had made it capable of doing mischief, to render it safe and innoxious.

In *Langridge v. Levy* the action was in case, and the declaration alleged that the defendant, by falsely and fraudulently warranting a gun to have been made by Nock and to be a good, safe, and secure gun, sold the gun to the plaintiff's father for the use of himself and his son, and that one of his sons, confiding in the warranty, used the gun, which burst and injured him. Plea not guilty and no warranty as alleged. The report is not very satisfactory. No evidence is reported of any warranty or statement except that the gun was an elegant twist gun by Nock. The judge left to the jury whether the defendant had warranted the gun to be by Nock and to be safe; whether it was in fact unsafe; and whether the defendant warranted it to be safe knowing that it was not so. The jury returned a general verdict for the plaintiff. It appears to have been argued that the plaintiff could recover wherever there is a breach of duty imposed on the defendant by contract or otherwise, and the plaintiff is injured by reason of its breach; by this is meant apparently that the duty need not be owed to the plaintiff, but that he can take advantage of the breach of a duty owed to a third party. This contention was negatived by the Court, who held, however, that the plaintiff could recover if a representation known to be false was made to a third person with the intention that a chattel should be used by the plaintiff, even though it does not appear that the defendant intended the false representation to be communicated to him; see per Parke B. The same view was adopted by the Exchequer Chamber, the use by the plaintiff being treated by the Court as one of the acts contemplated by the fraudulent defendant. It is unnecessary to consider whether the proposition can be supported in its widest form. It is sufficient to say that the case was based, as I think, in the pleading, and certainly in the judgment, on the ground of fraud, and it appears to add nothing of value positively or negatively to the present discussion. *Winterbottom v. Wright* was a case decided on a demurrer. The plaintiff had demurred to two of the pleas, as to which there was no decision by the Court; but on the hearing of the plaintiff's demurrer the Court, in accordance with the practice of the day, were entitled to consider the whole record, including the declaration, and, coming to the conclusion that this declaration disclosed no cause of action, gave judgment for the defendant: see Sutton's *Personal Actions at Common Law.* The advantage of the procedure is that we are in a position to know the precise issue at law which arose for determination. The declaration was in case, and alleged that the defendant had contracted with the Postmaster-General to provide the mail-coach to convey mails from Hartford to Holyhead and to keep the mails in safe condition; that Atkinson and others, with notice of the said contract, had contracted with the Postmaster-General to convey the road mail-coach from Hartford to Holyhead; and that the plaintiff, relying on the said first contract, hired himself to Atkinson to drive the mail-coach; but that the defendant so negligently conducted himself and so utterly disregarded his aforesaid contract that the defendant, having the means of knowing, and well knowing, all the aforesaid premises, the mail-coach, being in a dangerous condition, owing to certain latent defects and to no other cause, gave way, whereby the plaintiff was thrown from his seat and injured. It is to be observed that no negligence apart from breach of contract was alleged—in other words, no duty was alleged other than the duty arising out of the contract; it is not stated that the defendant knew, or ought to have known, of the latent defect. The argument of the defendant was that, on the face of the declaration, the wrong arose merely out of the breach of a contract, and that only a party to the contract could sue. The Court of Exchequer adopted that view, as clearly appears from the judgments of Alderson and Rolfe BB. There are *dicta* by Lord Abinger which are too wide as to an action of negligence being confined to cases of breach of a public duty. The actual decision appears to have been manifestly right; no duty to the plaintiff arose out of the contract; and the duty of the defendant under the contract with the Postmaster-General to put the coach in good repair could not have involved such direct relations with the servant of the persons whom the Postmaster-General employed to drive the coach as would give rise to a duty of care owed to such servant. We now come to *Longmeid v. Holliday*, the *dicta* in which have had considerable effect in subsequent decisions. In that case the declaration in case alleged that the plaintiff, Frederick Longmeid, had bought from the defendant, the maker and seller of "the Holliday lamp," a lamp to be used by himself and his wife Eliza in the plaintiff's shop; that the defendant induced the sale by the false and fraudulent warranty that the lamp was reasonably fit for the purpose; and that the plaintiff Eliza, confiding in the said warranty, lighted the lamp, which exploded, whereby she was injured. It is perhaps not an extravagant guess to suppose that the plaintiffs' pleader had read the case of *Langridge v. Levy.* The jury found all the facts for the plaintiffs except the allegation of fraud; they were not satisfied that the defendant knew of the defects. The plaintiff Frederick had already recovered damages on the contract of sale for breach of the implied warranty of fitness. The declaration made no averment of negligence. Verdict was entered at the trial by Martin B. for the plaintiff, but with liberty to the defendant to move to enter the verdict for him. A rule having been obtained, plaintiff's counsel sought to support the verdict on the ground that this was not an action for a breach of duty arising solely from contract, but for an injury resulting from conduct amounting to fraud. Parke B., who delivered the judgment of the Court, held that, fraud having been negatived, the action could not be maintained on that ground. He then went on to discuss cases in which a third person not a party to a contract may sue for damages sustained if it is broken. After dealing with the negligence of a surgeon, or of a carrier, or of a firm in breach of contract committing a nuisance on a highway, he deals with the case where any one delivers to another without notice an instrument in its nature dangerous, or under particular circumstances, as a loaded gun, and refers to *Dixon v. Bell*, though what this case has to do with contract it is difficult to see. He then goes on:

> But it would be going much too far to say that so much care is required in the ordinary intercourse of life between one individual and another, that, if a machine not in its nature dangerous—a carriage for instance—but which might become so by a latent defect entirely unknown although discoverable by the exercise of ordinary care, should be lent or given by one person, even by the person who manufactured it, to another, the former should be answerable to the latter for a subsequent damage accruing by the use of it.

It is worth noticing how guarded this *dictum* is. The case put is a machine such as a carriage, not in its nature dangerous, which might become dangerous by a latent defect entirely unknown. Then there is the saying, "although discoverable by the exercise of ordinary care," discoverable by whom is not said; it may include the person to whom the innocent machine is "lent or given." Then the *dictum* is confined to machines "lent or given" (a later sentence makes it clear that a distinction is intended between these words and "delivered to the purchaser under the contract of sale"), and the manufacturer is introduced for the first time, "even by the person who manufactured it." I do not for a moment believe that Parke B. had in his mind such a case as a loaf negligently mixed with poison by the baker which poisoned a purchaser's family. He is, in my opinion, confining his remarks primarily to cases where a person is seeking to rely upon a duty of care which arises out of a contract with a third party, and has never even discussed the case of a manufacturer negligently causing an article to be dangerous and selling it in that condition whether with immediate or mediate effect upon the consumer. It is noteworthy that he only refers to "letting or giving" chattels, operations known to the law, where the special relations thereby created have a particular bearing on the existence or non-existence of a duty to take care. Next in this chain of authority come *George v. Skivington* and *Heaven v. Pender*, which I have already discussed. The next case is *Earl v. Lubbock*. The plaintiff sued in the county court for personal injuries due to the negligence of the defendant. The plaintiff was a driver in the employ of a firm who owned vans. The defendant, a master wheelwright, had contracted with the firm to keep their vans in good and substantial repair. The allegation of negligence was that the defendant's servant had negligently failed to inspect and repair a defective wheel, and had negligently repaired the wheel. The learned county court judge had held that the defendant owed no duty to the plaintiff, and the Divisional Court (Lord Alverstone L.C.J. [*Lord Chief Justice*], Wills and Kennedy JJ.) and the Court of Appeal agreed with him. The Master of the Rolls, Sir R. Henn Collins, said that the case was concluded by *Winterbottom v. Wright*. In other words, he must have treated the duty as alleged to arise only from a breach of contract; for, as has been pointed out, that was the only allegation in *Winterbottom v. Wright*, negligence apart from contract being neither averted nor proved. It is true that he cites with approval the dicta of Lord Abinger in that case; but obviously I think his approval must be limited to those *dicta* so far as they related to the particular facts before the Court of Appeal, and to cases where, as Lord Abinger says, the law permits a contract to be turned into a tort. Stirling L.J., it is true, said that to succeed the plaintiff must bring his case within the proposition of the majority in *Heaven v. Pender*, that any one who, without due warning, supplies to others for use an instrument which to his knowledge is in such a condition as to cause danger is liable for injury. I venture to think that the Lord Justice is mistakenly treating a proposition which applies one test of a duty as though it afforded the only criterion.

Mathew L.J. appears to me to put the case on its proper footing when he says the argument of the plaintiff was that the defendant's servants had been negligent in the performance of the contract with the owners of the van, and that it followed as a matter of law that any one in this employment had a cause of action against the defendant. "It is impossible to accept such a wide proposition, and, indeed, it is difficult to see how, if it were the law, trade could be carried on." I entirely agree. I have no doubt that in that case the plaintiff failed to show that the repairer owed any duty to him. The question of law in that case seems very different from that raised in the present case. The case of *Blacker v. Lake & Elliot, Ld.* (1912), approaches more nearly the facts of this case. I have read and re-read it, having unfeigned respect for the authority of the two learned judges, Hamilton and Lush JJ., who decided it, and I am bound to say I have found difficulty in formulating the precise grounds upon which the judgment was given. The plaintiff had been injured by the bursting of a brazing lamp which he had bought from a shopkeeper who had bought it from the manufacturer, the defendant. The plaintiff had used the lamp for twelve months before the accident. The case was tried in the county court before that excellent lawyer the late Sir Howland Roberts. That learned judge had directed the jury that the plaintiff could succeed if the defendants had put upon the market a lamp not fit for use in the sense that a person working it with reasonable care would incur a risk which a properly constructed lamp would not impose upon him. The jury found that the lamp was defective by reason of an improper system of making an essential joint between the container and the vaporizer; that the defendants did not know that it was dangerous, but ought as reasonable men to have known it. Hamilton J. seems to have thought that there was no evidence of negligence in this respect. Lush J. expressly says so and implies—"I also think"—that Hamilton J. so thought. If so, the case resolves itself into a series of important *dicta*. Hamilton J. says that it has been decided in authorities from *Winterbottom v. Wright* to *Earl v. Lubbock* that the breach of the defendants' contract with A., to use care and skill in and about the manufacture or repair of an article, does not itself give any cause of action to B. when injured by the article proving to be defective in breach of that contract. He then goes on to say, how is the case of the plaintiffs any better when there is no contract proved of which there could be a breach. I think, with respect, that this saying does not give sufficient weight to the actual issues raised by the pleadings on which alone the older cases are an authority. If the issue raised was an alleged duty created by contract, it would have been irrelevant to consider duties created without reference to contract; and contract cases cease to be authorities for duties alleged to exist beyond or without contract. Moreover, it is a mistake to describe the authorities as dealing with the failure of care or skill in the manufacture of goods, as contrasted with repair. The only manufacturing case was *Longmeid v. Holliday*, where negligence was not alleged. Hamilton J. recognizes that *George v. Skivington* was a decision which, if it remained an authority, bound him. He says that, without presuming to say it was wrong, he cannot follow it, because it is in conflict with *Winterbottom v. Wright*. I find this very difficult to understand, for *George v. Skivington* was based upon a duty in the manufacturer to take care independently of contract, while *Winterbottom v. Wright* was decided on demurrer in a case where the alleged duty was based solely on breach of a contractual duty to keep in repair, and no negligence was alleged. Lush J. says in terms that there are only three classes of cases in which a stranger to a contract can sue for injury by a defective chattel: one is that of fraud; the second of articles dangerous or noxious in themselves, where the duty is only to warn; the third of public nuisance. He does not bring the cases represented by *Elliott v. Hall* (1885) (the defective coal wagon) within his classes at all. He says they belong to a totally different class, "where the control of premises or the management of a dangerous thing upon premises creates a duty." I have already pointed out that this distinction is unfounded in fact, for in *Elliott v. Hall*, as in *Hawkins v. Smith* (the defective sack), the defendant exercised no control over the article and the accident did not occur on his premises. With all respect, I think that the judgments in the case err by seeking to confine the law to rigid and exclusive categories, and by not giving sufficient attention to the general principle which governs the whole law of negligence in the duty owed to those who will be immediately injured by lack of care. The last case I need refer to is *Bates v. Batey & Co., Ld.*, where manufacturers of ginger-beer were sued by a plaintiff who had been injured by the bursting of a bottle of ginger-beer bought from a shopkeeper who had obtained it from the manufacturers. The manufacturers had bought the actual bottle from its maker, but were found by the jury to have been negligent in not taking proper means to discover whether the bottle was defective or not. Horridge J. found that a bottle of ginger-beer was not dangerous in itself, but this defective bottle was in fact dangerous; but, as the defendants did not know that it was dangerous, they were not liable, though by the exercise of reasonable care they could have discovered the defect. This case differs from the present only by reason of the fact that it was not the manufacturers of the ginger-beer who caused the defect in the bottle; but, on the assumption that the jury were right in finding a lack of reasonable care in not examining the bottle, I should have come to the conclusion that, as the manufacturers must have contemplated the bottle being handled immediately by the consumer, they owed a duty to him to take care that he should not be injured externally by explosion, just as I think they owed a duty to him to take care that he should not be injured internally by poison or other noxious thing. I do not find it necessary to discuss at length the cases dealing with duties where the thing is dangerous, or, in the narrower category, belongs to a class of things which are dangerous in themselves. I regard the distinction as an unnatural one so far as it is used to serve as a logical differentiation by which to distinguish the existence or non-existence of a legal right. In this respect I agree with what was said by Scrutton L.J. in *Hodge & Sons v. Anglo-American Oil Co.* (1922), a case which was ultimately decided on a question of fact.

> Personally, I do not understand the difference between a thing dangerous in itself, as poison, and a thing not dangerous as a class, but by negligent construction dangerous as a particular thing. The latter, if anything, seems the more dangerous of the two; it is a wolf in sheep's clothing instead of an obvious wolf.

The nature of the thing may very well call for different degrees of care, and the person dealing with it may well contemplate persons as being within the sphere of his duty to take care who would not be sufficiently proximate with less dangerous goods; so that not only the degree of care but the range of persons to whom a duty is owed may be extended. But they all illustrate the general principle.

Lord Atkin discusses several additional cases to support the position that a duty of care can exist independent of a contract, and that the duty of care in the case of inherently dangerous objects is a difference of degree, not of kind, from a duty stemming from objects which are made dangerous by neglect. However, he indicates that it is not easy to reconcile all the authorities on this issue. Lord Atkin considers briefly a famous American case before concluding that affirmation of a duty of care will provide much needed clarification of the law—a clarification which he believes "is in accordance with sound common sense."

Lord Thankerton

Lord Thankerton offers his brief opinion in support of a duty of care where he outlines the facts of the case, lays out the issue to be decided, and notes that he so entirely agrees with Lord Atkin's judgment that he cannot usefully add anything to it. He does proceed, however to discuss a case that is very similar to the one before them:

> An interesting illustration of similar circumstances is to be found in *Gordon v. M'Hardy* (1903), in which the pursuer sought to recover damages from a retail grocer on account of the death of his son by ptomaine poisoning, caused by eating tinned salmon purchased from the defender. The pursuer averred that the tin, when sold, was dented, but he did not suggest that the grocer had cut through the metal and allowed air to get in, or had otherwise caused injury to the contents. The action was held irrelevant, the Lord Justice-Clerk remarking:
>
> > I do not see how the defender could have examined the tin of salmon which he is alleged to have sold without destroying the very condition which the manufacturer had established in order to preserve the contents, the tin not being intended to be opened until immediately before use.
>
> Apparently in that case the manufacturers' label was off the tin when sold, and they had not been identified. I should be sorry to think that the meticulous care of the manufacturer to exclude interference or inspection by the grocer in that case should relieve the grocer of any responsibility to the consumer without any corresponding assumption of duty by the manufacturer.

Lord Thankerton offers additional passing remarks before expressing his support for the duty of care principle.

Lord Macmillan

In his lengthy opinion Lord Macmillan reviews the facts of the case and announces that there is no "unbroken and consistent current of decisions" denying what he regards to be the "reasonable and equitable" conclusion; namely, that there exists a duty of care. Rather, he suggests that the conflicting decisions reflect two rival principles that are finally brought to a head in this case: "On the one hand, there is the well established principle that no one other than a party to a contract can complain of a breach of contract. On the other hand, there is the equally well established doctrine that negligence apart from contract gives a right of action to the party injured by that negligence. ... " Much of his opinion, which is not reproduced here, focuses on revealing the inconsistent body of case law discussed by Lords Buckmaster and Atkin. Lord Macmillan then offers his justification for the duty of care:

Having regard to the inconclusive state of the authorities [*i.e., existing case law*] in the Courts below and to the fact that the important question involved is now before your Lordships for the first time, I think it desirable to consider the matter from the point of view of the principles applicable to this branch of law which are admittedly common to both English and Scottish jurisprudence.

The law takes no cognizance of carelessness in the abstract. It concerns itself with carelessness only where there is a duty to take care and where failure in that duty has caused damage. In such circumstances carelessness assumes the legal quality of negligence and entails the consequences in law of negligence. What, then, are the circumstances which give rise to this duty to take care? In the daily contacts of social and business life human beings are thrown into, or place themselves in, an infinite variety of relations with their fellows; and the law can refer only to the standards of the reasonable man in order to determine whether any particular relation gives rise to a duty to take care as between those who stand in that relation to each other. The grounds of action may be as various and manifold as human errancy; and the conception of legal responsibility may develop in adaptation to altering social conditions and standards. The criterion of judgment must adjust and adapt itself to the changing circumstances of life. The categories of negligence are never closed. The cardinal principle of liability is that the party complained of should owe to the party complaining a duty to take care, and that the party complaining should be able to prove that he has suffered damage in consequence of a breach of that duty. Where there is room for diversity of view, it is in determining what circumstances will establish such a relationship between the parties as to give rise, on the one side, to a duty to take care, and on the other side to a right to have care taken.

To descend from these generalities to the circumstances of the present case, I do not think that any reasonable man or any twelve reasonable men would hesitate to hold that, if the appellant establishes her allegations, the respondent has exhibited carelessness in the conduct of his business. For a manufacturer of aerated water to store his empty bottles in a place where snails can get access to them, and to fill his bottles without taking any adequate precautions by inspection or otherwise to ensure that they contain no deleterious foreign matter, may reasonably be characterized as carelessness without applying too exacting a standard. But, as I have pointed out, it is not enough to prove the respondent to be careless in his process of manufacture. The question is: Does he owe a duty to take care, and to whom does he owe that duty? Now I have no hesitation in affirming that a person who for gain engages in the business of manufacturing articles of food and drink intended for consumption by members of the public in the form in which he issues them is under a duty to take care in the manufacture of these articles. That duty, in my opinion, he owes to those whom he intends to consume his products. He manufactures his commodities for human consumption; he intends and contemplates that they shall be consumed. By reason of that very fact he places himself in a relationship with all the potential consumers of his commodities, and that relationship which he assumes and desires for his own ends imposes upon him a duty to take care to avoid injuring them. He owes them a duty not to convert by his own carelessness·an article which he issues to them as wholesome and innocent into an article which is dangerous to life and health. It is sometimes said that liability can only arise where a reasonable man would have foreseen and could have avoided the consequences of his act or omission. In the present case the respondent, when he manufactured his ginger-beer, had directly in contemplation that it would be consumed by members of the public. Can it be said that he could not be expected as a reasonable man to foresee that if he conducted his process of manufacture carelessly he might injure those whom he expected and desired to consume his ginger-beer? The possibility of injury so arising seems to me in no sense so remote as to excuse him from foreseeing it. Suppose that a baker, through carelessness, allows a large quantity of arsenic to be mixed with a batch of his bread, with the result that those who subsequently eat it are poisoned, could he be heard to say that he owed no duty to the consumers of his bread to take care that it was free from poison, and that, as he did not know that any poison had got into it, his only liability was for breach of warranty under his contract of sale to those who actually bought the poisoned bread from him? Observe that I have said "through carelessness," and thus excluded the case of a pure accident such as may happen where every care is taken. I cannot believe, and I do not believe, that neither in the law of England nor in the law of Scotland is there redress for such a case. The state of facts I have figured might well give rise to a criminal charge, and the civil consequence of such carelessness can scarcely be less wide than its criminal consequences. Yet the principle of the decision appealed from is that the manufacturer of food products intended by him for human consumption does not owe to the consumers whom he has in view any duty of care, not even the duty to take care that he does not poison them.

Lord Macmillan comments on a technical point about the relation of the law of Scotland to the law of England before proceeding with his justification. He repeats the passage (cited by Lord Buckmaster) from *Longmeid v. Holliday* where Baron Parke suggests that holding manufacturers responsible for unknown latent defects "would be going much too far."

I read this passage rather as a note of warning that the standard of care exacted in human dealings must not be pitched too high than as giving any countenance to the view that negligence may be exhibited with impunity. It must always be a question of circumstances whether the carelessness amounts to negligence, and whether the injury is not too remote from the carelessness. I can readily conceive that where a manufacturer has parted with his product and it has passed into other hands it may well be exposed to vicissitudes which may render it defective or noxious, for which the manufacturer could not in any view be held to be to blame. It may be a good general rule to regard responsibility as ceasing when control ceases. So, also, where between the manufacturer and the user there is interposed a party who has the means and opportunity of examining the manufacturer's product before he re-issues it to the actual user. But where, as in the present case, the article of consumption is so prepared as to be intended to reach the consumer in the condition in which it leaves the manufacturer, and the manufacturer takes steps to ensure this by sealing or otherwise closing the container so that the contents cannot be tampered with, I regard his control as remaining effective until the article reaches the consumer and the container is opened by him. The intervention of any exterior agency is intended to be excluded, and was in fact in the present case excluded. It is doubtful whether in such a case there is any redress against the retailer: *Gordon v. M'Hardy.*

The burden of proof must always be upon the injured party to establish that the defect which caused the injury was present in the article when it left the hands of the party whom he sues, that the defect was occasioned by the carelessness of that party, and that the circumstances are such as to cast upon the defender a duty to take care not to injure the pursuer. There is no presumption of negligence in such a case as the present, nor is there any justification for applying the maxim, *res ipsa loquitur* [*the thing speaks for itself*]. Negligence must be both averred and proved.

Lord Macmillan concludes by supporting the appeal in favour of a duty of care.

REASONING FROM PRINCIPLE

Morgentaler v. The Queen (1988)

The main question in this controversial Supreme Court of Canada case, *Morgentaler v. The Queen* (1988), was whether the abortion provisions of the *Criminal Code* (section 251) infringed the *Charter* "right of life, liberty and security of the person and the right not to be deprived thereof except in accordance with the principles of fundamental justice" (section 7). In a five-to-two decision, the majority decided that the abortion provisions did violate the *Charter*. Separate concurring opinions were written by Chief Justice Dickson, by Justice Beetz, and by Madame Justice Wilson; the minority opinion was written by Justice McIntyre. Excerpts from all but Justice Beetz's opinion are presented here. Many of the arguments in these opinions are based on reasoning from principle.

Chief Justice Dickson

In his opening remarks, Chief Justice Dickson stresses the need to distinguish political evaluation of legislation from constitutional review:

During argument before this Court, counsel for the Crown emphasized repeatedly that it is not the role of the judiciary in Canada to evaluate the wisdom of legislation enacted by our democratically elected representatives, or to second-guess difficult policy choices that confront all governments. In *Morgentaler v. The Queen* (1975) [*a pre-Charter abortion case also involving Dr. Morgentaler*], I stressed that the Court had "not been called upon to decide, or even to enter, the loud and continuous public debate on abortion." Eleven years later, the controversy persists, and it remains true that this Court cannot presume to resolve all of the competing claims advanced in vigorous and healthy public debate. Courts and legislators in other democratic societies have reached completely contradictory decisions when asked to weigh the competing values relevant to the abortion question. ... [*Refers to prominent American and European cases and legislation involving abortion.*]

But since 1975, and the first *Morgentaler* decision, the Court has been given added responsibilities. I stated in *Morgentaler* (1975) that

The values we must accept for the purposes of this appeal are those expressed by Parliament which holds the view that the desire of a woman to be relieved of her pregnancy is not, of itself, justification for performing an abortion.

Although no doubt it is still fair to say that courts are not the appropriate forum for articulating complex and controversial programmes of public policy, Canadian courts are now charged with the crucial obligation of ensuring that the legislative initiatives pursued by our Parliament and legislatures conform to the democratic values expressed in the *Canadian Charter of Rights and Freedoms.* As Justice McIntyre states in his reasons for judgment, "... the task of the Court in this case is not to solve nor seek to solve what might be called the abortion issue, but simply to measure the content of s.251 against the *Charter*." It is in this latter sense that the current *Morgentaler* appeal differs from the one we heard a decade ago.

The Chief Justice reviews relevant legislative and constitutional provisions before considering the appropriate approach to interpreting the *Charter*. Citing recent cases, he notes that "this Court has held consistently that the proper technique for the interpretation of *Charter* provisions is to pursue a 'purposive' analysis of the right guaranteed" which mean that it is to be understood "in the light of the interests it was meant to protect." In considering the kind of legislative review authorized by the need to conform with "principles of fundamental justice" the Chief Justice refers to comments by Supreme Court Justice Lamer in *Re B.C. Motor Vehicle Act* (1985) that these principles may involve a review of the fairness of either the procedures or the substance of a law. As the Chief Justice explains:

I have no doubt that s.7 does impose upon courts the duty to review the substance of legislation once it has been determined that the legislation infringes an individual's right to "life, liberty and security of the person." The section states clearly that those interests may only be impaired if the principles of fundamental justice are respected. Lamer J. emphasized, however, that the courts should avoid "adjudication of the merits of public policy." In the present case, I do not believe that it is necessary for the Court to tread the fine line between substantive review and the adjudication of public policy. As in the *Singh* (1985) case, it will be sufficient to investigate whether or not the impugned legislative provisions meet the procedural standards of fundamental justice.

Having cleared up preliminary questions about interpretation, the Chief Justice considers whether section 251 of the *Criminal Code* impairs the right to security of the person, as found in section 7 of the *Charter*. He suggests that "the law has long recognized that the human body ought to be protected from interference by others." Chief Justice Dickson then asks whether security of the person refers solely to the physical and bodily security of a person. Citing several cases, he concludes that it is not restricted to physical integrity but extends to the psychological effects on the individual.

I wish to reiterate that finding a violation of security of the person does not end the s.7 inquiry. Parliament could choose to infringe security of the person if it did so in a manner consistent with the principles of fundamental justice. The present discussion should therefore be seen as a threshold inquiry and the conclusions do not dispose definitively of all the issues relevant to s.7. With that caution, I have no difficulty in concluding that the encyclopedic factual submissions addressed to us by counsel in the present appeal establish beyond any doubt that s.251 of the *Criminal Code* is *prima facie* a violation of the security of the person of thousands of Canadian women who have made the difficult decision that they do not wish to continue with a pregnancy.

At the most basic, physical and emotional level, every pregnant woman is told by the section that she cannot submit to a generally safe medical procedure that might be of clear benefit to her unless she meets criteria entirely unrelated to her own priorities and aspirations. Not only does the removal of decision making power threaten women in a physical sense; the indecision of knowing whether an abortion will be granted inflicts emotional stress. Section 251 clearly interferes with a woman's bodily integrity in both a physical and emotional sense. Forcing a woman, by threat of criminal sanction, to carry a foetus to term unless she meets certain criteria unrelated to her own priorities and aspirations, is a profound interference with a woman's body and thus a violation of security of the person. Section 251, therefore, is required by the *Charter* to comport with the principles of fundamental justice.

The Chief Justice begins a lengthy reporting of evidence to document the physical and psychological stress imposed by existing abortion practices. He discusses the delays in obtaining abortions and the consequences of these delays:

These periods of delay may not seem unduly long, but in the case of abortion, the implications of any delay, according to the evidence, are potentially devastating. The first factor to consider is that different medical techniques are employed to perform abortions at different stages of pregnancy. The testimony of expert doctors at trial indicated that in the first twelve weeks of pregnancy, the relatively safe and simple suction dilation and curettage method of abortion is typically used in North America. From the thirteenth to the sixteenth week, the more dangerous dilation and evacuation procedure is performed, although much less often in Canada than in the United States. From the sixteenth week of pregnancy, the instillation method is commonly employed in Canada. This method requires the intra-amniotic introduction of prostoglandin, urea, or a saline solution, which causes a woman to go into labour, giving birth to a foetus which is usually dead, but not invariably so. The uncontroverted evidence showed that each method of abortion progressively increases risks to the woman. (See, e.g., Tyler, *et al.*, "Second Trimester Induced Abortion in the United States.")

The second consideration is that even within the periods appropriate to each method of abortion, the evidence indicated that the earlier the abortion was performed, the fewer the complications and the lower the risk of mortality. For example, a study emanating from the Centre for Disease Control in Atlanta confirmed that "D & E [*dilation and evacuation*] procedures performed at 13 to 15 weeks' gestation were nearly 3 times safer than those performed at 16 weeks or later." (Cates and Grimes, "Deaths from Second Trimester Abortion by Dilation and Evacuation: Causes, Prevention, Facilities" (1981). See also the *Powell Report.*) The Court was advised that because of their perceptions of risk, Canadian doctors often refuse to use the dilation and evacuation procedure from the thirteenth to sixteenth weeks and instead wait until they consider it appropriate to use the instillation technique. Even more revealing were the overall mortality statistics evaluated by Drs. Cates and Grimes. They concluded from their study of the relevant data that:

Anything that contributes to delay in performing abortions increases the complication rates by 15 to 30%, and the chance of dying by 50% for each week of delay.

These statistics indicate clearly that even if the average delay caused by s.251 *per arguendo* [*for the sake of argument*] is of only a couple of weeks' duration, the effects upon any particular woman can be serious and, occasionally, fatal.

It is no doubt true that the overall complication and mortality rates for women who undergo abortions are very low, but the increasing risks caused by delay are so clearly established that I have no difficulty in concluding that the delay in obtaining therapeutic abortions caused by the mandatory procedures of s.251 is an infringement of the purely physical aspect of the individual's right to security of the person. I should stress that the marked contrast between the relative speed with which abortions can be obtained at the government-sponsored community clinics in Quebec and in hospitals under the s.251 procedure was established at trial. The evidence indicated that at the government-sponsored clinics in Quebec, the maximum delay was less than a week. One must conclude, and perhaps underline, that the delay experienced by many women seeking a therapeutic abortion, be it of one, two, four, or six weeks duration, is caused in large measure by the requirements of s.251 itself.

The Chief Justice observes that the risk to the physical well-being of woman caused by the delays created by section 251 is, itself, sufficient to warrant inquiring whether the legislation is consistent with the principles of fundamental justice. However, he recognizes further infringement of security of the person arising from harm to the psychological integrity of women seeking abortions. He cites a Canadian Medical Association report and the testimony of medical experts to document the psychological impact upon women of the delays inherent in section 251 procedures. The Chief Justice then introduces a potential objection to the argument that section 251 is the source of these delays, and of the accompanying medical dangers and psychological stress.

In its supplementary factum [*statements of facts*] and in oral submissions, the Crown argued that evidence of what could be termed "administrative inefficiency" is not relevant to the evaluation of legislation for the purposes of s.7 of the *Charter*. The Crown argued that only evidence regarding the purpose of legislation is relevant. The assumption, of course, is that any impairment to the physical or psychological interests of individuals caused by s.251 of the *Criminal Code* does not amount to an infringement of security of the person because the injury is caused by practical difficulties and is not intended by the legislator.

The submission is faulty on two counts. First, as a practical matter it is not possible in the case of s.251 to erect a rigid barrier between the purposes of the section and the administrative procedures established to carry those purposes into effect. For example, although it may be true that Parliament did not enact s.251 intending to create delays in obtaining therapeutic abortions, the evidence demonstrates that the system established by the section for obtaining a therapeutic abortion certificate inevitably does create significant delays. It is not possible to say that delay results only from administrative constraints, such as limited budgets or a lack of qualified persons to sit on therapeutic abortion committees. Delay results from the cumbersome operating requirements of s.251 itself. (See, by way of analogy, *R. v. Therens.*) Although the mandate given to the courts under the *Charter* does not, generally speaking, enable the judiciary to provide remedies for administrative inefficiencies, when denial of a right as basic as security of the person is infringed by the procedure and administrative structures created by the law itself, the courts are empowered to act.

Secondly, were it nevertheless possible in this case to dissociate purpose and administration, this Court has already held as a matter of law that purpose is not the only appropriate criterion in evaluating the constitutionality of legislation under the *Charter*. In *R. v. Big M Drug Mart Ltd.* the Court stated that:

> ... both purpose and effect are relevant in determining constitutionality; either an unconstitutional purpose or an unconstitutional effect can invalidate legislation.

> Even if the purpose of legislation is unobjectionable, the administrative procedures *created by law* to bring that purpose into operation may produce unconstitutional effects, and the legislation should then be struck down.

The Chief Justice concludes that section 251 "forces women to carry a foetus to term contrary to their own priorities and aspirations and ... imposes serious delay causing increased physical and psychological trauma to those women who meet its criteria." He must determine, therefore, whether the infringement is in accordance with the principles of fundamental justice. Although he acknowledges that the "principles of fundamental justice" have both a substantive and a procedural component, Chief Justice Dickson sees no need to evaluate the substantive content of section 251 of the *Criminal Code*—his discussion focuses on the administrative structure and procedures for access to abortions.

> The procedure surrounding the defence is rather complex. A pregnant woman who desires to have an abortion must apply to the "therapeutic abortion committee" of an "accredited or approved hospital." Such a committee is empowered to issue a certificate in writing stating that in the opinion of a majority of the committee, the continuation of the pregnancy would be likely to endanger the pregnant woman's life or health. Once a copy of the certificate is given to a qualified medical practitioner who is not a member of the therapeutic abortion committee, he or she is permitted to perform an abortion on the pregnant woman and both the doctor and the woman are freed from any criminal liability.

The Chief Justice defines several key terms and notes: "Interestingly, the term 'health' is not defined for the purposes of s.251, so it would appear that the therapeutic abortion committees are free to develop their own theories as to when a potential impairment of a woman's 'health' would justify the granting of a therapeutic abortion certificate."

> As is so often the case in matters of interpretation, however, the straightforward reading of this statutory scheme is not fully revealing. In order to understand the true nature and scope of s.251, it is necessary to investigate the practical operation of the provisions. The Court has been provided with a myriad of factual submissions in this area. One of the most useful sources of information is the *Badgley Report*. The Committee on the Operation of the Abortion Law was established by Orders-in-Council of September 29, 1975 and its terms of reference instructed it to "conduct a study to determine whether the procedure provided in the Criminal Code for obtaining therapeutic abortions is operating equitably across Canada." Statistics were provided to the Committee by Statistics Canada and the Committee conducted its own research, meeting with officials of the departments of the provincial attorneys general and of health, and visiting hospitals throughout Canada. The Committee also commissioned national hospital, hospital staff, physician, and patient surveys. The overall conclusion of the Committee was that "The procedures set out for the operation of the Abortion Law are not working equitably across Canada." Of course, that conclusion does not lead to the necessary inference that s.251 procedures violate the principles of fundamental justice. Unfair functioning of the law could be caused by external forces which do not relate to the law itself.

> The *Badgley Report* contains a wealth of detailed information which demonstrates, however, that many of the most serious problems with the functioning of s.251 are created by procedural and administrative requirements established in the law. For example, the Badgley Committee noted that:

... the Abortion Law implicitly establishes a minimum requirement of three qualified physicians to serve on a therapeutic abortion committee, plus a qualified medical practitioner who is not a member of the therapeutic abortion committee, to perform the procedure.

The Committee went on to make the following observation:

Of the 1,348 civilian hospitals in operation in 1976, at least 331 hospitals had less than four physicians on their medical staff. In terms of the distribution of physicians, 24.6 percent of hospitals in Canada did not have a medical staff which was large enough to establish a therapeutic abortion committee and to perform the abortion procedure.

In other words, the seemingly neutral requirement of s.251(4) that at least four physicians be available to authorize and to perform an abortion meant in practice that abortions would be absolutely unavailable in almost one quarter of all hospitals in Canada.

The Chief Justice lists some of the impediments surrounding existing procedures, including the following:

Many Canadian hospitals do not provide all of the required services, thereby being automatically disqualified from undertaking therapeutic abortions. The *Badgley Report* stressed the remarkable limitations created by these requirements, especially when linked with the four-physician rule discussed above:

Of the total of 1,348 non-military hospitals in Canada in 1976, 789 hospitals, or 58.5 percent, were ineligible in terms of their major treatment functions, the size of their medical staff, or their type of facility to establish therapeutic abortion committees.

Moreover, even if a hospital is eligible to create a therapeutic abortion committee, there is no requirement in s.251 that the hospital need do so. The Badgley Committee discovered that in 1976, of the 559 general hospitals which met the procedural requirements of s.251, only 271 hospitals in Canada, or only 20.1 per cent of the total, had actually established a therapeutic abortion committee.

Even though the *Badgley Report* was issued ten years ago, the relevant statistics do not appear to be out of date. Indeed, Statistics Canada reported that in 1982 the number of hospitals with therapeutic abortion committees had actually fallen to 261. Even more recent data exists for Ontario. In the *Powell Report*, it was noted that in 1986 only fifty-four percent of accredited acute care hospitals in the province had therapeutic abortion committees. In five counties there were no committees at all. Of the ninety-five hospitals with committees, twelve did not do any abortions in 1986.

The *Powell Report* reveals another serious difficulty with s.251 procedures. The requirement that therapeutic abortions be performed only in "accredited" or "approved" hospitals effectively means that the practical availability of the exculpatory provisions of subs. (4) may be heavily restricted, even denied, through provincial regulation. In Ontario, for example, the provincial government promulgated O. Reg. 248/70 under *The Public Hospitals Act*. This regulation provides that therapeutic abortion committees can only be established where there are ten or more members on the active medical staff. A Minister of Health is not prevented from imposing harsher restrictions. During argument, it was noted that it would even be possible for a provincial government, exercising its legislative authority over public hospitals, to distribute funding for treatment facilities in such a way that no hospital would meet the procedural requirements of s.251(4). Because of the administrative structure established in s.251(4) and the related definitions, the "defence" created in the section could be completely wiped out.

A further flaw with the administrative system established in s.251(4) is the failure to provide an adequate standard for therapeutic abortion committees which must determine when a therapeutic abortion should, as a matter of law, be granted. Subsection (4) states simply that a therapeutic abortion committee may grant a certificate when it determines that a continuation of a pregnancy would be likely to endanger the "life or health" of the pregnant woman. It was noted above that "health" is not defined for the purposes of the section. The Crown admitted in its supplementary factum that the medical witnesses at trial testified uniformly that the "health" standard was ambiguous, but the Crown derives comfort from the fact that "the medical witnesses were unanimous in their approval of the broad World Health Organization definition of health." The World Health Organization defines "health" not merely as the absence of disease or infirmity, but as a state of physical, mental and social well-being.

I do not understand how the mere existence of a workable definition of "health" can make the use of the word in s.251(4) any less ambiguous when that definition is nowhere referred to in the section. There is no evidence that therapeutic abortion committees are commonly applying the World Health Organization definition. Indeed, the *Badgley Report* indicates that the situation is quite the contrary:

> There has been no sustained or firm effort in Canada to develop an explicit and operational definition of health, or to apply such a concept directly to the operation of induced abortion. In the absence of such a definition, each physician and each hospital reaches an individual decision on this matter. How the concept of health is variably defined leads to considerable inequity in the distribution and the accessibility of the abortion procedure.

Various expert doctors testified at trial that therapeutic abortion committees apply widely differing definitions of health. For some committees, psychological health is a justification for therapeutic abortion; for others it is not. Some committees routinely refuse abortions to married women unless they are in physical danger, while for other committees it is possible for a married woman to show that she would suffer psychological harm if she continued with a pregnancy, thereby justifying an abortion. It is not typically possible for women to know in advance what standard of health will be applied by any given committee.

The Chief Justice cites from the opinion of the Ontario High Court attesting to the lack of adequate guidelines for committees charged with determining when an abortion should legally be available. He concludes that "the absence of any clear legal standard to be applied by the committee in reaching its decision is a serious procedural flaw."

> The combined effect of all of these problems with the procedure stipulated in s.251 for access to therapeutic abortions is a failure to comply with the principles of fundamental justice. In *Re B.C. Motor Vehicle Act,* Lamer J. held that "the principles of fundamental justice are to be found in the basic tenets of our legal system." One of the basic tenets of our system of criminal justice is that when Parliament creates a defence to a criminal charge, the defence should not be illusory or so difficult to attain as to be practically illusory. The criminal law is a very special form of governmental regulation, for it seeks to express our society's collective disapprobation of certain acts and omissions. When a defence is provided, especially a specifically-tailored defence to a particular charge, it is because the legislator has determined that the disapprobation of society is not warranted when the conditions of the defence are met.

> Consider then the case of a pregnant married woman who wishes to apply for a therapeutic abortion certificate because she fears that her psychological health would

be impaired seriously if she carried the foetus to term. The uncontroverted evidence reveals that there are many areas in Canada where such a woman would simply not have access to a therapeutic abortion. She may live in an area where no hospital has four doctors; no therapeutic abortion committee can be created. Equally, she may live in a place where the treatment functions of the nearby hospitals do not satisfy the definition of "accredited hospital" in s.251(6). Or she may live in a province where the provincial government has imposed such stringent requirements on hospitals seeking to create therapeutic abortion committees that no hospital can qualify. Alternatively, our hypothetical woman may confront a therapeutic abortion committee in her local hospital which defines "health" in purely physical terms or which refuses to countenance abortions for married women. In each of these cases, it is the administrative structures and procedures established by s.251 itself that would in practice prevent the woman from gaining the benefit of the defence held out to her in s.251(4). ... [*The Chief Justice cites evidence that suggests these problems actually occur.*]

The Crown argues in its supplementary factum that women who face difficulties in obtaining abortions at home can simply travel elsewhere in Canada to procure a therapeutic abortion. That submission would not be especially troubling if the difficulties facing women were not in large measure created by the procedural requirements of s.251 itself. If women were seeking anonymity outside their home town or were simply confronting the reality that it is often difficult to obtain medical services in rural areas, it might be appropriate to say "let them travel." But the evidence establishes convincingly that it is the law itself which in many ways *prevents* access to local therapeutic abortion facilities. The enormous emotional and financial burden placed upon women who must travel long distances from home to obtain an abortion is a burden created in many instances by Parliament. Moreover, it is not accurate to say to women who would seem to qualify under s.251(4) that they can get a therapeutic abortion as long as they are willing to travel. Ms. Carolyn Egan, administrative co-ordinator of the Birth Control and Venereal Disease Centre of Toronto, testified that many hospitals in Toronto had been forced to establish arbitrary abortion quotas, and that some Toronto hospitals restricted access to women inside the geographical area the hospitals were designated to serve. A woman from outside Toronto could run into serious difficulties attempting to procure a therapeutic abortion in that city ... [*cites more examples*].

A majority of this Court held in *R. v. Jones* (1986) that

> The provinces must be given room to make choices regarding the type of administrative structure that will suit their needs unless the use of such structure is in itself so manifestly unfair, having regard to the decisions it is called upon to make, as to violate the principles of *fundamental* justice [*emphasis in original*].

Similarly, Parliament must be given room to design an appropriate administrative and procedural structure for bringing into operation a particular defence to criminal liability. But if that structure is "so manifestly unfair, having regard to the decisions it is called upon to make, as to violate the principles of *fundamental* justice," that structure must be struck down. In the present case, the structure—the system regulating access to therapeutic abortions—is manifestly unfair. It contains so many potential barriers to its own operation that the defence it creates will in many circumstances be practically unavailable to women who would *prima facie* qualify for the defence, or at least would force such women to travel great distances at substantial expense and inconvenience in order to benefit from a defence that is held out to be generally available.

The Chief Justice concludes "that the procedures created in s.251 of the *Criminal Code* for obtaining a therapeutic abortion do not comport with the principles of fundamental justice." He then considers whether section 1 of the *Charter* can "salvage" section 251 of the *Criminal Code*. He notes that a law which infringes any section of the *Charter* can be saved under section 1 only if (1) the objective of the provision is "of sufficient importance to warrant overriding a constitutionally protected right or freedom" and (2) the means chosen in overriding the right are reasonable and demonstrably justified in a free and democratic society. As established in *R. v. Oakes* (1986), the Chief Justice explains that the second step, that of assessing the proportionality of the means to the end, requires meeting three conditions:

> First, the means chosen to achieve an important objective should be rational, fair and not arbitrary. Second, the legislative means should impair as little as possible the right or freedom under consideration. Third, the effects of the limitation upon the relevant right or freedom should not be out of proportion to the objective sought to be achieved.

The Chief Justice considers a side issue, before returning to the two-step assessment required by section 1 of the *Charter*.

> I have no difficulty in concluding that the objective of s.251 as a whole, namely, to balance the competing interests identified by Parliament, is sufficiently important to meet the requirements of the first step in the *Oakes* inquiry under s.1. I think the protection of the interests of pregnant women is a valid governmental objective, where life and health can be jeopardized by criminal sanctions. Like Beetz and Wilson JJ., I agree that protection of foetal interests by Parliament is also a valid governmental objective. It follows that balancing these interests, with the lives and health of women a major factor, is clearly an important governmental objective. As the Court of Appeal stated, "the contemporary view [is] that abortion is not always socially undesirable behavior."

> I am equally convinced, however, that the means chosen to advance the legislative objectives of s.251 do not satisfy any of the three elements of the proportionality component of *R. v. Oakes*. The evidence has led me to conclude that the infringement of the security of the person of pregnant women caused by s.251 is not accomplished in accordance with the principles of fundamental justice. It has been demonstrated that the procedures and administrative structures created by s.251 are often arbitrary and unfair. The procedures established to implement the policy of s.251 impair s.7 rights far more than is necessary because they hold out an illusory defence to many women who would *prima facie* qualify under the exculpatory provisions of s.251(4). In other words, many women whom Parliament professes not to wish to subject to criminal liability will nevertheless be forced by the practical unavailability of the supposed defense to risk liability or to suffer other harm such as a traumatic late abortion caused by the delay inherent in the s.251 system. Finally, the effects of the limitation upon the s.7 rights of many pregnant women are out of proportion to the objective sought to be achieved. Indeed, to the extent that s.251(4) is designed to protect the life and health of women, the procedures it establishes may actually defeat that objective. The administrative structures of s.251(4) are so cumbersome that women whose health is endangered by pregnancy may not be able to gain a therapeutic abortion, at least without great trauma, expense and inconvenience.

> I conclude, therefore, that the cumbersome structure of subs. (4) not only unduly subordinates the s.7 rights of pregnant women but may also defeat the value Parliament itself has established as paramount, namely, the life and health of the

mother. As I have noted, counsel for the Crown did contend that one purpose of the procedures required by subs. (4) is to protect the interests of the foetus. State protection of foetal interests may well be deserving of constitutional recognition under s.1. Still, there can be no escape from the fact that Parliament has failed to establish either a standard or a procedure whereby any such interests might prevail over those of the woman in a fair and non-arbitrary fashion.

Section 251 of the *Criminal Code* cannot be saved, therefore, under s.1 of the *Charter*.

The Chief Justice addresses an issue raised by comments to the jury made by Dr. Morgentaler's lawyer, and then concludes by summarizing the majority position.

Madame Justice Wilson

In her opinion, Madame Justice Wilson raises a more fundamental issue than the assessment of the procedural fairness of section 251 of the *Criminal Code*. As she suggests, "At the heart of this appeal is the question whether a pregnant woman can, as a constitutional matter, be compelled by law to carry the foetus to term." She notes that Chief Justice Dickson and Justice Beetz (the other two judges on the majority position) conclude that the legislation is invalid because the procedures for obtaining abortions fail to comply with the principles of fundamental justice. Madame Justice Wilson believes that before deciding this issue it is necessary to consider whether or not the very restriction of a woman's access to abortion is, itself, unconstitutional.

If a pregnant woman cannot, as a constitutional matter, be compelled by law to carry the foetus to term against her will, a review of the procedural requirements by which she may be compelled to do so seems pointless. Moreover, it would, in my opinion, be an exercise in futility for the legislature to expend its time and energy in attempting to remedy the defects in the procedural requirements unless it has some assurance that this process will, at the end of the day, result in the creation of a valid criminal offence. I turn, therefore, to what I believe is the central issue that must be addressed.

Madame Justice Wilson then asks: "Does s.251 of the *Criminal Code*, which limits the pregnant woman's access to abortion, violate her right to life, liberty and security of the person within the meaning of s.7?"

Leaving aside for the moment the implications of the section for the foetus and addressing only the s.7 right of the pregnant woman, it seems to me that we can say with a fair degree of confidence that a legislative scheme for the obtaining of an abortion which exposes the pregnant woman to a *threat* to her security of the person would violate her right under s.7. Indeed, we have already stated in *Singh v. Minister of Employment and Immigration*, that security of the person even on the purely physical level must encompass freedom from the *threat* of physical punishment or suffering as well as freedom from the actual punishment or suffering itself. In other words, the fact of exposure is enough to violate security of the person. I agree with the Chief Justice and Beetz J. who, for differing reasons, find that pregnant women are exposed to a threat to their physical and psychological security under the legislative scheme set up in s.251 and, since these are aspects of their security of the person, their s.7 right is accordingly violated. But this, of course, does not answer the question whether even the ideal legislative scheme, assuming that it is one which poses no threat to the physical and psychological security of the person of the pregnant woman, would be valid under s.7. I say this for two reasons: (1) because s.7 encompasses more than the right to security of the person; it speaks also of the right to liberty, and (2) because security of the person may encompass more than physical and psychological security; this we have yet to decide.

It seems to me, therefore, that to commence the analysis with the premise that the s.7 right encompasses only a right to physical and psychological security and to fail to deal with the right to liberty in the context of "life, liberty and security of the person" begs the central issue in the case. If either the right to liberty or the right to security of the person or a combination of both confers on the pregnant woman the right to decide for herself (with the guidance of her physician) whether or not to have an abortion, then we have to examine the legislative scheme not only from the point of view of fundamental justice in the procedural sense but in the substantive sense as well. I think, therefore, that we must answer the question: what is meant by the right to liberty in the context of the abortion issue? Does it, as Mr. Manning [the lawyer for Dr. Morgentaler] suggests, give the pregnant woman control over decisions affecting her own body? If not, does her right to security of the person give her such control? I turn first to the right to liberty.

Madame Justice Wilson quotes from Chief Justice Dickson about the need to interpret constitutional rights generously in light of their purpose, and then she inquires into the purpose of the *Charter* in general and of the right to liberty in particular.

The *Charter* is predicated on a particular conception of the place of the individual in society. An individual is not a totally independent entity disconnected from the society in which he or she lives. Neither, however, is the individual a mere cog in an impersonal machine in which his or her values, goals and aspirations are subordinated to those of the collectivity. The individual is a bit of both. The *Charter* reflects this reality by leaving a wide range of activities and decisions open to legitimate government control while at the same time placing limits on the proper scope of that control. Thus, the rights guaranteed in the *Charter* erect around each individual, metaphorically speaking, an invisible fence over which the state will not be allowed to trespass. The role of the courts is to map out, piece by piece, the parameters of the fence.

The *Charter* and the right to individual liberty guaranteed under it are inextricably tied to the concept of human dignity. Professor Neil MacCormick, *Legal Right and Social Democracy: Essays in Legal and Political Philosophy,* speaks of liberty as "a condition of human self-respect and of that contentment which resides in the ability to pursue one's own conception of a full and rewarding life." He says:

> To be able to decide what to do and how to do it, to carry out one's own decisions and accept their consequences, seems to me essential to one's self-respect as a human being, and essential to the possibility of that contentment. Such self-respect and contentment are in my judgment fundamental goods for human beings, the worth of life itself being on condition of having or striving for them. If a person were deliberately denied the opportunity of self-respect and that contentment, he would suffer deprivation of his essential humanity.

Dickson C.J. in *R. v. Big M Drug Mart Ltd.* makes the same point:

> It should also be noted, however, that an emphasis on individual conscience and individual judgment also lies at the heart of our democratic political tradition. The ability of each citizen to make free and informed decisions is the absolute prerequisite for the legitimacy, acceptability, and efficacy of our system of self-government. It is because of the centrality of the rights associated with freedom of individual conscience both to basic beliefs about human worth and dignity and to a free and democratic political system that American jurisprudence has emphasized the primacy or firstness of the First Amendment. It is this same

centrality that in my view underlies their designation in the *Canadian Charter of Rights and Freedoms* as fundamental. They are the *sine qua non* [*the indispensable feature*] of the political tradition underlying the *Charter*.

It was further amplified in Dickson C.J.'s discussion of *Charter* interpretation in *R. v. Oakes*:

> A second contextual element of interpretation of s.1 is provided by the words "free and democratic society." Inclusion of these words as the final standard of justification for limits on rights and freedoms refers the Court to the very purpose for which the *Charter* was originally entrenched in the Constitution: Canadian society is to be free and democratic. The Court must be guided by the values and principles essential to a free and democratic society which I believe embody, to name but a few, respect for the inherent dignity of the human person, commitment to social justice and equality, accommodation of a wide variety of beliefs, respect for cultural and group identity, and faith in social and political institutions which enhance the participation of individuals and groups in society. The underlying values and principles of a free and democratic society are the genesis of the rights and freedoms guaranteed by the *Charter* and the ultimate standard against which a limit on a right or freedom must be shown, despite its effect, to be reasonable and demonstrably justified.

The idea of human dignity finds expression in almost every right and freedom guaranteed in the *Charter*. Individuals are afforded the right to choose their own religion and their own philosophy of life, the right to choose with whom they will associate and how they will express themselves, the right to choose where they will live and what occupation they will pursue. These are all examples of the basic theory underlying the *Charter*, namely that the state will respect choices made by individuals and, to the greatest extent possible, will avoid subordinating these choices to any one conception of the good life.

Thus, an aspect of the respect for human dignity on which the *Charter* is founded is the right to make fundamental personal decisions without interference from the state. This right is a critical component of the right to liberty. Liberty, as was noted in *Singh*, is a phrase capable of a broad range of meaning. In my view, this right, properly construed, grants the individual a degree of autonomy in making decisions of fundamental personal importance.

This view is consistent with the position I took in the case of *R. v. Jones*. One issue raised in that case was whether the right to liberty in s.7 of the *Charter* included a parent's right to bring up his children in accordance with his conscientious beliefs. In concluding that it did I stated:

> I believe that the framers of the Constitution in guaranteeing "liberty" as a fundamental value in a free and democratic society had in mind the freedom of the individual to develop and realize his potential to the full, to plan his own life to suit his own character, to make his own choices for good or ill to be non-conformist, idiosyncratic and even eccentric—to be, in today's parlance, "his own person" and accountable as such. John Stuart Mill described it as "pursuing our own good in our own way." This, he believed, we should be free to do "so long as we do not attempt to deprive others of theirs or impede their efforts to obtain it." He added:
>
> > Each is the proper guardian of his own health, whether bodily *or* mental and spiritual. Mankind are greater gainers by suffering each other to live as seems good to themselves than by compelling each to live as seemsgood to the rest.

Liberty in a free and democratic society does not require the state to approve the personal decisions made by its citizens; it does, however, require the state to respect them.

This conception of the proper ambit of the right to liberty under our *Charter* is consistent with the American jurisprudence on the subject. While care must undoubtedly be taken to avoid a mechanical application of concepts developed in different cultural and constitutional contexts, I would respectfully agree with the observation of my colleague, Estey J., in *Law Society of Upper Canada v. Skapinker* (1984):

> With the *Constitution Act, 1982* comes a new dimension, a new yardstick of reconciliation between the individual and the community and their respective rights, a dimension which, like the balance of the Constitution, remains to be interpreted and applied by the Court.

> The courts in the United States have had almost two hundred years experience at this task and it is of more than passing interest to those concerned with these new developments in Canada to study the experience of the United States courts.

Madame Justice Wilson reviews a number of American cases from 1920 until 1973 in the which the U.S. Supreme Court upheld the fundamental freedom of individuals to direct their own lives.

> For our purposes the most interesting developments in this area of American law are the decisions of the Supreme Court in *Roe v. Wade*, and its sister case *Doe v. Bolton* (1973). In *Roe v. Wade* the Court held that a pregnant woman has the right to decide whether or not to terminate her pregnancy. This conclusion, the majority stated, was mandated by the body of existing law ensuring that the state would not be allowed to interfere with certain fundamental personal decisions such as education, child-rearing, procreation, marriage and contraception. The Court concluded that the right to privacy found in the Fourteenth Amendment guarantee of liberty "... is broad enough to encompass a woman's decision whether or not to terminate her pregnancy."

> This right was not, however, to be taken as absolute. At some point the legitimate state interests in the protection of health, proper medical standards, and pre-natal life would justify its qualification. Professor Tribe, *American Constitutional Law* (1978), conveniently summarizes the limits the Court found to be inherent in the woman's right. I quote:

>> Specifically, the Court held that, because the woman's right to decide whether or not to end a pregnancy is fundamental, only a compelling interest can justify state regulation impinging in any way upon that right. During the first trimester of pregnancy, when abortion is less hazardous in terms of the woman's life than carrying the child to term would be, the state may require only that the abortion be performed by a licensed physician; no further regulations peculiar to abortion as such are compellingly justified in that period.

>> After the first trimester, the compelling state interest in the mother's health permits it to adopt reasonable regulations in order to promote safe abortions— but requiring abortions to be performed in hospitals, or only after approval of another doctor or committee in addition to the woman's physician, is impermissible, as is requiring that the abortion procedure employ a technique that, however preferable from a medical perspective, is not widely available.

Once the fetus is viable, in the sense that it is capable of survival outside the uterus with artificial aid, the state interest in preserving the fetus becomes compelling, and the state may thus proscribe its premature removal (i.e., its abortion) except to preserve the mother's life or health.

The decision in *Roe v. Wade* was re-affirmed by the Supreme Court in *City of Akron v. Akron Centre for Reproductive Health Inc.* (1983), and again, though by a bare majority, in *Thornburgh v. American College of Obstetricians and Gynecologists* (1986). In *Thornburgh*, Blackburn J., speaking for the majority, identifies the core value which the American courts have found to inhere in the concept of liberty. He states:

Our cases long have recognized that the Constitution embodies a promise that a certain private sphere of individual liberty will be kept largely beyond the reach of government . ... [citations omitted]. That promise extends to women as well as to men. Few decisions are more personal and intimate, more properly private, or more basic to individual dignity and autonomy, than a woman's decision—with the guidance of her physician and within the limits specified in *Roe*—whether to end her pregnancy. A woman's right to make that choice freely is fundamental. Any other result, in our view, would protect inadequately a central part of the sphere of liberty that our law guarantees equally to all.

In my opinion, the respect for individual decision-making in matters of fundamental personal importance reflected in the American jurisprudence also informs the Canadian *Charter*. Indeed, as the Chief Justice pointed out in *R. v. Big M Drug Mart Ltd.*, beliefs about human worth and dignity "are the *sine qua non* of the political tradition underlying the *Charter*." I would conclude, therefore, that the right to liberty contained in s.7 guarantees to every individual a degree of personal autonomy over important decisions intimately affecting their private lives.

The question then becomes whether the decision of a woman to terminate her pregnancy falls within this class of protected decisions. I have no doubt that it does. This decision is one that will have profound psychological, economic and social consequences for the pregnant woman. The circumstances giving rise to it can be complex and varied and there may be, and usually are, powerful considerations militating in opposite directions. It is a decision that deeply reflects the way the woman thinks about herself and her relationship to others and to society at large. It is not just a medical decision; it is a profound social and ethical one as well. Her response to it will be the response of the whole person.

It is probably impossible for a man to respond, even imaginatively, to such a dilemma not just because it is outside the realm of his personal experience (although this is, of course, the case) but because he can relate to it only by objectifying it, thereby eliminating the subjective elements of the female psyche which are at the heart of the dilemma. As Noreen Burrows has pointed out in her essay on "International Law and Human Rights: The Case of Women's Rights," in *Human Rights: From Rhetoric to Reality,* the history of the struggle for human rights from the eighteenth century on has been the history of men struggling to assert their dignity and common humanity against an overbearing state apparatus. The more recent struggle for women's rights has been a struggle to eliminate discrimination, to achieve a place for women in a man's world, to develop a set of legislative reforms in order to place women in the same position as men. It has *not* been a struggle to define the rights of women in relation to their special place in the societal structure and in relation to the biological distinction between the two sexes. Thus, women's needs and aspirations are only now being translated into protected rights. The right to reproduce or not to reproduce which is in issue in this case is one such right and is properly perceived as an integral part of modern woman's struggle to assert *her* dignity and worth as a human being.

Given then that the right to liberty guaranteed by s.7 of the *Charter* gives a woman the right to decide for herself whether or not to terminate her pregnancy, does s.251 of the *Criminal Code* violate this right? Clearly it does. The purpose of the section is to take the decision away from the woman and give it to a committee. Furthermore, as the Chief Justice correctly points out, the committee bases its decision on "criteria entirely unrelated to [the pregnant woman's] priorities and aspirations." The fact that the decision whether a woman will be allowed to terminate her pregnancy is in the hands of a committee is just as great a violation of the woman's right to personal autonomy in decisions of an intimate and private nature as it would be if a committee were established to decide whether a woman should be allowed to continue her pregnancy. Both these arrangements violate the woman's right to liberty by deciding for her something that she has the right to decide for herself.

Madame Justice Wilson briefly discusses the way in which the *Criminal Code* provisions infringe the security of the person before considering whether section 7 "principles of fundamental justice" have been respected.

Does s.251 deprive women of their right to liberty and to security of the person "in accordance with the principles of fundamental justice"? I agree with Lamer J. who stated in *Re B.C. Motor Vehicle Act* that the principles of fundamental justice "cannot be given any exhaustive content or simple enumerative definition, but will take on concrete meaning as the courts address alleged violations of s.7." In the same judgment Lamer J. also stated:

> In other words, the principles of fundamental justice are to be found in the basic tenets of our legal system. They do not lie in the realm of general public policy but in the inherent domain of the judiciary as guardian of the justice system. Such an approach to the interpretation of "principles of fundamental justice" is consistent with the wording and structure of s.7, the context of the section, i.e., ss.8 to 14, and the character and larger objects of the *Charter* itself. It provides meaningful content for the s.7 guarantee all the while avoiding adjudication of policy matters.

While Lamer J. draws mainly upon ss.8 to 14 of the *Charter* to give substantive content to the principles of fundamental justice, he does not preclude, but seems rather to encourage, the idea that recourse may be had to other rights guaranteed by the *Charter* for the same purpose. The question, therefore, is whether the deprivation of the s.7 right is in accordance not only with procedural fairness (and I agree with the Chief Justice and Beetz J. for the reasons they give that it is not) but also with the fundamental rights and freedoms laid down elsewhere in the *Charter*.

This approach to s.7 is supported by comments made by La Forest J. in *Lyons v. The Queen* (1987). He urged that the rights enshrined in the *Charter* should not be read in isolation. Rather, he states:

> ... the *Charter* protects a complex of interacting values, each more or less fundamental to the free and democratic society that is Canada (*R. v. Oakes*), and the particularization of rights and freedoms contained in the *Charter* thus represents a somewhat artificial, if necessary and intrinsically worthwhile attempt to structure and focus the judicial exposition of such rights and freedoms. The necessity of structuring the discussion should not, however, lead us to overlook the importance of appreciating the manner in which the amplification of the content of each enunciated right and freedom imbues and informs our understandings of the value structure sought to be protected by the *Charter* as

a whole and, in particular, of the content of the other specific rights and freedoms it embodies.

I believe, therefore, that a deprivation of the s.7 right which has the effect of infringing a right guaranteed elsewhere in the *Charter* cannot be in accordance with the principles of fundamental justice.

In my view, the deprivation of the s.7 right with which we are concerned in this case offends s.2(a) of the *Charter*. I say this because I believe that the decision whether or not to terminate a pregnancy is essentially a moral decision, a matter of conscience. I do not think there is or can be any dispute about that. The question is: whose conscience? Is the conscience of the woman to be paramount or the conscience of the state? I believe, for the reasons I gave in discussing the right to liberty, that in a free and democratic society it must be the conscience of the individual. Indeed, s.2(a) makes it clear that this freedom belongs to "everyone," i.e., to each of us individually.

Madame Justice Wilson quotes at length from Chief Justice Dickson's comments in *R. v. Big M Drug Mart Ltd.* on the nature and importance of the right enshrined in section 2(a), including his observations that:

... The values that underlie our political and philosophic traditions demand that every individual be free to hold and to manifest whatever beliefs and opinions his or her conscience dictates, provided *inter alia* only that such manifestations do not injure his or her neighbours or their parallel rights to hold and manifest beliefs and opinions of their own ... [*further references to the Chief Justice's remarks*].

As is pointed out by Professor C.E.M. Joad: *Guide to the Philosophy of Morals and Politics*, the role of the state in a democracy is to establish the background conditions under which individual citizens may pursue the ethical values which in their view underlie the good life. He states:

For the welfare of the state is nothing apart from the good of the citizens who compose it. It is no doubt true that a State whose citizens are compelled to go right is more efficient than one whose citizens are free to go wrong. But what then? To sacrifice freedom in the interests of efficiency, is to sacrifice what confers upon human beings their humanity. It is no doubt easy to govern a flock of sheep; but there is no credit in the governing, and, if the sheep were born as men, no virtue in the sheep.

Professor Joad further emphasizes that individuals in a democratic society can never be treated "merely as means to ends beyond themselves" because:

To the right of the individual to be treated as an end, which entails his right to the full development and expression of his personality, all other rights and claims must, the democrat holds, be subordinated. I do not know how this principle is to be defended any more than I can frame a defence for the principles of democracy and liberty. ... [*refers to and cites other remarks by Professor Joad*]

It seems to me, therefore, that in a free and democratic society "freedom of conscience and religion" should be broadly construed to extend to conscientiously-held beliefs, whether grounded in religion or in a secular morality. Indeed, as a matter of statutory interpretation, "conscience" and "religion" should not be treated as tautologous if capable of independent, although related, meaning. Accordingly, for the state to take sides on the issue of abortion, as it does in the impugned legislation by making it a criminal offence for the pregnant woman to exercise one of her options, is not only to endorse but also to enforce, on pain of a further loss of liberty through actual imprisonment, one conscientiously-held view at the expense of another. It is to deny freedom of conscience to some, to treat them as means to an end, to deprive them, as Professor MacCormick puts it, of their "essential humanity." Can this comport with fundamental justice? Was Blackmun J. not correct when he said in *Thornburgh*:

> A woman's right to make that choice freely is fundamental. Any other result ... would protect inadequately a central part of the sphere of liberty that our law guarantees equally to all.

> Legislation which violates freedom of conscience in this manner cannot, in my view, be in accordance with the principles of fundamental justice within the meaning of s.7.

Madame Justice Wilson concludes her opinion by arguing why section 251 of the *Criminal Code* cannot be saved under section 1 of the *Charter*.

Justice McIntyre

In the sole dissenting opinion, endorsed by Justice La Forest, Justice McIntyre argues that the *Criminal Code* provisions on abortion are consistent with the *Charter*. He opens with a summary of the relevant legislation and a discussion of the role of the courts in reviewing legislation. Justice McIntyre stresses that "the courts must confine themselves to such democratic values as are clearly found and expressed in the *Charter* and refrain from imposing or creating other values so based."

> It follows, then, in my view, that the task of the Court in this case is not to solve nor seek to solve what might be called the abortion issue, but simply to measure the content of s.251 against the *Charter*. While this may appear to be self-evident, the distinction is of vital importance. If a particular interpretation enjoys no support, express or reasonably implied, from the *Charter*, then the Court is without power to clothe such an interpretation with constitutional status. It is not for the Court to substitute its own views on the merits of a given question for those of Parliament. The Court must consider not what is, in its view, the best solution to the problems posed; its role is confined to deciding whether the solution enacted by Parliament offends the *Charter*. If it does, the provision must be struck down or declared inoperative, and Parliament may then enact such different provisions as it may decide.

Justice McIntyre quotes from the famous American jurist Oliver Wendell Holmes about the need for judicial restraint:

> I think the proper course is to recognize that a state legislature can do whatever it sees fit to do unless it is restrained by some express prohibition in the Constitution of the United States or of the State, and that Courts should be careful not to extend such prohibitions beyond their obvious meaning by reading into them conceptions of public policy that the particular Court may happen to entertain.

In summarizing the American position on constitutional review, Justice McIntyre cites a 1963 U.S. case: "We have returned to the constitutional proposition that courts do not substitute their social and economic beliefs for the judgment of legislative bodies, who are elected to pass laws."

> It is essential that this principle be maintained in a constitutional democracy. The Court must not resolve an issue such as that of abortion on the basis of how many judges may favour "pro-choice" or "pro-life." To do so would be contrary to sound principle and the rule of law affirmed in the preamble to the *Charter* which must mean that no discretion, including a judicial discretion, can be unlimited. But there is a problem, for the Court must clothe the general expression of rights and freedoms

contained in the *Charter* with real substance and vitality. How can the Courts go about this task without imposing at least some of their views and predilections upon the law? This question has been the subject of much discussion and comment. Many theories have been postulated but few have had direct reference to the problem in the Canadian context. In my view, this Court has offered guidance in this matter. In such cases as *Hunter v. Southam Inc.,* and *R. v. Big M Drug Mart Ltd.*, it has enjoined what has been termed a "purposive approach" in applying the *Charter* and its provisions. I take this to mean that the Courts should interpret the *Charter* in a manner calculated to give effect to its provisions, not to the idiosyncratic view of the judge who is writing. This approach marks out the limits of appropriate *Charter* adjudication. It confines the content of *Charter* guaranteed rights and freedoms to the purposes given expression in the *Charter*. Consequently, while the courts must continue to give a fair, large and liberal construction to the *Charter* provisions, this approach prevents the Court from abandoning its traditional adjudicatory function in order to formulate its own conclusions on questions of public policy, a step which this Court has said on numerous occasions it must not take. That *Charter* interpretation is to be purposive necessarily implies the converse: it is not to be "non-purposive." A court is not entitled to define a right in a manner unrelated to the interest which the right in question was meant to protect. I endeavoured to formulate an approach to the problem in *Reference Re Public Service Employee Relations Act* (1987), in these words:

> It follows that while a liberal and not overly legalistic approach should be taken to constitutional interpretation, the *Charter* should not be regarded as an empty vessel to be filled with whatever meaning we might wish from time to time. The interpretation of the *Charter,* as of all constitutional documents, is constrained by the language, structure and history of the constitutional text, by constitutional tradition, and by the history, traditions, and underlying philosophies of our society.

The approach, as I understand it, does not mean that judges may not make some policy choices when confronted with competing conceptions of the extent of rights or freedoms. Difficult choices must be made and the personal views of judges will unavoidably be engaged from time to time. The decisions made by judges, however, and the interpretations that they advance or accept must be plausibly inferable from something in the *Charter*. It is not for the courts to manufacture a constitutional right out of whole cloth. I conclude on the question by citing and adopting the following words, although spoken in dissent, from the judgment of Harlan J. in *Reynolds v. Sims* (1964), which, in my view, while stemming from the American experience, are equally applicable in a consideration of the Canadian position. Harlan J. commented on the:

> ... current mistaken view of the Constitution and the constitutional function of this Court. This view, in a nutshell, is that every major social ill in this country can find its cure in some constitutional "principle," and that this Court should take the lead in promoting reform when other branches of government fail to act. The Constitution is not a panacea for every blot upon the public welfare, nor should this Court, ordained as a judicial body, be thought of as a general haven for reform movements. The Constitution is an instrument of government, fundamental to which is the premise that in a diffusion of governmental authority lies the greatest promise that this Nation will realize liberty for all its citizens. This Court, limited in function in accordance with that premise, does not serve its high purpose when it exceeds its authority, even to satisfy justified impatience with the slow workings of the political process. For when, in the name of constitutional interpretation, the Court *adds* something to the Constitution that

was deliberately excluded from it, the Court in reality substitutes its view of what should be so for the amending process.

Justice McIntyre turns to consider the positions held by Chief Justice Dickson and Madame Justice Wilson on the constitutionality of the *Criminal Code* provisions on abortion.

The judgment of my colleague, Wilson J., is based upon the proposition that a pregnant woman has a right, under s.7 of the *Charter,* to have an abortion. The same concept underlies the judgment of the Chief Justice. He reached the conclusion that a law which forces a woman to carry a foetus to term, unless certain criteria are met which are unrelated to her own priorities and aspirations, impairs the security of her person. That, in his view, is the effect of s.251 of the *Criminal Code.* He has not said in specific terms that the pregnant woman has the right to an abortion, whether therapeutic or otherwise. In my view, however, his whole position depends for its validity upon that proposition and that interference with the right constitutes an infringement of her right to security of the person. It is said that a law which forces a woman to carry a foetus to term unless she meets certain criteria unrelated to her own priorities and aspirations interferes with security of her person. If compelling a woman to complete her pregnancy interferes with security of her person, it can only be because the concept of security of her person includes a right not to be compelled to carry the child to completion of her pregnancy. This, then, is simply to say that she has a right to have an abortion. It follows, then, that if no such right can be shown, it cannot be said that security of her person has been infringed by state action or otherwise.

All laws, it must be noted, have the potential for interference with individual priorities and aspirations. In fact, the very purpose of most legislation is to cause such interference. It is only when such legislation goes beyond interfering with priorities and aspirations, and abridges rights, that courts may intervene. If a law prohibited membership in a lawful association it would be unconstitutional, not because it would interfere with priorities and aspirations, but because of its interference with the guaranteed right of freedom of association under s.2(d) of the *Charter.* Compliance with the *Income Tax Act* has, no doubt, frequently interfered with priorities and aspirations. The taxing provisions are not, however, on that basis unconstitutional, because the ordinary taxpayer enjoys no right to be tax free. Other frustrations may be found. In my view, it is clear that before it could be concluded that any enactment infringed the concept of security of the person, it would have to infringe some underlying right included in or protected by the concept. For the appellants to succeed here, then, they must show more than an interference with priorities and aspirations; they must show the infringement of a right which is included in the concept of security of the person.

The proposition that woman enjoy a constitutional right to have an abortion is devoid of support in the language of s.7 of the *Charter* or any other section. While some human rights documents, such as the American Convention on Human Rights, 1969, expressly address the question of abortion, the *Charter* is entirely silent on the point. It may be of some significance that the *Charter* uses specific language in dealing with other topics, such as voting rights, religion, expression and such controversial matters as mobility rights, language rights and minority rights, but remains silent on the question of abortion which, at the time the *Charter* was under consideration, was as much a subject of public controversy as it is today. Furthermore, it would appear that the history of the constitutional text of the *Charter* affords no support for the appellants' proposition.

Justice McIntyre refers to the Minutes of the Special Joint Committee of Senate and House of Commons on the Constitution of Canada where the government explained that it did not wish to see the courts make use of the *Charter* to second-guess legislative decisions on issues such as abortion and capital punishment. Justice McIntyre then outlines the history of abortion legislation from early English law until the passing of the latest changes in the *Criminal Code* in 1969 to indicate that "that there has never been a general right to abortion in Canada."

> There has always been clear recognition of a public interest in the protection of the unborn and there has been no evidence or indication of any general acceptance of the concept of abortion at will in our society. It is to be observed as well that at the time of adoption of the *Charter* the sole provision for an abortion in Canadian law was that to be found in s.251 of the *Criminal Code*. It follows then, in my view, that the interpretive approach to the *Charter*, which has been accepted in this Court, affords no support for the entrenchment of a constitutional right of abortion.
>
> As to an asserted right to be free from any state interference with bodily integrity and serious state-imposed psychological stress, I would say that to be accepted, as a constitutional right, it would have to be based on something more than the mere imposition, by the State, of such stress and anxiety. It must, surely, be evident that many forms of government action deemed to be reasonable, and even necessary in our society, will cause stress and anxiety to many, while at the same time being acceptable exercises of government power in pursuit of socially desirable goals. The very facts of life in a modern society would preclude the entrenchment of such a constitutional right. Governmental action for the due governance and administration of society can rarely please everyone. It is hard to imagine a governmental policy or initiative which will not create significant stress or anxiety for some and, frequently, for many members of the community. Governments must have the power to expropriate land, to zone land, to regulate its use and the rights and conditions of its occupation. The exercise of these powers is frequently the cause of serious stress and anxiety. In the interests of public health and welfare, governments must have and exercise the power to regulate, control—and even suppress—aspects of the manufacture, sale and distribution of alcohol and drugs and other dangerous substances. Stress and anxiety resulting from the exercise of such powers cannot be a basis for denying them to the authorities. At the present time there is great pressure on governments to restrict—and even forbid—the use of tobacco. Government action in this field will produce much stress and anxiety among smokers and growers of tobacco, but it cannot be said that this will render unconstitutional control and regulatory measures adopted by governments. Other illustrations abound to make the point.

Justice McIntyre explains that any infringement of the right of security of the person would have to be more than a matter of stress or strain: "A breach of the right would have to be based upon an infringement of some interest which would be of such nature and such importance as to warrant constitutional protection." To support his view that abortion has achieved this stature, Justice McIntyre refers to the following comment by a lower court judge who heard the *Morgentaler* case: "bearing in mind the statutory prohibition against abortion in Canada which has existed for over 100 years, it could not be said that there is a right to procure an abortion so deeply rooted in our traditions and way of life as to be fundamental. A woman's only right to an abortion at the time the *Charter* came into force would accordingly appear to be that given to her by s-s. (4) of s.251."

It is for these reasons I would conclude, that save for the provisions of the *Criminal Code,* which permit abortion where the life or health of the woman is at risk, no right of abortion can be found in Canadian law, custom or tradition, and that the *Charter,* including s.7, creates no further right. Accordingly, it is my view that s.251 of the *Code* does not in its terms violate s.7 of the *Charter.* Even accepting the assumption that the concept of security of the person would extend to vitiating a law which would require a woman to carry a child to the completion of her pregnancy at the risk of her life or health, it must be observed that this is not our case. As has been pointed out, s.251 of the *Code* already provides for abortion in such circumstances.

Justice McIntyre then considers arguments that section 251 of the *Criminal Code* fails to secure procedural fairness.

It is pointed out that therapeutic abortions are available only in accredited or approved hospitals, that hospitals so accredited or approved may or may not appoint abortion committees, and that "health" is defined in vague terms which afford no clear guide to its meaning. Statistically, it was said that abortions could be lawfully performed in only twenty per cent of all hospitals in Canada. Because abortions are not generally available to all women who seek them, the argument goes, the defence is illusory, or practically so, and the section therefore fails to comport with the principles of fundamental justice.

Precise evidence on the questions raised is, of course, difficult to obtain and subject to subjective interpretation depending upon the views of those adducing it. Much evidence was led at trial based largely on the Ontario experience. Additional material in the form of articles, reports and studies was adduced, from which the Court was invited to conclude that access to abortion is not evenly provided across the country and that this could be the source of much dissatisfaction. While I recognize that in constitutional cases a greater latitude has been allowed concerning the reception of such material, I would prefer to place principal reliance upon the evidence given under oath in court in my considerations of the factual matters. Evidence was adduced from the chairman of a therapeutic abortion committee at a hospital in Hamilton, where in 1982 eleven hundred and eighty-seven abortions were performed, who testified that of all applications received by his committee in that year less than a dozen were ultimately refused. Refusal in each case was based upon the fact that a majority of the committee was not convinced that "the continuation of the pregnancy would be detrimental to the woman's health." All physicians who performed abortions under the *Criminal Code* provisions admitted in cross-examination that they had never had an application for a therapeutic abortion on behalf of the patient ultimately refused by an abortion committee. No woman testified that she personally had applied for an abortion anywhere in Canada and had been refused, and no physician testified to his participation in such an application. In 1982, the Province of Ontario had ninety-nine hospitals with abortion committees. In that year in Ontario, hospitals performed 31,379 abortions and thirty-six of those hospitals performed more than two hundred in one year. There were seventeen hospitals with abortion committees in metropolitan Toronto and they performed 16,706 abortions in 1982, nine of them performing more than one thousand abortions each. In 1982 all ten provinces and both territories had at least one hospital with an abortion committee. The evidence was not as clear as to the situation in rural or more remote areas. It would be reasonable to assume that access to abortion would have been more difficult outside of the principal inhabited areas. This situation, however, is common to the delivery of all health-care services. Significantly, the testimony and exhibits entered at trial reflect that even in the more permissive abortion regime in the United States there is a similar problem of access. Ten years after the decision in *Roe v. Wade* (1973), only slight gains in access had been made in rural areas. It is also worth noting that the evidence adduced at trial, comparing the respective abortion regimes in Canada and the United States, reveals other significant parallels. For example, there is a close parallel in the two countries concerning such matters as the stage in the pregnancy at which abortions are performed and the procedures used to perform abortions at the respective stages. There is also a high degree of similarity in the two countries regarding the percentages and methods of abortion performed in the crucial early trimester. In both countries, it appears that many of the problems that have arisen in relation to abortion reflect the more general reality that medical services are subject to budgetary, time, space and staff constraints. With abortion, in particular, matters are further complicated by the fact that many physicians regard abortions as unethical and refuse to perform them. In all, the extent to which the statutory procedure contributes to the problems connected with procuring an abortion is anything but clear. Accordingly, even if one accepts that it would be contrary to the principles of fundamental justice for Parliament to make available a defence which, by reason of its terms, is illusory or practically so, it cannot, in my view, be said that s.251 of the *Code* has had that effect.

It would seem to me that a defence created by Parliament could only be said to be illusory or practically so when the *defence is not available in the circumstance in which it is held out as being available*. The very nature of the test assumes, of course, that it is for Parliament to define the defence and, in so doing, to designate the terms and conditions upon which it may be available. The Chief Justice has said in his reasons:

> The criminal law is a very special form of governmental regulation, for it seeks to express our society's collective disapprobation of certain acts and omissions. When a defence is provided, especially a specifically-tailored defence to a particular charge, it is because the legislator has determined that the disapprobation of society is not warranted when the conditions of the defence are met.

From this comment, I would suggest it is apparent that the Court's role is not to second-guess Parliament's policy choice as to how broad or how narrow the defence should be. The determination of when "the disapprobation of society is not warranted" is in Parliament's hands. The Court's role when the enactment is attacked on the basis that the defence is illusory is to determine whether the defence is available in the circumstances in which it was intended to apply. Parliament has set out the conditions, in s.251(4), under which a therapeutic abortion may be obtained, free from criminal sanction. It is patent on the face of the legislation that the defence is circumscribed and narrow. It is clear that this was the Parliamentary intent and it was expressed with precision. I am not able to accept the contention that the defence has been held out to be generally available. It is, on the contrary, carefully tailored and limited to special circumstances. Therapeutic abortions may be performed only in certain hospitals and in accordance with certain specified provisions. It could only be classed as illusory or practically so if it could be found that it does not provide lawful access to abortions in circumstances described in the section. No such finding should be made upon the material before this Court. The evidence will not support the proposition that significant numbers of those who meet the conditions imposed in s.251 of the *Criminal Code* are denied abortions.

It is evident that what the appellants advocate is not the therapeutic abortion referred to in s.251 of the *Code*. Their clinic was called into being because of the perceived inadequacies of s.251. They propose and seek to justify "abortion on demand." The defence in s.251(4) was not intended to meet the views of the appellants and provide a defence at large which would effectively repeal the operative subsections of s.251 Some feel strongly that s.251 is not adequate in today's society. Be that as it may, it does not follow that the defence provisions of s.251(4) are illusory. They represent the legislative choice on this question and, as noted, it has not been shown that therapeutic abortions have not been available in cases contemplated by the provision.

It was further argued that the defence in s.251(4) is procedurally unfair in that it fails to provide an adequate standard of "health" to guide the abortion committees which are charged with the responsibility for approving or disapproving applications for abortions. It is argued that the meaning of the word "health" in s.251(4) is so vague as to render the subsection unconstitutional. This argument was, in my view, dealt with fully and effectively in the Court of Appeal. I accept and adopt the following passage from the judgment of that court:

> Counsel for the respondent in his attack on s.251 also argued that the section was void for "vagueness." The argument under this head was that the concepts of "health" and "miscarriage" in s.251(4) yield an arbitrary application being so vague and uncertain that it is difficult to understand what conduct is proscribed. It is fundamental justice that a person charged with an offence should know with sufficient particularity the nature of the offence alleged.

> There was a far-ranging discussion by the respondents' counsel on the concept of "health" and the meaning of the term "miscarriage"; the way in which courts deal with the vagueness in the interpretation of municipal by-laws, and an extensive examination of American authorities.

> In this case, however, from a reading of s.251 with its exception, there is no difficulty in determining what is proscribed and what is permitted. It cannot be said that no sensible meaning can be given to the words of the section. Thus, it is for the courts to say what meaning the statute will bear. Counsel was unable to give the Court any authority for holding a statute void for uncertainty. In any event, there is no doubt the respondents knew that the acts they proposed and carried out were in breach of the section. The fact that they did not approve of the law in this regard does not make it uncertain. They could have no doubt but that the procuring of a miscarriage which they proposed (and we agree with the trial judge that the phrase "procuring a miscarriage" is synonymous with "performing an abortion"), could only be carried out in an accredited or approved hospital after the securing of the required certificate in writing from the therapeutic abortion committee of that hospital.

Finally, this Court has dealt with the matter. Dickson J. (as he then was), speaking for the majority in *Morgentaler* (1975) in concluding a discussion of s.251(4) of the *Criminal Code*, said:

> Whether one agrees with the Canadian legislation or not is quite beside the point. Parliament has spoken unmistakably in clear and unambiguous language.

In the same case, Laskin C.J., while dissenting on other grounds, said:

> The contention under point 2 is equally untenable as an attempt to limit the substance of legislation in a situation which does not admit of it. In submitting that the standard upon which therapeutic abortion committees must act is uncertain and subjective, counsel who make the submission cannot find nourishment for it even in *Doe v. Bolton*. There it was held that the prohibition of abortion by a physician except when "based upon his best clinical judgment that an abortion is necessary" did not prescribe a standard so vague as to be constitutionally vulnerable. *A fortiori* [*even more so*], under the approach taken here to substantive due process, the argument of uncertainty and subjectivity fails. It is enough to say that Parliament has fixed a manageable standard

because it is addressed to a professional panel, the members of which would be expected to bring a practised judgment to the question whether "continuation of the pregnancy ... would or would be likely to endanger ... life or health."

In my opinion, then, the contention that the defence provided in s.251(4) of the *Criminal Code* is illusory cannot be supported. From evidence adduced by the appellants, it may be said that many women seeking abortions have been unable to get them in Canada because s.252(4) fails to respond to this need. Section 251(4) was designed to meet specific circumstances. Its aim is to restrict abortion to cases where the continuation of the pregnancy would, or would likely, be injurious to the life or health of the woman concerned, not to provide unrestricted access to abortion. It was to meet this requirement that Parliament provided for the administrative procedures to invoke the defence in subs. (4). This machinery was considered adequate to deal with the type of abortion Parliament had envisaged. When, however, as the evidence would indicate, many more would seek abortions on a basis far wider than that contemplated by Parliament, any system would come under stress and possibly fail. It is not without significance that many of the appellants' clients did not meet the standard set or did not seek to invoke it and that is why their clinic took them in. What has confronted the scheme has been a flood of demands for abortions, some of which could meet the tests of s.251(4) and many which could not. In so far as it may be said that the administrative scheme of the Act has operated inefficiently, a proposition which may be highly questionable, it is caused principally by forces external to the statute, the external circumstances being a general demand for abortion. It is not open to a court, in my view, to strike down a statutory provision on this basis.

Justice McIntyre then reviews his answers to the issues raised by the case, and offers concluding observations about the need to leave questions of public policy to the legislators.

SECTION FOUR:

REFERENCES

Notes

PREFACE

1   Both Moore (1981, p. 154) and Morawetz (1990, pp. 36-37) refer to endless preoccupation with theories of judicial reasoning. Scholars have generally assumed commonality in the fundamental structure of judicial reasoning in legal systems within the Anglo-American tradition. See, for example, Casswell (1982, p. 132), Dworkin (1986, pp. 1-44), and MacCormick (1978, pp. 11-12). This is not to deny important differences among these jurisdictions. For example, Honore (1983, pp. 48-49) suggests that American and British judges' authority to overrule long-standing precedents may differ because of different constitutional arrangements.

CHAPTER 1: JUDICIAL TYRANNY OR ENDANGERED INSTITUTION?

2   There has been a spate of "grand theories" about the appropriate role of the judiciary within a constitutional democracy (Tushnet, 1988, p. 1). Dworkin (1986, p. 11) writes: "No department of state is more important than our courts, and none is so thoroughly misunderstood by the governed ... [P]opular opinion about judges and judging is a sad affair of empty slogans, and I include the opinions of many working lawyers and judges when they are writing or talking about what they do." The bitter debate over the proposed appointment of Robert Bork as United States Supreme Court justice raised fundamental questions about judges' legitimate role in applying the U.S. Constitution. See, for example, Dworkin (1984, 1985, 1987). Richards (1979, p. 1395) believes that American jurisprudence is in the midst of a major "paradigm shift," and Wolfe (1986, p. 321) thinks that American constitutional law is in a "most unsettled state." Waluchow (1994, p. 2) characterizes jurisprudence as being in a state of "chaos."

3   Kovesi (1971) uses the term "formal" in a similar way. Formal theorizing is not identical with "formalism," which is a particular formal theory of legal reasoning that describes judicial decisions in terms of straightforward, deductive inferences from uncontroversial legal rules or standards. Hart's conception of law as a collection of primary and secondary rules is an example of a formal theory. Formal theorizing is descriptive, in that it must faithfully portray the recognized practices of a given system, but it also has a normative dimension—it explains what practitioners would do if they operated in accordance with the norms prescribed by their system. MacCormick (1978, pp. 12-13) describes his (formal) theory of judicial reasoning as "an attempt to explicate and explain the criteria as to what constitutes a good or a bad, an acceptable or an unacceptable type of argument in law." Formal theories account for "proper" rather than "typical" behaviour. This distinction underlies the following remarks by Raz (1983, p. 181) concerning his theory of precedent: "My observations are meant to be faithful to the accepted theory of practice rather than to the practice itself. Their aim is to explain the way judges and legal scholars regard the working of the doctrine of precedent. Only an empirical study going beyond the examination of the law reports could record to what extent the actual practice conforms to these theories." The normative dimension of formal theories, unlike that of evaluative theories, does not imply a justification or evaluation of the norms embedded in a given system: the most plausible formal theory about legal practice need not presume that particular laws, or the system generally, are ethically defensible. In other words, although a formal theory implies normative conceptions of judicial responsibility, it does not assess

the ethical merits of these *legal* obligations. MacCormick (1978, p. 13) offers a compatible observation: "My conclusions therefore present a double face: they are both in their own right normative and yet I believe them to describe norms actually operative within the systems under study." See Waluchow (1990) for a discussion of the kinds of normative forces implied by legal theories and Case (1993) for a discussion of formal and other types of legal theories.

4   The phrase mechanical "application of iron rules" was coined by Frederick Pollock and Frederic William Maitland in their classic text, *History of English Law* (cited in Kennedy, 1973, p. 392). In commenting on those who criticize the mechanical application position, Dworkin (1980, pp. 15-16) notes that their difficulty is in finding practitioners who actually adhered to the position: "So far they have had little luck in caging and exhibiting mechanical jurisprudents (all specimens captured—even Blackstone and Joseph Beale—have had to be released after careful reading of their texts)."

5   Canadian references are to Russell (1983, p. 52), Fulford (1986, p. 9), and Madame Justice Claire L'Heureux-Dube's comments in McCormick and Greene (1990, p. 228). See also Mandel (1994, pp. 39-71). The British legislator's comment, made in 1954 by Health Minister Aneurin Bevan, is cited in Jowell (1986, p. 7). The comments by U.S. Presidential hopeful Pat Buchanan are found in McCarthy (1996, p. 17); the other American references are to Tushnet (1983, pp. 787-789; 1988, pp. 16-17) and Agresto (1984, pp. 9-13).

6   Bishop Benjamin Hoadly's remarks are found in Gray (1966, p. 195).

7   Reference is to Holmes (1966, p. 176).

8   Cited in Hutchinson (1987, p. 358). Hutchinson believes the popular view about constitutional decisions, that they have a great impact on our lives, is exaggerated. He suggests that the U.S. abortion and school segregation decisions, touted as celebrated instances of constitutional social reform, changed very little. Ultimately, his arguments fail because his yardsticks for measuring impact are narrow. For example, Hutchinson would have us believe that the *Roe v. Wade* [1973] 410 U.S. 113 decision had no impact because the total number of abortions was not altered significantly; the only change was in the percentage of abortions that were legal (p. 372). I doubt that Hutchinson's assessment of the modest significance of this decision is shared by the millions of American women who have avoided the additional trauma, humiliation, and financial costs of illegal abortions, by the doctors who are currently practicing only because they were not barred for performing illegal abortions, or by the countless women who are alive or unimpaired because of access to the significantly safer procedures provided by legal abortion facilities.

9   Reference is to Petter and Hutchinson (1989, p. 532).

10 Attributed to former U.S. Chief Justice Evans Hughes (Fulford, 1986, p. 7). The famous English constitutional authority A.V. Dicey offered a less ambiguous account: "Parliament is supreme legislator, but from the moment Parliament has uttered its will as law giver, that will becomes subject to the interpretation put upon it by the judges" (cited in Bradley, 1985, p. 27).

11 Reference is to Morton (1989, p. 2). The cases are *Morgentaler v. The Queen* [1988] 1 S.C.R. 30 and *Borowski v. Attorney General of Canada* [1989] 1 S.C.R. 342.

12 Reference is to MacGuigan (1967, pp. 660-661). For a critique of this narrow view of constitutional adjudication, see Weiler (1974, pp. 168-169).

13 The comments by *Maclean's* editor Kevin Doyle (1988) were about *Morgentaler v. The Queen* [1988] 1 S.C.R. 30.

14 *Morgentaler v. The Queen* [1988] 1 S.C.R. 30 at pp. 171-172. More extended excerpts from Madame Justice Wilson's opinion and the opinions of other judges in *Morgentaler* are found in Chapter 9.

15 Reference is to Heard (1991, p. 291).

16 Reference is to Petter and Hutchinson (1989, pp. 543-544).

17 Reference is to Monahan (1987, pp. 96-97).

18 These comments are from a review of Justice Richard Neely's book by Graham Hughes (1981). Significantly, the reviewer notes that Justice Neely's analysis ignores the fact that judges have "much more to look at than a laconic constitutional text" and rigid concepts which are frozen in time—"Justice Neely holds too narrow a notion of the job that concepts do in reasoning. Fidelity to precedent is not exhibited, as he seems to think, by a mechanical reproduction of past decisions. Indeed such a wooden refusal to change would be a sign of

disrespect for the vitality of the constitutional principles involved" (Hughes, 1981, pp. 42-43). According to British Columbia Chief Justice McEachern, "One of the most serious misconceptions that troubles the judiciary is the apparent belief on the part of many that judges decide cases in accordance with personal views and values" (1996, p. A15).

19   Reference is to Laskin (1978, p. 120).

20   McCormick and Greene (1990, pp. 211-246). Williams (1982, pp. 76-77) suggests that it is inevitable—it is "simply human nature"—that "in extreme and unusual circumstances" judges will find a way to circumvent an undesirable conclusion. Significantly, Williams expresses doubts about this being a common occurrence. For a discussion of "authorized" divisions within the law, see Case (1993) and Sartorius (1971, p. 160).

21   Reference is to Griswold (1960, p. 92).

22   Reference is to Dickson (1982, pp. 2, 7, 8). Similar sentiments were expressed by Lord Bingham, the newly appointed British Lord Chief Justice (1996, p. 11).

23   See, for example, Heard (1991) and Morton, Russell, and Withey (1992).

24   Laskin's remarks, which are quotations from Lord Macmillan, are cited in Robins (1979, p. 27).

25   Madame Justice Wilson makes a similar point in *Operation Dismantle v. The Queen* [1985] 1 S.C.R. 441 at p. 472 when she suggests: "because the effect of the appellant's action is to challenge the government's defense policy, it is tempting to say that the Court should in the same way refuse to involve itself. However, I think this would be to miss the point, to fail to focus on the question which is before us. The question before us is not whether the government's defense policy is sound but whether or not it violates the appellant's rights under s. 7 of the *Charter of Rights and Freedoms.*"

26   Reference is to Morton (1984, p. 8). British Columbia Chief Justice McEachern regards political pressure to "reform" the judiciary fuelled by public dissatisfaction to be "the greatest threat to traditional legal values, including the rule of law and judicial independence" (1996, p. A15).

27   See Tribe (1985, pp. 47-50) and Pilon (1990, pp. 13-14). The U.S. Congress has some power to overturn Supreme Court rulings on the Constitution and more extensive power to override decisions regarding federal statutes.

28   Dworkin (1987, pp. 36-39) surmises that: "the debate over Bork, like the debate over Roosevelt's plan left the public in no doubt that the issue was one of constitutional principles, and no senator could have justified his vote on any other grounds." Perhaps the most famous instance of this form of near tampering was President Roosevelt's threat in 1937 to pack the Supreme Court with fifteen judges to secure passage of his New Deal legislation (Hughes, 1981, p. 43). President Taft is reported to have written that the most significant domestic issue facing American electors in the Harding-Cox presidential race was whose Supreme Court appointments would be most desirable (Black, 1969, p. 41). The references to *Time* are from Lacayo (1988, p. 21).

29   Reference is to Laskin (1978, pp. 120-121).

30   Reference is to Luban (1987, p. 11). Simply having a particular political affiliation does not imply judicial prejudice. In applauding the appointment of Anthony Kennedy over Robert Bork, Dworkin (1987, p. 42) notes that while both are "conservative," Bork was rightly rejected because his views on judicial reasoning were inconsistent with acceptable practice. Although he disagrees with many of Kennedy's decisions, Dworkin admires his "intellectual discipline" and "lawyerlike, principled" approach to judicial decision making.

31   See, for example, Morton (1989) and Bindman (1986). Supreme Court appointments in Canada have been influenced to some extent by candidates' political and religious affiliations (Snell & Vaughan, 1985, pp. 82, 85, 129). The federal government has repeatedly been accused of appointing judges with centrist leanings (Snell & Vaughan, 1985, pp. 23, 33-34). Calls for pre-screening of judges' "political philosophies" regularly follow on the heels of controversial *Charter* cases (see, for example, Beatty, 1995, p. A17).

32   Reference is to Morton, Russell, and Withey (1992, pp. 45-46). Cameron (1994, p. 189) reports that fifty percent of judicial appointments during the 1985-1989 term of Prime Minister Mulroney went to well-known Conservative Party members.

33   The comments cited are found in Sartorius (1971, p. 160) and Agresto (1984, p. 161).

34   These comments are by Anderson (1980, p. 459). See Snell and Vaughan (1985, pp. 241-242) for evidence of the public's blaming of the courts for the results in *Murdoch v. Murdoch*

[1975] 1 S.C.R. 423. Not everyone would agree that the judges did not have the authority to overrule the existing legislation. Whether or not the *Murdoch* decision was legally required is largely irrelevant. The point of the example is that public assessment of the judiciary hinges on public approbation of its results, not on its conformity to standards of judicial reasoning. The underlying issue is whether or not we want to encourage judges to deviate from what they believe to be the *legally* most defensible resolution of the cases before them.

35   Hook's comment is cited by Fulford (1986, p. 9). The phrase about taking judicial duty seriously is found in Burton (1992, p. 162). The earlier comment about the limits of judicial benevolence is by Jowell (1985, p. 18). Burton (1992, p. 255) makes a similar point about the inappropriateness of criticizing judges for doing their job, even when applying the law leads to unwanted results.

CHAPTER 2: RULES OF APPLICATION

36   Waluchow (1980, p. 191) uses the phrase "normative standard" as equivalent to the term "rule." Gottlieb (1968, p. 40) suggests that any normative utterance that can be expressed in the form "In circumstances X, Y is required/permitted" functions as a rule, and that "every device for guiding a decision *can be restated in the form of a rule*" (p. 43). Significantly, in a later work, Hart (1982, p. 18) moves away from use of the term "rule" and refers instead to "authoritative legal reasons" which "constitute legal guides to action and legal standards of evaluation." Hart's newer language more explicitly supports the account of rule-governed application of law offered here. Schauer's (1992, pp. 1-16) broad understanding of "rule" is similar to my use. Even writers such as MacCormick (1990, p. 545) who draw a distinction between rules and standards recognize that "It is by incorporation in a rule that the relevant standard is made the law's standard." For a discussion of legal rules as reasons for acting, see Burton (1992, pp. 27-34).

37   Reference is to Hart (1967b, p. 271). Farrar (1984, p. 52) characterizes the cumulative effect of discrete reasons justifying a legal decision as "the legs of a chair not the links of a chain." See, also, Bodenheimer (1969, pp. 378ff.), Gottlieb (1968, p. 71), Holmes (1966, p. 184), Levenbook (1984, p. 16), Lloyd (1981, pp. 268-269), Lyons (1985, pp. 327-328), MacCormick (1978, pp. 11-12), Sartorius (1968, p. 178), and Stone (1964, p. 327).

38   Reference is found in *Quebec Association of Protestant School Boards v. Attorney-General of Quebec (No. 2)* [1982] 140 D.L.R. (3d) 33 at pp. 79-88.

39   The reference to conductive reasoning is from Govier (1985, p. 260). For a discussion of judicial responsibility to decide the case as argued before them, see MacCormick (1978, pp. 122-123), Weiler (1968, p. 416), and Read (1986, p. 163). For example, in *Hunter v. Southam* [1984] 2 S.C.R. 145 at p. 169, the Supreme Court of Canada refused to consider whether the provisions of the *Combines Investigation Act* could be salvaged under the reasonable limits section of the *Charter* because the Crown had not argued the point. See Chapter 7 for the actual judicial opinion and a reconstruction of the conflicting arguments offered by majority and dissenting judges in *Riggs v. Palmer.*

40   Reference is to Hart (1961, pp. 77-96). The theory of judicial reasoning I propose comes out of the legal positivist tradition, specifically Hart's explication of law as a union of primary and secondary rules. Whether or not my theory of legal reasoning qualifies as a legal positivist theory depends entirely on one's conception of legal positivism. The notion has been used in so many different ways (Hart, 1958, 1961, p. 253; Lyons, 1984, p. 50; Raz, 1983b, p. 37) that the label "legal positivism" may indicate very little about a theory (Hart, 1967a, p. 418; MacCormick, 1978, p. 240). The theory of judicial reasoning I propose meets Hart's "minimal" condition of legal positivism, which requires proponents to assert that "unless the law itself provides to the contrary, the fact that a legal rule is iniquitous or unjust does not entail that it is invalid or not law" (Hart, 1967a, p. 419). This does not imply, as Lyons (1984, pp. 58-59) suggests, that the only "moral" standards appropriately appealed to by judges in deciding a case must be *explicitly* stated in law. Hart (1961, pp. 200-201) rejects this requirement and, elsewhere (Hart, 1967a), suggests legal positivism claims that "no reference to justice or other moral values enters into the *definition* of law" (emphasis added), although judges and legislators often entertain moral considerations (p. 419). Lyons (1984, p. 49) finds this

interpretation of legal positivism implausible because he believes that almost no one, including a "natural law" theorist, would deny Hart's minimal condition. While it would be hard to find contemporary opponents, this minimal condition apparently was denied by notable jurists such as Lord Blackstone (Hart, 1958, p. 594). On the other hand, my theory would not qualify under Raz's (1983b, pp. 27-52) explication of legal positivism in terms of what he calls "the strong source thesis"—that tests for identification of the existence and content of laws depend exclusively on social facts and can be applied without resort to moral argument. This account of legal positivism implies that cases involving almost *any* judgment in applying law are law-making, not law-identifying situations. For example, Raz (1983b, p. 181) holds the counterintuitive view that application of statutes containing value-laden terms such as "unreasonable" necessarily require law-making discretion. Lyons (1984, pp. 54-57) discounts positivism, as Raz understands it, as an implausible theory of law.

41   Hart (1961, p. 144) explicitly states that judicial reasoning is beyond the scope of his book. Where he does deal with the topic his account is, at best, incomplete. In easy or "core" cases, judicial application of a law is governed by the settled meaning of law (Hart, 1961, pp. 140-141). The settled meaning is essentially a product of the legal and ordinary meaning of the wording and of the obvious purpose of the law (Hart, 1967b, p. 271). In controversial or "penumbra" cases, judges are expected to impartially balance competing considerations—"individual and social interests, social and political aims, and standards of morality and justice" (1967b, p. 271). Or, as he says elsewhere (1961), it may only be possible to expect that the decision be a "reasoned product of impartial choice" (p. 200). Hart's vague articulation of standards in penumbra situations represents a significant gap in his theory of law. Waluchow (1994, p. 76) suggests that Hart "seriously underestimated" the importance of secondary rules of adjudication. Although my account of judicial reasoning differs from Hart's brief explication, I regard my work as a complement to his conception of law as a system of primary and secondary rules.

Another category of rules of adjudication, which I do not address, covers the rules governing how the facts of a case are to be established. These rules deal with admissibility of evidence, hearsay, reliability of witnesses and establishing reasonable doubt. Sartorius (1989, p. 45) suggests that Hart's model needs a further type of secondary rule, "rules of enforcement," which authorize and regulate judges' sanction-imposing powers. My focus is on reasoning about application of law, not on determination of facts or imposition of sanctions.

42   See Bell (1985, pp. 23, 27, 35), Levenbook (1984, pp. 4-5), and MacCormick (1978, pp. 11-12).

43   Reference is to *International Fund for Animal Welfare v. The Queen* [1987] 30 C.C.C. (3d) 80. See Mackie (1984, p. 164). Taylor (1961, p. 12) supports the distinction between the weight of a standard and the implications for a standard. He refers to this as a difference between the "relative precedence" and "degree of fulfillment" of standards. Vlastos (1962, pp. 60-62) claims that maximization of protected interests and rights is a requirement of justice: "given any two levels of production of goods known to be possible in given circumstances, then, other things being equal, the higher should be preferred on grounds of justice."

44   References are to *Dennis v. United States* [1951] 341 U.S. 494 at p. 501 and to *Operation Dismantle Inc. v. The Queen* [1985] 1 S.C.R. 441 at pp. 451-454.

45   Reference is to *Grey v. Pearson* [1857] 6 H.L.Cas. 61 at p. 106.

46   *Daniels and Daniels v. White & Sons and Tarbard* [1938] 4 All E.R. 258 is discussed in MacCormick (1978, pp. 19-33).

47   Reference is to Hart (1961, p. 119). Significantly, Hart (1949, p. 183) recognizes that application of a law even in straightforward situations cannot be simply a matter of deductive inference. See Moore (1981) for a discussion of the additional premises need to subsume fact patterns within the scope of a law.

48   The case is *Attorney General v. Edison Telephone Company* [1881] 6 Q.B.D. 244. Similarly, live broadcasts and videotapes were held not to be protected under the *Copyright Act* since the technology they used was not a photographic process.

49   Reference is to Peck (1987, p. 12).

50   The case is *Hunter v. Southam* [1984] 2 S.C.R. 145 at pp. 154ff.

CHAPTER 3: CONTROLLED JUDGMENT

51   Waluchow's most recent discussion of judicial discretion can be found in Chapter 7 of his book, *Inclusive Legal Positivism* (1994).

52   The case, *Royal College of Nursing v. Department of Health* [1981] A.C. 800; 814, is discussed in Bell (1985, pp. 88-93). Extended excerpts from both the Court of Appeal and House of Lords decisions are found in Chapter 9.

53   The references in *Royal College of Nursing v. Department of Health* [1981] A.C. 800 are found at pp. 825, 827, 829, 831, 838. Significantly, neither dissenting nor majority judges argued that one policy was more desirable, politically speaking, than the other. See, for example, Lord Edmund-Davies' remarks in dissent (at p. 831). Bell (1985, p. 92) admits as much when he concedes that "it would be fair to say that there is little evidence of consideration given to *wide-ranging social implications* of any interpretation" (emphasis added).

54   Mechanical application of law differs from the exercise of judgment since the latter requires forming an opinion or notion "by exercising the mind upon it," *Black's Law Dictionary* (Fifth edition). Some writers do not appear to recognize a middle position—what I call "controlled judgment." Witness the dichotomy in McCormick and Greene's (1990, p. 122) definitions of the two options open to judges: "By *discretion* we mean the extent to which the judges saw the process as requiring a significant degree of arbitrary personal choice or judgment, as opposed to a mechanical process in which the answer simply presents itself when the right buttons are pushed."

55   The distinction between discretion and controlled judgment is adapted from Dworkin's discussion of strong and weak discretion (1980, pp. 31-39) and Waluchow's very helpful discussion of "having discretion" and "exercising discretion" (1980, p. 89; 1983, p. 333; 1994, pp. 201-213). Judges *have* discretion if there is not a uniquely correct legal answer for every dispute. Judges *exercise* discretion either if they *believe* that there is not a uniquely correct answer, or if they *believe* that they cannot ascertain the correct answer. The difference between having and exercising discretion is that according to the latter "the proposition that judges lack strong discretion does not mean that all cases are fully controlled by binding legal standards; only that judges are required by the legal system always to proceed on the assumption that they are" (Waluchow, 1980, p. 67). Dworkin agrees that strong judicial discretion (i.e., exercising discretion) is unacceptable: "The law may not be a seamless web; but the plaintiff is entitled to ask the judge to treat it as if it were" (1980, p. 116). See also Waluchow (1983, pp. 325-328). On "interstitial legislation," see Bell (1985, pp. 17-20).

56   For a discussion of "judgment," see Green (1971, p. 178). Controlled judgment does not require a uniquely correct legal answer to every dispute; rather, judges must merely *believe* that there is a legally best answer, and that they can ascertain it. Burton (1992) offers a similar theory of judicial reasoning, called "the good faith thesis," which argues that judges are bound to uphold the law by acting only on legally warranted reasons even when there is no single correct answer. Hart (1977, pp. 139-140) conjectures that Dworkin's thesis will be attacked most for its insistence that "even if there is no way of demonstrating which of two conflicting solutions, both equally well warranted by the existing law, is correct, still there must always be a single correct answer awaiting discovery." For a critique of Dworkin's arguments regarding the possibility of a uniquely correct answer for every case, see Waluchow (1980, pp. 263-278; 1990, pp. 191ff.).

57   Waluchow (1980, pp. 101-102) reports that Justice Holmes wrote that sometimes judges must exercise "the sovereign prerogative of choice" and that Justice Cardozo wrote "Every judge must be conscious of times when a free exercise of will, directed to set purpose to the furtherance of the common good, determined the form and the tendency of a rule which at that moment took its origin in one creative act."

58   Reference is to Dworkin (1980, pp. 32-33).

59   Bell (1985, p. 27) writes that: "The notion of judicial discretion is often connected with the idea that there are 'gaps' in the law and that, when the law runs out, the judges are free to exercise a degree of personal choice. Given that the legal materials are more extensive than simply the [primary] rules of the system, the number of situations is less than might first appear."

60   This repudiation of Lord Denning occurs in *Davis and Johnson* [1978] 1 All E.R. 1132 at pp. 1137, 1139. Elsewhere, MacCormick (1978, p. 242) refers to Lord Denning as a "strong-minded maverick" and Waluchow (1990, p. 70) mentions Denning's propensity to "seek justice despite the law." For disclosures by Canadian judges of their deviation from the law, see McCormick and Greene (1990, pp. 229-246). Significantly, although somewhat ambiguously, these authors claim that Canadian judges make law "only reluctantly and only where they have no other options" (p. 245).

61   See Dworkin (1987) and Hughes (1981). In *Rathwell v. Rathwell* [1979] 2 S.C.R. 436, Justice Dickson comments on divisions within matrimonial property law. For a more general discussion of divisions within judicial practices, see Case (1993, pp. 126-128).

62   Disputes of this sort often have no further levels of appeal. As Hart (1961, p. 149) suggests: "The truth may be that, when courts settle previously unimagined questions concerning the most fundamental constitutional rules, they *get* their authority to decide them accepted after the questions have arisen and the decision has been given. Here all that succeeds is success." See also Eekelaar's (1973, pp. 37ff.) discussion of the possibility of rule-governed judicial decisions in extreme situations such as court decisions following a revolution.

CHAPTER 4: REASONING FROM INTERPRETIVE GUIDELINES

63   Reference is to Gottlieb (1968, p. 95).

64   This view of interpretation builds on the notion of performative utterances. See Austin (1970) for the inaugural work on performatives. Coval and Smith (1986, pp. 117-118) make use of performatives in accounting for rules of recognition. For other discussions of legislative intention, see Dworkin (1985, pp. 38-54; 1986, pp. 315-327), Gall (1983, p. 253), Llewellyn (1960, p. 218), Moore (1981, pp. 246-270), Payne (1956, p. 111), Tushnet (1988, pp. 23-45), and Willis (1938, p. 3). The duty to apply the "legislative intent" has variously been characterized as the uniformly acknowledged proper function of Canadian courts (Nova Scotia Commissioners, 1975, p. 218), an article of faith among American lawyers (Murphy, 1975, p. 1299), a fundamental rule in English law (Payne, 1956, p. 96), and a constitutional tenet of Anglo-American legal systems (Kernochan, 1976, p. 346). It is important to distinguish the broader, fundamental tenet from a more specific, literal sense of "legislative intention." The latter refers to actual intentions that legislators had in passing the legislation and the former refers to a legal fiction. Payne (1956, pp. 97-98) suggests "the legislature, being a composite body, cannot have a single state of mind and so cannot have a single intention." MacCallum (1966, pp. 769-775) argues that Payne merely demonstrates that legislatures may not always have a common intention. Willis (1938, p. 3) calls legislative intention a "very slippery phrase."

65   The first quotation is by de Sloovere, cited in MacCallum (1966, p. 781). Justice Frankfurter's comments are cited in Johnson (1978, p. 430). See also Gottlieb (1968, pp. 100-101). Willis (1938, p. 17) reported that the general presumption against interpreting statutes so as to interfere with individual liberty has been used to justify decisions that are clearly at odds with what the legislators had actually intended.

66   Each rule has countless implied exceptions. For example, it is understood that "where the law imposes a duty to act, noncompliance with the duty will be excused where compliance is physically impossible" (Coval & Smith, 1986, p. 63).

67   Reference is to Willis (1938, p. 1). See also Zander (1980, pp. 37, 82).

68   Reference is to Murphy (1975, p. 1299).

69   *In Re Meaning of the Word Persons* [1928] S.C.R. 276, Chief Justice Anglin wrote that provisions of the *B.N.A. Act* (now the *Constitution Act, 1867*) "bear today the same construction which the courts would, if then required to pass upon them, have given to them when they were first enacted. If the phrase 'qualified person' in s. 24 includes women today, it has so included them since 1867" (at p. 282). This approach to constitutional interpretation was rejected, and the Supreme Court decision was overturned, by the Privy Council in Lord Sankey's famous "living tree" opinion (*Edwards v. Attorney General of Canada* [1930] A.C. 124). On the frozen concept approach, see Hart (1961, p. 126) and Hogg (1982, p. 10). I use the term "frozen concept" somewhat arbitrarily to refer to a plain meaning approach that

limits the meaning of words to what they plainly meant at the time the legislation was passed. It might be suggested that originalism espouses a frozen concept approach, although some original intention proponents would allow terms to acquire a more modern meaning if doing so in the given situation better effected the legislators' intentions. For example, Hogg (1987, p. 96) suggests that a "progressive" approach to interpretation in light of changing social conditions may be consistent with drafters' original intentions.

70   Reference is to *Witthuhn v. Minister of National Revenue* [1955] 55 D.T.C. 174. The American version of the plain meaning rule approximates what in Canada and Britain is known as the golden meaning rule. For example, citing a Canadian judicial opinion, Willis (1938, p. 10) reports that the plain meaning rule directs that "if the precise words used are plain and unambiguous in their ordinary sense ... we are bound to construe them in their ordinary sense, even though it leads ... to an absurdity or a manifest injustice." Gall (1983, pp. 253-254) uses identical words in his textbook on the Canadian legal process. Zander (1980, pp. 37-38) offers a similar account of the rule in Britain. This Anglo-Canadian account is to be compared with an American definition of the plain meaning rule as cited from a leading case: "where the language of an enactment is clear and construction according to its terms does not lead to absurd or impracticable consequences, the words employed are to be taken as the final expression of the meaning intended" (Murphy, 1975, p. 1299). See also Johnson (1978, p. 417).

71   Cited with approval by Willis (1938, p. 12); the statement appears in *Grey v. Pearson* [1857] 6 H.L.Cas. 61 at p. 106.

72   Reference is to Bell (1985, p. 85). The mischief rule was first formulated in *Heydon's Case* [1584] 3 Co. Rep. 7b.

73   For a critical discussion of originalism, see Dworkin (1984; 1985, pp. 33ff.).

74   Reference is to *R. v. Big M Drug Mart* [1985] 18 D.L.R. (4th) 321 at pp. 359-360.

75   Reference is to Kernochan (1976, pp. 343, 351).

76   See Willis (1938, pp. 14-15) and also Lord Diplock in *Black Clawson International Ltd. v. Papierwerke Waldorf-Ascheffenburg A.G.* [1975] A.C. 591 at p. 638.

77   See Gibson (1986, p. 45) and Posner (1982).

78   Reference is to *Law Society of Upper Canada v. Skapinker* [1984] 9 D.L.R. (4th) 161 at p. 179.

79   See Elliot (1982, pp. 18-22).

80   Reference is to *R v. Videoflicks Ltd.* [1984] 5 O.A.C. 1 at p. 20.

81   Reference is to Kernochan (1976, p. 335) and Saxon (cited in Gottlieb, 1968, p. 91).

82   MacCormick (1978, p. 207) and Llewellyn (1960, p. 521). See also Peck (1987, p. 13).

83   Cited by Llewellyn (1960, pp. 522-529).

84   Reference is to Gibson (1986, p. 44). My explication of interpretive conventions is consistent with Llewellyn's account of competing interpretive rules. He sought to debunk the view that "there is only one single correct meaning" of a statute (1960, p. 521) and to help "cease driving about some compelling 'legislative intent' which flatly controls the court, even in cases where no such intent existed or can be found" (p. 528). Notwithstanding their inconclusiveness, Llewellyn regarded them as "needed tools of argument" (p. 521). An example of judicial attention to the *cumulative* weight of arguments arising from interpretive rules is the Saskatchewan Court of Appeal's rejection of the inclusion of a foetus within the meaning of "person" in *Borowski v. Canada* [1987] 56 Sask. R. 129.

85   See, for example, Willis (1938, pp. 11-13), Payne (1956, p. 111), Murphy (1975, pp. 1301-1302), and Bell (1985, p. 92).

86   See Willis (1938, pp. 2, 11-16, 21). The Canadian reference is to Gall (1983, p. 253) and the American reference is to Murphy (1975, p. 1315). The U.S. decision in *United States v. American Trucking Associations* [1940] 310 U.S. 534 at p. 545 is taken as deciding that evidence of legislative intention was admissible even though the meaning of the words seemed clear on "superficial examination."

87   The theory is basically from Willis (1938, pp. 15-17) with support from Kernochan (1976, pp. 345, 356-357).

88   *Holy Trinity Church v. United States* [1892] 143 U.S. 457 is discussed in Johnson (1978, p. 420). It is reported that the British rule on legislative history is that it "should be used not at all or only with the greatest restraint" (Dickinson, cited in Murphy, 1975, p. 1316). Elliot

(1982, p. 19) suggests that the traditional Anglo-Canadian rule that "the Parliamentary history of legislation is not a permissible aid in construing a statute" has been relaxed in Canada.

89   The expression was used by Lord Denning in *Davis v. Johnson* [1978] 1 All E.R. 841 at p. 857 in reference to the possibility that exceptions to the doctrine of *stare decisis* had reduced it to mere guidance. For U.S. cases that subsequently made use of legislative history, see Murphy (1975, p. 1031).

90   Reference is to Driedger (1981, p. 780). MacCormick (1978, pp. 207-208) offers a largely compatible view. He argues that there is a presumption in favour of applying statutes in their more "obvious" meaning and treats appeals to the golden rule and the mischief rule (defined in terms of legislators' actual objectives) as exceptions to the plain meaning rule. Later, with a reference to the English authority Rupert Cross, he suggests that "the 'literal rule' may be overridden by the other 'rules' provided the statutory words can bear a meaning other than the more obvious one" (MacCormick, 1978, p. 210).

91   Reference is to MacCormick, (1978, p. 208). This explanation also helps to account for Murphy's (1975) complaints about continuing references in judicial opinions to plain meaning after 1940 when the U.S. Supreme Court delivered the supposed death blow to the plain meaning rule. The Court's decision was not an abandonment of judicial concern for interpreting statutes in light of their plain meaning but an extension of the basic rule to allow evidence from legislative history to be used in that deliberation.

CHAPTER 5: REASONING FROM PRIOR CASES

92   Reference is to Alexander (1989, p. 3).

93   Cross is cited in MacCormick (1978, p. 215). See also Simpson (1961, p. 163) and MacCormick (1978, p. 83).

94   This point is made by Simpson (1961, pp. 162ff.). For this reason alone, application of a *ratio* cannot hinge on the meaning of the specific words used by the judge to formulate the *ratio*. Reference is to *R. v. Therens* [1985] 1 S.C.R. 613.

95   Reference is to Levi (1964, p. 266).

96   *Steel v. Glasgow Iron and Steel Co.* [1944] S.C. 237 is discussed by MacCormick (1978, pp. 161-165).

97   Lord Wright's metaphor is cited by Dickson (1982, p. 3). On the matter of deciding only those issues before the court, see Levi (1964, pp. 268-269), MacCormick (1978, p. 160), and Simpson (1961, p. 160).

98   Dworkin (1980, p. 112) claims that judges merely declare rules that are immanent in the law. See also Levi's (1949, pp. 20-25) account of Justice Cardozo's opinion in the classic American negligence case *MacPherson v. Buick* [1916] 217 N.Y. 382. Raz (1983b, pp. 185ff.) implicitly acknowledges that judges often claim that they are applying an unwritten law, but believes that they are being less than candid about their exercise of law-making powers. Significantly, Raz (1983b, p. 188) recognizes the distinction between the *ratio* of a case and its formulation. Witness his comment that "it is unreasonable to attribute great weight to the actual formulation of the rule in the hands of the court." However, Raz treats this as a problem of the courts being "a little careless in formulating rules" and not, as I have suggested, that the *ratio* of a case is a partial formulation of an underlying, never-to-be-fully-developed rule. If a judge were to speculate about the complete rule formulation at the time of the initial case, that formulation would never be identical to the full rule formulation that actually develops. There are several reasons for this difference: (1) all the hypothetical cases a judge might consider may not actually come before the courts, (2) the initial judge or subsequent judges may make mistakes, and (3) changes in statutory, constitutional, or common law between the time of the initial case and the final formulation will legitimately alter the initial rule.

99   Raz (1983b, p. 208) and MacCormick (1978, pp. 213ff.) assert that following a precedent is essentially a form of rule interpretation, not a matter of analogical reasoning. MacCormick (1978, p. 83) suggests that his discussion of *Donoghue* shows that "in deciding a particular case [judges] should act only in accordance with some ruling which covers not only the particular case but all other possible cases which are like cases just because they would be covered by the same ruling." Raz (1983b, p. 202) writes: "A court relies on analogy whenever

it draws on similarities and differences between the present case and previous cases which are not binding precedents applying to the case ... [A]rgument by analogy is not a method of discovering which rules are legally binding because of the doctrine of precedent. That discovery requires nothing more than an interpretation of the precedent to establish its *ratio*. Analogical argument is a form of justification of new rules laid down by the courts in the exercise of their law-making discretion."

100   The 1970 case is *Home Office v. Dorset Yacht Co.* [1970] A.C. 1004 at p. 1054. Levi (1949, p. 7) notes a judge is not free to "ignore the results of a great number of cases which he cannot explain under a remade rule." MacCormick (1974a, p. 222) suggests that "To enunciate a principle is to make sense of a cluster of rules." However, MacCormick (1978, p. 126) incorrectly believes that formulating a general principle is "a real effort of the creative imagination." In "expressing the underlying common purpose of a specific set of rules" a judge does more than "simply find and state the rationale of the rules; to a greater or lesser degree, he makes them rational by stating a principle capable of embracing them, and he uses that as a necessary jumping-off point for a novel decision, which can now be represented as one already 'covered' by 'existing' law." MacCormick arrives at this assessment because he believes that unless a case is directly covered by a rule it must be an extension of the law (1978, p. 107). Therefore, if a common law principle is used to justify situations which were not expressly established by prior decisions, then the new formulation of the principle must be a creative (i.e., "law-making") action.

101   Lord Wilberforce's remarks are in *Anns, Merton London Borough Council* [1978] A.C. 728 at pp. 751-752 (H.L.) and are cited in Coval and Smith (1986, pp. 113-114). See Justice Dickson's reasoning in *Harrison v. Carswell* [1975] 6 W.W.R. 673 at p. 675. The judges' reasoning in *Home Office v. Dorset Yacht Co.* [1970] A.C. 1004, which applied the duty of care principle, supports this position. Interestingly, two of the five judges in that case rejected the presumption of a duty of care. Bell (1985, pp. 43-46) provides the following summary of the opinion. Lord Dilhorne (in sole dissent) denied that Lord Atkin's principle was one of general applicability and, instead, required specific authority for any liability to the plaintiff. (As he found no authority, he concluded there was no liability.) Lord Diplock "started with no basic principle, but thought that the judges should first identify the characteristics common to the cases where a duty of care has already been found and, by this inductive process, produce a general statement of what does give rise to a duty of care." The three remaining judges accepted the presumption that a duty of care should apply unless there were compelling reasons to the contrary. In arguing that there were no compelling reasons, Lord Morris "was content to describe the process of extending liability in negligence as one of finding a sufficient analogy with previous cases of liability." Lords Pearson and Reid concluded that the issues required the "balancing of social interests"—an evaluation that Bell calls "policy determination" and I refer to as reasoning from principle. As I have suggested, reasoning from principle is required when judges conclude that there are inconclusive reasons for asserting that prior cases establish a precedent for the present case.

102   There is a modest difference in the rules of reasoning from prior cases—dealing with the onus of support—when common law principles are invoked. Judges commonly refer to a general presumption in connection with well-established common law principles, but not in connection with a *ratio* that has not often been reaffirmed. The widespread adoption of a principle in many cases warrants an assumed relevant similarity between situations that, on the face of it, appear similar. This is not surprising. In reasoning from prior cases it is generally difficult to positively establish that cases are similar: the focus is typically on confirming and refuting arguments for distinguishing cases. Increasingly as a common law principle is reaffirmed, the onus of support shifts to those who believe that a subsequent case should be distinguished from the body of cases which gave rise to the principle.

103   Citing several examples, MacCormick (1978, p. 222) suggests that a failure to consider an issue in sufficient depth or to provide good reasons for a conclusion reduces the authority that subsequent judges will ascribe to the decision.

104   Reference is to Raz (1983b, p. 184).

105   Reference is to Stone (1959, pp. 603ff.). Stone suggests that judges must exercise a "fresh creative decision" when deciding at which levels of generality to describe the rule established

by a case (p. 615). This challenge presents a problem solely for those who believe that a prior case decides a subsequent case only when the material facts of the subsequent case fall within the scope of the prior case's *ratio*. Proponents of this view see the level of generality of the *ratio* as determining the range of subsequent cases that are bound by the prior decision. Goodhart (1930, pp. 80-81), Lloyd (1981, p. 278), and Raz (1983b, pp. 180ff.) fall in this camp. Proponents of this view often draw a distinction between "direct" and "analogous" precedent (Goodhart, 1930, pp. 80-81). A prior case would be a direct precedent for a current case only if the prior and current case were identical in all their material facts. Analogous precedent refers to cases where the material facts of a current case are merely relevantly similar to the facts of a prior case. The distinction between direct and analogous precedent disguises the fact that even the so-called direct precedents require analogical reasoning—strictly speaking, no two sets of material facts are identical.

106   See *Donoghue v. Stevenson* [1932] A.C. 562 at pp. 578, 579, 599. MacCormick (1978, p. 216) admits that "Even if a doubt could have been raised whether that [the *Donoghue*] ruling covered all manufacturers of consumer goods as *per* Lord Atkin, or only manufacturers of articles of food and drink as *per* Lord Macmillan, it would have been immaterial to the instant case which concerned lemonade."

107   MacCormick appears to be aware of this point. In an earlier article, he wrote that "the binding rules derived from these and other precedents [referring to *Donoghue* and another case] are relatively narrow and specific in terms" (1974a, p. 221). He also acknowledges that "every law student knows" that the neighbour principle (the principle about the relationship required for a duty of care to exist between an agent and an injured party) is *obiter dictum* not a *ratio* because it is more broadly stated than is necessary to decide the case (1978, p. 157). See also Lord Halsbury's comments in *Quinn v. Leathem* [1901] A.C. 25 at p. 39: "every judgment must be read as applicable to the particular facts proved, or assumed to be proved, since the generality of the expressions which may be found there are not intended to be expositions of the whole law, but governed and qualified by the particular facts of the case in which such expressions are found ... [A] case is only an authority for what it actually decides."

108   Reference is to Burton (1985, p. 40). Williams (1982, p. 73) suggests that the criteria judges rely upon to establish permissible limits of abstraction include "common sense" and "a feeling for what the law ought to be."

109   See Raz (1983b, pp. 197ff.) and Bell (1985, pp. 17ff.).

110   Lloyd's (1981, p. 270) discussion of *Candler v. Crane, Christmas & Co.* [1951] 2 K.B. 164 is found in *The Idea of Law*.

111   Burton (1985, p. 36) asserts that if reasoning from prior cases is analogical reasoning, it cannot be explained in terms of applying pre-existing rules. Raz believes that whenever the rule established in a prior case is "extended" to cover a new situation judges are necessarily exercising discretion. Significantly, Raz (1983b, pp. 208-209) wonders why judges do not more clearly distinguish between occasions when they apply law and when they create law.

112   I am not denying that in the early history of Anglo-American common law, judges were clearly authorized to exercise discretion in adjudicating disputes (Sartorius, 1971, p. 151). Others, like Simpson (1961, p. 157) and Frank (1958), claim that judges currently have law-making powers. It is interesting to note the range of metaphors which have been used to try to capture what Justice Dickson (1982, p. 5) referred to as a judicial and legislative partnership in the law-making process: Lord Haldane likens the judicial role to "fleshing out the bare bones" of enacted law (cited in MacGuigan, 1967, p. 660), Kelsen refers to statutes as "semi-manufactured products" (cited in Gottlieb, 1968, p. 88), and Dworkin (1986, p. 228) introduced the metaphor of judges as "chain novelists."

113   Reference is to Dickson (1982, p. 6).

114   Reference is to Gottlieb (1968, p. 88).

115   Raz (1983b, pp. 189ff.) advances this argument.

116   Weiler (1974, pp. 63-64) refers to the decision in *Fleming v. Atkinson* [1959] S.C.R. 513 as "judicial innovation" and "an intelligent change," whereas the majority of the Court denied that the English common law immunity from stray cattle was ever the common law of Ontario.

117   Justice Cardozo's comments in *MacPherson v. Buick* [1916] 217 N.Y. 382 are cited by Levi (1949, p. 21) and Waluchow (1980, p. 213). Weiler (1968, p. 423) explains that gradual changes in law alter the relevance of differences between apparently like cases. It is useful to remember the earlier comment that a change in the legal definition of a word alters the rule that a statute lays down even if the formulation remains unchanged. Lawful changes in the complete rule underlying a case occur even though the case is not explicitly mentioned or applied. In *Gideon v. Wainwright* [1963] 372 U.S. 335 at p. 348, the Supreme Court considered whether the American Constitution guaranteed persons accused of serious crimes a right to be provided with a lawyer if they could not afford to hire one. At the time the right to counsel was first raised in court, the right extended only to persons accused of capital crimes (i.e., cases for which the death penalty may be imposed). Subsequent changes in constitutional case law were seen to alter the legitimacy of limiting the right to capital crimes. For example, in connection with military trials, an earlier Court repudiated the distinction between capital and non-capital crimes. Thus, what initially might have been a relevant distinction between capital and serious non-capital crimes, ceased to be so because of subsequent changes in other areas of the law.

CHAPTER 6: REASONING FROM PRINCIPLE

118   This description by Keating (1987, p. 534) is in reference to claims about principled reasoning advanced by Dworkin.
119   Reference is to Vlastos (1962, p. 53).
120   Reference is to Wechsler (1959, p. 15). Apparently, the view that judicial decisions must be principled is widely held (Altman, 1986, p. 218). Levi (1964, p. 273) regrets Wechsler's use of the term "neutral" because of the confusion it has caused. As Tushnet (1988, p. 46) explains, principles cannot be neutral in content because they provide support for one side or the other in a dispute. Earlier, Tushnet (1983, p. 805) noted that "neutral" refers to "judicial indifference to who the winner is." For general discussions of principles, see Taylor (1961, pp. 40-47) and Hare (1972).
121   Reference is found in *Egerton v. Earl Brownlow* [1852] 4 H.L.Cas. 1 at p. 196.
122   Reasoning from principle is not an inevitable way of resolving disputes when the meaning of words or prior cases fail to provide conclusive results. For example, Bell (1985, p. 18) points out that the 1907 *Swiss Civil Code* authorizes a judge to decide "according to the rule which he would enact if he were legislator." The judicial evaluation of competing considerations is often referred to as a "balancing test" (Petter & Hutchinson, 1989, pp. 543-544). For discussions of evaluating legal principles in light of legal standards, see Bell (1985, pp. 22-39), Gottlieb (1968, pp. 74-77), Hart (1961, p. 200; 1967b, p. 271), MacCormick (1978, pp. 149-150), and Wechsler (1959, 1964).
123   One case was cited by the Court in *R. v. Big M Drug Mart Ltd.* [1985] 18 D.L.R. (4th) 321 at p. 352, but it appears to provide authority for the undesirability of litigating the same question more than once and not to indicate the validity of the shifting purpose principle *per se*.
124   Reference is to Hare (1952, p. 65).
125   See Coombs (1980, 1990). I do not claim that these exhaust the ways that judges "test" the acceptability of adopting a principle to resolve a given case, although they certainly are very commonly used means.
126   Reference is to *R. v. Bryant* [1984] 6 O.A.C. 118 at p. 122.
127   Reference is to *Davis v. Johnson* [1978] 1 All E.R. 841 at p. 863.
128   This report of the reasoning in *McCulloch v. Maryland* [1819] 4 Wheat. 316 is from Bodenheimer (1969, p. 385).
129   References are to *M. v. Director of Child Welfare* [1986] 47 Alta. L.R. (2d) 380 at pp. 394-395, 395-396.
130   This report of the reasoning in *Express Newspapers v. McShane* [1980] A.C. 672 is from Bell (1985, pp. 87-88).
131   Reference is to *Miranda v. Arizona* [1966] 384 U.S. 439 at p. 537.
132   Clearly, conclusions about hypothetical situations are regarded as *obiter dicta*. See Wechsler (1964, pp. 297-298) and Goodhart (1930, p. 179). In *R. v. Big M Drug Mart Ltd.* [1985] 18

D.L.R. (4th) 321 at p. 351, the Supreme Court confronted a case that an earlier court had cited as a paradigm infringement of religious freedom. The earlier court's observation about the then-hypothetical situation was not binding on the later court. For critics of this test, see Levi (1964, pp. 274-275) and Tushnet (1983, p. 810).

133 Reference is to *Morgentaler v. The Queen* [1988] S.C.R. 30 at p. 76.

134 Reference is to *Donoghue v. Stevenson* [1932] A.C. 562 at p. 620.

135 Reference is to *Riggs v. Palmer* [1889] 115 N.Y. 506 at pp. 511-512.

136 Singer (1958, p. 162) refers to this as the generalization argument: "if the consequences of everyone's acting in a certain way would be undesirable, then no one has the right to act in that way without a reason or justification." The references to "floodgates" and "parade of horribles" are from Bell (1985, p. 70) and Bodenheimer (1969, p. 378), respectively. An *in terrorem* argument (an argument predicting terrible consequences) is cited in *PPG Industries Canada Ltd. v. Attorney General of Canada* [1983] 42 B.C.L.R. 334 at p. 344.

137 Reference is to *Morgentaler v. The Queen* [1988] S.C.R. 30 at p. 78.

138 *London Street Tramways v. London County Council* [1898] A.C. 375 at p. 380. This case is offered solely to illustrate the judicial use of this test; the test may not have been properly applied in this case. An argument based on repeated instances has force only if there is no non-arbitrary way to distinguish the present case from a rash of like cases with undesirable consequences. It is arguable that the clearly unfair consequences in this case warrant a review which would not set a precedent for reviewing *every* previously decided case.

139 *McCulloch v. Maryland* [1819] 4 Wheat. 316 at p. 432.

140 See Sartorius (1968, pp. 175-177; 1971, pp. 154-155), Lloyd (1981, p. 135), and Coval and Smith (1986, p. 74). Levenbook (1984) argues that some principles may be legal principles by virtue of their being presupposed by the point of law generally.

141 References are to *Miranda v. Arizona* [1966] 384 U.S. 439 at pp. 459-462, 537-539.

142 The arguments are found in *Law Society of Upper Canada v. Skapinker* [1984] 9 D.L.R. (4th) 161 at pp. 170-175.

143 For Dworkin, judicial reasoning is, at heart, political interpretation (1986, pp. 87ff., 254-258, 410). It is interpretive because judges adjudicate by constructing a theory about what the law requires in a given instance. Particularly in difficult cases, but also in easier cases, judges confront rival explanations of what the law requires and they must select the best from among these plausible alternatives (pp. 264-266). To do so responsibly, judges must interpret what would be consistent with the legal system as a whole, or at least with an area or field of law. The correct disposition of a case must fit with the relevant statutes, prior decisions, and judicial practices. However, alternative dispositions of a case may "fit" with different interpretations of the relevant legal phenomena. As with interpretations of literature, interpretations of social practices such as law require that the final arbiter decide which set of values ascribed by the varying interpretations shows the enterprise in its best light, all things considered (pp. 45ff.). This is so because different plausible interpretations often impute different values or functions to a particular legal system or area of law (pp. 52-53).

The best interpretation of the law in a particular case depends, in the final analysis, on the judge's assessment of the most acceptable reasons for the continued existence of the legal system (pp. 87ff.). Although this is a "political" judgment, it is not identical to the decision a legislator might make in deciding what the law should be. Judicial decision making must conform to special requirements arising from the role judges play in the legal system (pp. 379-380). Dworkin's analysis of the British and American legal systems leads him to ascribe four fundamental ideals to legal practice in these jurisdictions: justice, fairness, procedural due process, and integrity (pp. 164-167). These values provide the criteria for distinguishing among rival plausible interpretations of the law.

Dworkin calls his theory "law as integrity" (p. 94) because, in his opinion, this virtue is the overarching ideal of Anglo-American legal practice (p. 400). This requires that any interpretation of the law reflect, as much as actual practice allows, a coherent justification of the practice as a whole. More specifically, for judges adopting Dworkin's explication of the virtues, it means that the best interpretation of what the law requires will be the one that provides the most coherent arrangement of "justice," "fairness," and "procedural due process" attributable to the legal practice in which the judge operates (pp. 164-167, 225, 404-405).

For example, in discussing *McLoughlin v. O'Brian* [1983] 1 A.C. 410, Dworkin explains: "Deciding whether the law grants Mrs. McLoughlin compensation for her injury, for example, means deciding whether legal practice is seen in a better light if we assume the community has accepted the principle that people in her position are entitled to compensation" (pp. 225-226).

144 References are to Dworkin (1980, pp. 64-65, 340-344).

145 Reference is to *Quebec Association of Protestant School Boards v. Attorney-General of Quebec (No. 2)* [1982] 140 D.L.R. (3d) 33 at p. 62. Dworkin appears not to recognize this point. In discussing disputed interpretations of prior cases in *McLoughlin v. O'Brian* [1983] 1 A.C. 410, Dworkin has his hypothetical judge, Hercules, offer six "interpretations of the precedent cases even before he reads them" (1986, p. 240). In testing out these interpretations Hercules is instructed to consider "whether a single political official *could* [emphasis added] have given the verdicts of the precedent cases if that official were consciously and coherently enforcing the principles that form the interpretation" (p. 242).

146 This last point is supported by MacCormick (1978, p. 166). The likelihood of profoundly different justifications being offered for any particular rule or practice is one explanation why judges are not authorized to resort to further levels of "political" justification (Raz, 1985b, pp. 22-24).

147 It is implausible to expect that laws covering diffuse aspects of political life, passed by countless different bodies espousing opposing political ideologies, will share a sufficiently coherent justification to be useful in providing direction in controversial cases (Altman, 1986, pp. 216-227). Hart (1978, p. 2) suggests that "any morally tolerable account" of criminal punishment practices must characterize them as compromises "between distinct and partly conflicting principles." Hart also suggests that the law of contract exhibits "a plurality of features which can only be understood as a compromise between partly discrepant principles" (p. 10). Harry Kalven, cited as one of America's most insightful legal scholars, is reported to believe that U.S. constitutional law is "a sprawling body of judge-made law fashioned out of the gradual accretion of individual judgments" and to doubt whether "any theory or underlying philosophy could embrace the motley array of problems that courts actually confront in applying First Amendment law to life" (Schmidt, 1988, p. 12).

148 Local priority is a scaled-down version of coherence which recognizes that individual areas of law may be governed by their own set of legal standards. In other words, an acceptable principle may not contradict established principles in that area of law (Dworkin, 1986, p. 250).

149 See Dworkin (1986, pp. 126-128).

150 Dworkin (1986, pp. 176-186) seems aware that his justification of integrity does not fit with actual legal practice. He quickly shifts to justifying the notion of integrity in terms of its desirability as a theory (cf. pp. 134, 191-192, 404). A number of critics challenge Dworkin's appeal to overall coherence on the grounds that it is an impractical and undesirable recommendation (Mackie, 1984; Raz, 1985a; Shiner, 1986). For a fuller account of the inadequacies of Dworkin's theory as a faithful account of judicial practice, see Case (1993).

CHAPTER 7: *RIGGS v. PALMER*

151 See *Holy Trinity Church v. United States* [1892] 143 U.S. 456 at p. 457.

152 Reference is to *Riggs v. Palmer* [1889] 115 N.Y. 506 at p. 511.

153 See Dworkin (1986, pp. 15-20, 87-88) for his most recent discussion of the *Riggs* case.

154 Dworkin's (1980, pp. 28-29) formulation of the principle appears to overstate the principles that were actually cited in the case. For a discussion of the particular rules that might be subsumed under Dworkin's principle, see Coval and Smith (1986, p. 80). Justice Earl's primary reason is based on the argument, cited above, from "rational interpretation"—that legislators could not reasonably be assumed to have intended to allow persons who murdered their benefactors to inherit. Ironically, since this argument is inconsistent with Dworkin's view of the best theory of statutory interpretation, he must ultimately characterize the judge's actual reason as an anomaly (Dworkin, 1986, p. 417).

155 Dworkin's (1986, p. 18) account of the dissenting opinion is equally unsatisfactory. He offers several arguments in support of that judge's theory of "literal" interpretation, only one of which is mentioned in the opinion. Furthermore, that reason—the double punishment argument—is not a reason for adopting a theory of literal interpretation of statutes, but a consequence of interpreting the statute literally.

156 This formulation of Coval and Smith's rule is found in Timmis (1988, p. 414).

157 Critics have challenged their account on other grounds, including their justification for claiming that maximizing agency exhausts what is important in law (Cassels, 1988; Timmis, 1988).

158 Coval and Smith (1986, p. 80) offer a possible counter-argument to this objection. They cite a case where the assignees of a life insurance policy on an executed felon were prevented from collecting because the court was concerned that enforcing the policy might remove a deterrent to criminal activity—namely, it might alleviate a criminal's concern to look after his family. My point is simply that it is not obvious that the potential loss of deterrence clearly outweighs the other consequences. Consider, for example, the injustice of denying a family the right to collect on a life insurance policy that had been in force for years solely because the father was executed for a crime.

CHAPTER 8: *DAVIS v. JOHNSON*

159 See Moles (1987, pp. 260-261). Moles' most general purpose in discussing this case, and two other cases, is to show the inadequacy of Hart's account of rule application in terms of core and penumbra cases. Although I agree that Hart's account of secondary rules is inadequate, I believe that judicial reasoning is rule governed.

160 The case reference is *Young v. Bristol Aeroplane Co.* [1944] 2 All E.R. 293.

161 See *Davis v. Johnson* [1978] 1 All E.R. 1132 at p. 1133. Since the doctrine of precedent does not bind a higher court, the House of Lords was clearly entitled to overrule the Court of Appeal's decision.

162 The case reference is *Seward v. The Vera Cruz* [1881-5] All E.R. 216.

163 Another line of argument was offered, which was to by-pass *Young* altogether and distinguish *Davis* from the earlier cases. This suggestion is mentioned by Sir George Baker, rejected explicitly by two others, and not entertained by the remaining two. It does not avoid the dilemma that creates the problem of interest to us, because it does not touch upon the legitimacy of rejecting the received doctrine of precedent.

164 Lord Justice Cumming-Bruce was the only judge who considered the earlier two cases to be properly decided. Therefore, his argument is hypothetical.

165 The quotation is found in Fiss (1982, p. 748).

166 Reference is to Moles (1987, p. 165).

167 It is unclear whether the House of Lords approved of Lord Shaw's decision in *Davis* or merely accepted that his exception would not undermine the doctrine of precedent. Lord Justice Shaw's view was that a subsequent reversal of the incorrect decision would not readdress the injustice perpetuated during the interim period on those women who would be forced for financial reasons to stay with their abusive mates.

168 The reversal of the House of Lords' position in 1966 was not adopted in the context of a case but was issued as a practice statement ([1966] 1 W.L.R. 1234). As such it is not, in the strict sense, a judicial precedent, although it clearly was accepted as a binding pronouncement.

169 See Lord Salmon in *Davis v. Johnson* [1978] 1 All E.R. 1133 at p. 1153.

CHAPTER 9: SELECTED JUDICIAL OPINIONS

170 See Case (1993) for a more extensive discussion of the criteria for assessing theories of authorized legal practice.

Study Questions

CHAPTER 1—JUDICIAL TYRANNY OR ENDANGERED INSTITUTION?

1. In your own words, explain the difference between *authorized* and *actual* judicial practice. Why it is important to distinguish between these two notions?
2. Why should we be concerned to separate a judicial mandate to *apply* law from a judicial mandate to *make* law?
3. How is it possible that judges could go beyond the explicit wording of a provision and still be "applying a law according to the law"?
4. What arguments are offered to suggest that judges must inevitably resort to personal or political values when deciding highly controversial cases?
5. In your own words, describe the explanations offered in the chapter that counter the so-called judicial resort to personal and political values (i.e., that support a rule-governed account of judicial reasoning). Which of these explanations do you find compelling and which are unconvincing? Explain your answers.
6. Drawing on your own knowledge and from commentaries of judicial decisions in newspapers and other media, describe the problem with and concerns over judicial tyranny. Can these criticisms of the judiciary be explained adequately in terms of the rule-governed account of judicial practice offered in this chapter?
7. What is meant by the suggestion that the judiciary is the Achilles heel of our legal system? Do you agree with this characterization? Explain your answer.
8. It is claimed "Courts that act politically will come to be treated politically." What does this statement mean? Do you agree with this claim? Why or why not?
9. It is suggested that the legal profession and the lay public must "take seriously the judicial duty to uphold the law." Do you think that this proposal adequately protects against the doubled-edged threats of judicial tyranny and an endangered judicial system?
10. What additional concerns or questions do you have about the nature and exercise of the judicial role in our legal system?

CHAPTER 2—RULES OF APPLICATION

1 What does it mean to say that judicial reasoning is a form of conductive reasoning?
2 Explain in your own words the three kinds of arguments or modes of reasoning employed by judges in applying law.
3 Using examples of your own, explain the difference between primary and secondary rules.
4 In your own words, define the four types of secondary rules identified in this chapter.
5 Using your own words, explain the role of argument-validating rules in judicial reasoning.
6 Using your own words, explain the role of argument-verifying rules in judicial reasoning.
7 Using your own words, explain the role, and different types, of argument-weighting rules.
8 Analyze Chief Justice Dickson's actual opinion in the *Morgentaler* case (found in Chapter 9) in terms of the types of rules (i.e., validating, verifying, weighting) that he replied upon.
9 Using an example from the text, explain what is meant by the following statement: "A legal rule is recognized as correctly covering a set of particular situations only if we accept implicitly that second-level rules regulate the scope of coverage, or the *denotation*, of the primary rule."
10 Explain the "specificity threshold" of a law. Given the concerns about judicial tyranny, is it wise to deliberately make rules general? Explain your answer.

CHAPTER 3—CONTROLLED JUDGMENT

1 In your own words, explain the notion of judicial discretion as defined in the text.
2 What is meant by the suggestion that judicial decisions are *controlled* by legal criteria?
3 What is the difference between deciding an issue *according to the law* and deciding an issue *within the law*? Why is the latter a form of judicial discretion?
4 Do you agree that a judicial decision can be controlled by law and still not have a single correct conclusion?
5 It is claimed that even if the law provides explicit criteria for its application, it is still possible that judges will have to exercise discretion when applying the law in specific instances. The converse is also claimed: even if the law does not provide explicit criteria for its application, it is still possible that judges will not have to exercise discretion when applying the law in specific instances. Explain how both of these scenarios are possible.

6　With reference to the *Big M Drug Mart* case explain how rules of application can be altered in rule-governed ways.

7　What concerns or questions do you have about the notion of controlled judgment as an explanation of the rule-governed nature of judicial reasoning?

CHAPTER 4—REASONING FROM INTERPRETIVE GUIDELINES

1　Why is the notion of legislative intention a legal fiction—that is, why is it not identical with the actual intentions of the legislators?

2　Explain the following statement: a law's meaning is not "the conclusion that the legislature would have arrived at, but one which the legislature by the text has authorized the courts to find."

3　Using an example not found in the text, discuss the difference between a *rule* and a *rule formulation*.

4　What is the difference between a *letter of the law* and a *spirit of the law* focus?

5　Explain the six basic interpretive approaches. List the advantages and disadvantages of each.

6　Briefly discuss each of the four categories of minor interpretive rules.

7　Categorize each of the arguments in the *PPG Industries* case (found in Chapter 9) according to one of the four categories of minor interpretive rules.

8　What is the relation between the basic interpretive approaches and the minor interpretive rules?

9　Why are the apparent contradictions between many of the minor interpretive guidelines not necessarily a problem for a rule-governed account of judicial reasoning?

10　How can shifts in the basic interpretive approaches be accommodated in a rule-governed account of judicial reasoning? Do you find this explanation convincing? Why or why not?

CHAPTER 5—REASONING FROM PRIOR CASES

1　In your own words, explain the difference between analogous reasoning and the subsumption of a particular case under a judge-made general law.

2　What is the difference between *reference to precedent* and *reasoning from prior cases*?

3　What is the *ratio* of a case and why is its precise formulation always approximate?

4　What is involved in deciding that a prior case should be followed? Explain the comment that reasoning from prior cases is a "moving classification scheme."

5　What is involved in deciding that a prior case should be distinguished?

6 A case can be said to have authority only over what is required to decide the issues before the court. What significance does this secondary rule have for the accumulation of various cases into a common law principle?

7 How do argument-weighting rules apply in reasoning from prior cases?

8 How can the fact that judges will identify inconsistent *rationes* from the same case be reconciled with a rule-governed account of judicial reasoning?

9 What is the difference between accepting a precedent on *legally settled* distinctions as opposed to *legally desirable* distinctions?

10 How can claims that judges *make* law be reconciled with a rule-governed account of reasoning from prior cases? Do you find these explanations convincing? Why or why not?

CHAPTER 6—REASONING FROM PRINCIPLE

1 In your own words, explain what it means to *decide on principle.* How is this different from what is often referred to as a *policy decision*?

2 What is the difference between *appealing to a principle* and *reasoning from principle*?

3 How does reasoning from principle avoid the problem that arises when judges appear to run out of settled legal rules upon which to decide a case?

4 In your own words with reference to examples, explain what is involved in testing a principle by assessing its *consistency with fundamental principles*.

5 In your own words with reference to examples, explain what is involved in testing a principle by assessing its *consequences for all parties*.

6 In your own words with reference to examples, explain what is involved in testing a principle by assessing its *consequences in new cases*.

7 In your own words with reference to examples, explain what is involved in testing a principle by assessing its *consequences for repeated instances*.

8 Why is it important that reasoning from principle be done in light of legally recognized values?

9 Explain the notion of legally embedded standards. Provide a few examples not found in the text. How is Dworkin's account of embedded standards different from the conception argued for in the text?

10 What questions or concerns do you have about the ability of the three forms of reasoning to account for the judicial mandate to "declare the law, not to give it"?

CHAPTER 7—CASE STUDY: *RIGGS v. PALMER*

1 Check that the summary of Justice Earl's arguments accurately reflects the reasoning in the actual majority opinion. Are there any omissions or additions? Would you have characterized any arguments differently?

2 Check that the summary of Justice Gray's arguments accurately reflects the reasoning in the actual dissenting opinion. Are there any omissions or additions? Would you have characterized any arguments differently?

3 On the basis of the actual opinion, how adequate is the justification in the Commentary of the rule-governed nature of the reasoning in the *Riggs* case? What questions or reservations do you have about the extent to which legal standards, as opposed to extra-legal values, controlled each judge's conclusions?

4 On the basis of the actual opinion, assess the critique of Dworkin's account of the reasoning in the *Riggs* case.

5 On the basis of the actual opinion, assess the critique of Coval and Smith's account of the reasoning in the *Riggs* case.

6 Which interpretation of the law in the *Riggs* case do you regard as the most defensible? Write your own opinion on the most compelling reasons for your decision and on any counter-arguments to the opposing position.

7 After completing question #6, comment on the extent to which your decision was impartial and controlled by legal standards.

CHAPTER 8—CASE STUDY: *DAVIS v. JOHNSON*

1 Using the format found in Chapter 7, summarize each reason and the supporting rule(s) of application (cited or implied) for each of the five opinions in the Court of Appeal decision in *Davis v. Johnson*.

2 Using the format found in Chapter 7, summarize each reason and the supporting rule(s) of application (cited or implied) for the two presented opinions in the House of Lords decision in *Davis v. Johnson*.

3 On the basis of the actual opinion, how adequate is the justification in the Commentary of the rule-governed nature of the reasoning in the *Davis* case? What questions or reservations do you have about the extent to which legal standards, as opposed to extra-legal values, controlled the judges' conclusions?

4 Which position on binding precedent in the *Davis* case do you regard as the most defensible? Write your own opinion on the most compelling reasons for your decision and on any counter-arguments to the opposing position.

5 After completing question #4, comment on the extent to which your decision was impartial and controlled by legal standards.

CHAPTER 9—SELECTED JUDICIAL OPINIONS

1 To explore reasoning from interpretive guidelines, select either the Court of Appeal or the House of Lords decision in *Royal College of Nursing v. Department of Health and Social Security*, and write your own opinion outlining the most compelling reasons for your decision and any counter-arguments to the opposing position.

2 Using reasoning from prior cases, write your own opinion in *Donoghue v. Stevenson* outlining the most compelling reasons for your decision and any counter-arguments to the opposing position.

3 Using the Classification of Material Facts format from Chapter 5, identify from the opinions by Lords Buckmaster, Atkin, and Thankerton, in *Donoghue v. Stevenson* the material facts for each of the following cases:
   Langridge v. Levy
   Longmeid v. Holliday
   Winterbottom v. Wright
   George v. Skivington
   Francis v. Cockrell
   Heaven v. Pender
   Le Lievre v. Gould
   Earl v. Lubbock
   Bates v. Batey & Co., Ld.
   Mullen v. Barr & Co.
   Cunnington v. Great Northern Ry. Co.
   Hawkins v. Smith
   Dixon v. Bell
   Blacker v. Lake & Elliot, Ld.
   Gordon v. M'Hardy
   When their description of the material facts differs, list both Lord Buckmaster's and Lord Atkin's versions. Identify the *ratio* or *rationes* established in each of the above cases.

4 For each argument based on reasoning from principle found in Chief Justice Dickson's opinion in the *Morgentaler* case, identify which of the four principle tests they represent.

5 Using reasoning from principle, write your own opinion in *Morgentaler v. The Queen* outlining the most compelling reasons for your decision and any counter-arguments to the opposing position. .

6 Select any case and comment on the extent to which the actual opinions support or contradict the account of rule-governed judicial reasoning presented in the text.

7 On the basis of the opinions presented in Chapter 9, comment in specific terms on the difficulties judges face in deciding complex, controversial cases in a rule-governed manner.

8   On the basis of the opinions presented in Chapter 9, what concerns or questions do you have about the notion of controlled judgment as an explanation of the rule-governed nature of judicial reasoning?

9   Comment on how your own perceptions of the nature and exercise of the judicial role in our legal system have changed as a result of the arguments and examples presented in this book.

Table of Cases

AMERICAN

BRITISH

CANADIAN

Bibliography

Agresto, John. (1984). *The Supreme Court and constitutional democracy.* Ithaca, NY: Cornell University Press.

Alexander, Larry. (1989). Constrained by precedent. *Southern California Law Review, 63*(1), 1-64.

Altman, Andrew. (1986). Legal realism, critical legal studies, and Dworkin. *Philosophy and Public Affairs, 15*(3), 205-235.

Anderson, Doris. (1980). The Supreme Court and women's rights. *Supreme Court Law Review, 1*, 457-460.

Austin, J. L. (1970). *How to do things with words.* New York: Oxford University Press.

Beatty, David. (1995, October 9). Order in the Supreme Court! Ad-hockery is running wild. *The Globe and Mail*, p. A17.

Bell, John. (1985). *Policy arguments in judicial decisions.* Oxford: Clarendon Press.

Bell, Richard S. (1972). Understanding the model of rules: Toward a reconciliation of Dworkin and positivism. *Yale Law Journal, 81*, 912-948.

Bindman, Stephen. (1986, April 17). Supreme Court judges taking Charter seriously. *The Ottawa Citizen*, p. A4.

Black, Hugo LaFayette. (1969). *A constitutional faith.* New York: Knopf.

Bodenheimer, Edgar. (1969). A neglected theory of legal reasoning. *Journal of Legal Education, 21*, 373-402.

Bradley, A. W. (1985). The sovereignty of Parliament—in perpetuity? In Jeffrey Jowell & Dawn Oliver (Eds.), *The changing constitution* (pp. 23-47). Oxford: Clarendon Press.

Burton, Steven J. (1985). *An introduction to law and legal reasoning.* Boston: Little, Brown and Company.

Burton, Steven J. (1992). *Judging in good faith.* New York: Cambridge University Press.

Cameron, Stevie. (1994). *On the take: Crime, corruption and greed in the Mulroney years.* Toronto: Macfarlane Walter & Ross.

Case, Roland. (1993) Theorizing about law. *Canadian Journal of Law and Jurisprudence, 6*(1), 113-138.

Cassels, James. (1988). Liberal presuppositions. *University of Toronto Law Journal, 38*, 378-411.

Casswell, Donald. (1982). A prescriptive model for decision-making in the Supreme Court of Canada. *Ottawa Law Review, 14*, 126-151.

Coombs, Jerrold R. (1980). Validating moral judgments by principle testing. In D. Cochrane & M. Manley-Casimir (Eds.), *Development of moral reasoning: Practical approaches* (pp. 30-55). New York: Praeger.

Coombs, Jerrold R. (1990). Critical thinking and law-related reasoning. In J. R. Coombs, S. Parkinson, & R. Case (Eds.), *Ends in view: An analysis of the goals of law-related education* (pp. 109-121). Vancouver: Centre for the Study of Curriculum and Instruction (University of British Columbia) and Centre for Education, Law and Society (Simon Fraser University).

Coval, S. C., & Smith, Joseph C. (1986). *Law and its presuppositions: Actions, agents and rules.* London: Routledge & Kegan Paul.

Dickson, Brian. (1982). The judiciary—law interpreters or law-makers. *Manitoba Law Journal, 12*, 1-8.

Doyle, Kevin. (1988, February 8). The supreme authority. *Maclean's*, p. 2.

Driedger, E. A. (1981). Statutes: The mischievous literal golden rule. *Canadian Bar Review, 59*, 780-786.

Dworkin, Ronald. (1980). *Taking rights seriously.* Cambridge, MA: Harvard University Press.

Dworkin, Ronald. (1984, November 8). Reagan's justice. *New York Review of Books*, pp. 27-31.

Dworkin, Ronald. (1985). *A matter of principle.* Cambridge, MA: Harvard University Press.

Dworkin, Ronald. (1986). *Law's empire.* Cambridge, MA: Harvard University Press.

Dworkin, Ronald. (1987, December 17). From Bork to Kennedy. *New York Review of Books*, pp. 36-42.

Dyer, Clare. (1996, July 28). Bingham defends judges. *Guardian Weekly*, p. 11.

Eekelaar, J. M. (1973). Principles of revolutionary legality. In A. W. B. Simpson (Ed.), *Oxford essays in jurisprudence* (pp. 22-43). Oxford: Clarendon Press.

Elliot, Robin. (1982). Interpreting the Charter: Use of the earlier versions as an aid. *University of British Columbia Law Review* (Charter Edition), 11-57.

Farrar, John H. (1984). *Introduction to legal method.* London: Sweet & Maxwell.

Fiss, Owen M. (1982). Objectivity and interpretation. *Stanford Law Review, 34*, 739-763.

Frank, Jerome. (1958). *Law and the modern mind.* New York: Anchor Books.

Frankfurter, Felix. (1947). Some reflections on the reading of statutes. *Columbia Law Review, 47*, 527-546.

Fulford, Robert. (1986, December). Charter of wrongs. *Saturday Night*, pp. 7-9.

Gall, Gerald. (1983). *The Canadian legal system* (Second edition). Toronto: Carswell.

Gibson, Dale. (1986). *The law of the Charter: General principles.* Toronto: Carswell.

Goodhart, Arthur L. (1930). Determining the ratio decidendi of a case. *Yale Law Journal, 40*, 161-183.

Gottlieb, Gideon. (1968). *The logic of choice.* London: Allen and Unwin.

Govier, Trudy. (1985). *A practical study of argument.* Belmont, CA: Wadsworth.

Gray, John Chipman. (1966). The judge as law-giver. In M. P. Golding (Ed.), *The nature of law: Readings in legal philosophy* (pp. 188-196). New York: Random House.

Green, Thomas F. (1966). Teaching, acting, and behaving. In Israel Scheffler (Ed.), *Philosophy and education: Modern readings* (pp. 115-135). Boston: Allyn & Bacon.

Griswold, Erwin N. (1960). Forward: Of time and attitudes—Professor Hart and Judge Arnold. *Harvard Law Review, 74*, 81-94.

Hare, R. M. (1952). *The language of morals.* London: Clarendon Press.

Hare, R. M. (1972). Principles. *Aristotelian Society Proceedings, 73*, 1-18.

Hart, H. L. A. (1949). The ascription of responsibility and rights. *Aristotelian Society Proceedings, 44*, 171-194.

Hart, H. L. A. (1958). Positivism and the separation of law and morals. *Harvard Law Review, 71*, 593-629.

Hart, H. L. A. (1961). *The concept of law.* Oxford: Clarendon Press.

Hart, H. L. A. (1967a). Legal positivism. In Paul Edwards (Ed.), *Encyclopedia of philosophy* (Vol. 4, pp. 418-420). New York: Macmillan/Free Press.

Hart, H. L. A. (1967b). Problems of philosophy of law. In Paul Edwards (Ed.), *Encyclopedia of philosophy* (Vol. 6, pp. 264-276). New York: Macmillan/Free Press.

Hart, H. L. A. (1977). American jurisprudence through English eyes: The nightmare and the noble dream. *Georgia Law Review, 11*, 969-989.

Hart, H. L. A. (1978). *Punishment and responsibility: Essays in the philosophy of law.* Oxford: Clarendon Press.

Hart, H. L. A. (1982). *Essays on Bentham: Jurisprudence and political theory.* Oxford: Clarendon Press.

Heard, Andrew D. (1991). The Charter in the Supreme Court of Canada: The importance of which judge hears an appeal. *Canadian Journal of Political Science, 24*(2), 289-307.

Hogg, Peter W. (1982). A comparison of the Canadian Charter of Rights and Freedoms with the Canadian Bill of Rights. In Walter Tarnopolsky & Gerald-A. Beaudoin (Eds.), *The Canadian Charter of Rights and Freedoms: Commentary* (pp. 1-23). Toronto: Carswell.

Hogg, Peter W. (1987). The Charter of Rights and American theories of interpretation. *Osgoode Hall Law Journal, 25*, 87-113.

Holmes, Oliver Wendell. (1966). The law as predictions of what courts will do. In M. P. Golding (Ed.), *The nature of law: Readings in legal philosophy* (pp. 175-187). New York: Random House.

Honore, Tony. (1983). The role of the judge. In M. A. Stewart (Ed.), *Law, morality and rights* (pp. 43-50). Boston: Reidel Publishing.

Hughes, Graham. (1968). Rules, policy and decision making. *Yale Law Journal, 77*, 411-439.

Hughes, Graham. (1981, November 10). Are justices just? *New York Review of Books*, pp. 41-43.

Hutchinson, Allan C. (1987). Charter litigation and social change: Legal battles and social war. In Robert J. Sharpe (Ed.), *Charter litigation* (pp. 357-381). Toronto: Butterworths.

Johnson, John W. (1978). Retreating from the common law? The grudging reception of legislative history by American appellate courts in the early twentieth century. *Detroit College of Law Review, 3*, 413-431.

Jowell, Jeffrey. (1985). The rule of law today. In Jeffrey Jowell & Dawn Oliver (Eds.), *The changing constitution* (pp. 3-22). Oxford: Clarendon Press.

Keating, Gregory C. (1987). Justifying Hercules: Ronald Dworkin and the rule of law. *American Bar Foundation Research Journal, 2 & 3*, 525-535.

Kennedy, Duncan. (1973). Legal formalism. *Journal of Legal Studies, 2*(2), 351-398.

Kernochan, John M. (1976). Statutory interpretation: An outline of method. *Dalhousie Law Journal, 3*, 331-366.

Kovesi, Julius. (1971). *Moral notions.* London: Routledge & Kegan Paul.

Lacayo, Richard. (1988, July 11). A slam-dunk decision. *Time*, pp. 20-21.

Laskin, Bora. (1978). Judicial integrity and the Supreme Court of Canada. *Law Society Gazette, 12*, 116-121.

Levenbook, Barbara Baum. (1984). On universal relevance in legal reasoning. *Law and Philosophy, 3*, 1-23.

Levi, Edward. (1949). *An introduction to legal reasoning.* Chicago: University of Chicago Press.

Levi, Edward. (1964). The nature of judicial reasoning. In Sidney Hook (Ed.), *Law and philosophy: A symposium* (pp. 263-281). New York: New York University Press.

Llewellyn, Karl. (1960). *The common law traditions.* Boston: Little, Brown.

Lloyd, Dennis. (1981). *The idea of law: A repressive evil or a social necessity?* Markham, ON: Penguin Books.

Luban, David. (1987). Judicial activism vs. judicial restraint: A closer look at the Bork nomination. *Philosophy & Public Policy, 7*, 9-12.

Lyons, David. (1984). Moral aspects of legal theory. In Marshall Cohen (Ed.), *Ronald Dworkin and contemporary jurisprudence* (pp. 49-69). Totowa, NJ: Rowman & Allanheld.

Lyons, David. (1985). Derivability, defensibility, and the justification of judicial decisions. *Monist, 68*, 325-346.

Mac Callum, Gerald C., Jr. (1966). Legislative intent. *Yale Law Journal, 75*, 754-787.

MacCormick, Neil. (1974a). "Principles" of law. *Juridical Review, 19*, 217-226.

MacCormick, Neil. (1974b). Law as institutional fact. *Law Quarterly Review, 90*, 102-129.

MacCormick, Neil. (1978). *Legal reasoning and legal theory.* Oxford: Clarendon Press.

MacCormick, Neil. (1990). Reconstruction after deconstruction: A response to Critical Legal Studies. *Oxford Journal of Legal Studies, 10*(4), 539-558.

MacGuigan, Mark R. (1967). Precedent and policy in the Supreme Court. *Canadian Bar Review, 45,* 627-665.

Mackie, John. (1983). Rules and reason. In M. A. Stewart (Ed.), *Law, morality and rights* (pp. 31-42). Boston: Reidel Publishing.

Mackie, John. (1984). The third theory of law. In Marshall Cohen (Ed.), *Ronald Dworkin and contemporary jurisprudence* (pp. 161-170). Totowa, NJ: Rowman & Allanheld.

Mandel, Michael. (1994). *The Charter of Rights and the legalization of politics in Canada* (Revised edition). Toronto: Thompson Educational Publishing.

McCarthy, Coleman. (1996, July 28). A death sentence on human dignity. *Guardian Weekly,* p. 17.

McCormick, Peter, & Greene, Ian. (1990). *Judges and judging: Inside the Canadian judicial system.* Toronto: James Lorimer.

McEachern, Allan. (1996, August 28). Our judges are sorely tested. *Vancouver Sun,* p. A15.

Moles, Robert N. (1987). *Definition and rule in legal theory: A reassessment of H. L. A. Hart and the positivist tradition.* Oxford: Basil Blackwell.

Monahan, Patrick J. (1987). Judicial review and democracy: A theory of judicial review. *University of British Columbia Law Review, 21*(1), 87-164.

Moore, Michael S. (1981). The semantics of judging. *Southern California Law Review, 54*(2), 151-294.

Morawetz, Thomas. (1990). The epistemology of judging: Wittgenstein and deliberative practices. *Canadian Journal of Law and Jurisprudence, 3,* 35-55.

Morton, F. L. (1984, June). *Charting the Charter—year one: A statistical analysis.* Paper presented at the annual meeting of the Canadian Political Science Association, Guelph, ON.

Morton, F. L., Russell, Peter H., & Withey, Michael J. (1992). The Supreme Court's first one hundred Charter of Rights decisions: A statistical analysis. *Osgoode Hall Law Journal, 30*(1), 1-56.

Morton, Ted. (1989, February 20). Charter changed justices' role: Their selection needs review. *Financial Post,* p. 2.

Murphy, Arthur W. (1975). Old maxims never die: The "plain-meaning rule" and statutory interpretation in the "modern" federal courts. *Columbia Law Review, 75,* 1299-1317.

Nova Scotia Commissioners. (1975). A comparative study of the admissibility of extrinsic evidence. *Uniform Law Conference of Canada Proceedings* (pp. 218-248). Halifax: Nova Scotia Law Society.

Payne, Douglas. (1956). The intention of the legislature in the interpretation of statutes. *Current Legal Problems, 9,* 96-112.

Paterson, Alan. (1982). *The law lords.* London: Macmillan Press.

Peck, Sidney R. (1987). An analytical framework for the application of the Canadian Charter of Rights and Freedoms. *Osgoode Hall Law Journal, 25,* 1-85.

Petter, Andrew, & Hutchinson, Allan C. (1989). Rights in conflict: The dilemma of Charter legitimacy. *University of British Columbia Law Review, 23*(3), 531-548.

Pilon, Roger. (1990). Losing liberty through judicial restraint. *Philosophy & Public Policy, 10*(1), 12-15.

Posner, Richard. (1982). Economics, politics, and the reading of statutes and the constitution. *University of Chicago Law Review, 49,* 263-291.

Raz, Joseph. (1983a). *The concept of a legal system: An introduction to the theory of legal system* (Second edition). Oxford: Clarendon Press.

Raz, Joseph. (1983b). *The authority of law: Essays on law and morality.* Oxford: Clarendon Press.

Raz, Joseph. (1984). Legal principles and the limits of law. In Marshall Cohen (Ed.), *Ronald Dworkin and contemporary jurisprudence* (pp. 73-87). Totowa, NJ: Rowman & Allanheld.

Raz, Joseph. (1985a). Authority, law and morality. *Monist, 68,* 295-324.

Raz, Joseph. (1985b). Authority and justification. *Philosophy and Public Affairs, 14,* 3-29.

Read, William. (1986). *Legal thinking: Its limits and tensions*. Philadelphia: University of Pennsylvania Press.

Richards, David A. J. (1979). Human rights and the moral foundations of the substantive criminal law. *Georgia Law Review, 13*, 1395-1447.

Russell, Peter. (1983). The political purposes of the Canadian Charter of Rights and Freedoms. *Canadian Bar Review, 6*, 30-54.

Sartorius, Rolf. (1968). The justification of the judicial decision. *Ethics, 78*, 171-187.

Sartorius, Rolf. (1971). Social policy and judicial legislation. *American Philosophical Quarterly, 8*, 151-160.

Sartorius, Rolf. (1989). Positivism and the foundations of legal authority. In Ruth Gavison (Ed.), *Issues in contemporary legal philosophy: The influence of H. L. A. Hart* (pp. 43-61). Oxford: Clarendon Press.

Schauer, Frederick. (1992). *Playing by the rules: A philosophical examination of rule-based decision-making in law and in life*. Oxford: Clarendon Press.

Schmidt, Benno C., Jr. (1988, February 21). A nation without heretics. *New York Review of Books*, p. 12.

Shiner, Roger A. (1986). Review of *A matter of principle*. *Cambridge Law Journal, 45*, 511-515.

Simpson, A. W. B. (1961). The "ratio decidendi" of a case and the doctrine of binding precedent. In A. G. Guest (Ed.), *Oxford essays in jurisprudence* (pp. 148-175). London: Oxford University Press.

Singer, Marcus G. (1958). Moral rules and principles. In A. I. Meldon (Ed.), *Essays in moral philosophy* (pp. 160-197). Seattle: University of Washington Press.

Snell, James G., & Vaughan, Frederick. (1985). *The Supreme Court of Canada: History of the institution*. Toronto: University of Toronto Press.

Stone, Julius. (1959). The ratio of the ratio decidendi. *Modern Law Review, 22*, 597-620.

Stone, Julius. (1964). *Legal systems and lawyers' reasonings*. Sydney, Australia: Maitland Publications.

Taylor, Paul. (1961). *Normative discourse*. Englewood Cliffs, NJ: Prentice-Hall.

Timmis, Mark V. (1988). Review of *Law and its presuppositions*. *University of Toronto Law Journal, 38*, 412-420.

Tribe, Laurence H. (1985). *Constitutional choices*. Cambridge, MA: Harvard University Press.

Tushnet, Mark. (1983). Following the rules laid down: A critique of interpretivism and neutral principles. *Harvard Law Review, 96*, 781-827.

Tushnet, Mark. (1988). *Red, white, and blue: A critical analysis of constitutional law*. Cambridge, MA: Harvard University Press.

Vlastos, Gregory. (1962). Justice and equality. In Richard B. Brandt (Ed.), *Social justice* (pp. 31-72). Englewood Cliffs, NJ: Prentice-Hall.

Waluchow, Wilfrid J. (1980). *Adjudication and discretion*. Unpublished doctoral dissertation, Oxford University, Oxford.

Waluchow, Wilfrid J. (1983). Strong discretion. *Philosophical Quarterly, 33*, 321-339.

Waluchow, Wilfrid J. (1985). Hart, legal rules and palm tree justice. *Law and Philosophy, 4*, 41-70.

Waluchow, Wilfrid J. (1986). Herculean positivism. *Oxford Journal of Legal Studies, 5*, 187-210.

Waluchow, Wilfrid J. (1990). The "forces" of law. *Canadian Journal of Law and Jurisprudence, 3*(1), 51-67.

Waluchow, Wilfrid J. (1994). *Inclusive legal positivism*. Oxford: Clarendon Press.

Wechsler, Herbert. (1959). Toward neutral principles of constitutional law. *Harvard Law Review, 73*, 1-35.

Wechsler, Herbert. (1964). The nature of judicial reasoning. In Sidney Hook (Ed.), *Law and philosophy: A symposium* (pp. 290-300). New York: New York University Press.

Weiler, Paul. (1968). Two models of judicial decision-making. *Canadian Bar Review, 46,* 406-471.

Weiler, Paul. (1974). *In the last resort: A critical study of the Supreme Court of Canada.* Toronto: Carswell/Methuen.

Williams, Glanville. (1982). *Learning the law.* London: Stevens.

Willis, John. (1938). Statute interpretation in a nutshell. *Canadian Bar Review, 17,* 1-27.

Wolfe, Christopher. (1986). *The rise of modern judicial review: From constitutional interpretation to judge-made law.* New York: Basic Books

Zander, Michael. (1980). *The law-making process.* London: Weidenfeld & Nicolson.

Index

Page numbers for cases cited are indicated in the Table of Cases